71 0261540 1
UNIVERSITY

The People and the Party System

The People and the Party System

The referendum and electoral reform in British politics

VERNON BOGDANOR
Fellow of Brasenose College, Oxford

CAMBRIDGE UNIVERSITY PRESS
Cambridge
London New York New Rochelle
Melbourne Sydney

Published by the Press Syndicate of the University of Cambridge
The Pitt Building, Trumpington Street, Cambridge CB2 1RP
32 East 57th Street, New York, NY 10022, USA
296 Beaconsfield Parade, Middle Park, Melbourne 3206, Australia

First published 1981

Printed in Great Britain at
The Pitman Press, Bath

Library of Congress catalogue card number: 81–3895

British Library Cataloguing in Publication Data

Bogdanor, Vernon
The people and the party system.
1. Elections – Great Britain
I. Title
324.2'1'0941 JN956

ISBN 0 521 24207 x hard covers
ISBN 0 521 28525 9 paperback

For R.B.   J.E.B.
P.S.R.B.   A.M.D.B.

With thanks

The constitution does not exist for the benefit of parties, but of citizens

J. S. MILL

Contents

Preface

This book argues that many of Britain's political problems, and therefore her economic decline, can be explained as the result of a rigid party system which inhibits instead of encouraging popular involvement in politics. It is intended for the general reader as well as the specialist.

I have been greatly helped by Enid Lakeman, former Director of the Electoral Reform Society, who allowed me to use the Society's library, answered numerous queries on proportional representation and gave me permission to use the diagrams in Figure 1 on p. 186. Richard Holme and Hilary Muggridge of the National Committee for Electoral Reform gave me unlimited access to their voluminous supply of press cuttings, as well as generous hospitality.

David Butler, *doyen* of British electoral studies, with characteristic generosity, has helped me from the inception of this book, and Philip Williams has gone through the text with enormous care and suggested many valuable improvements.

I would also like to thank Sir Max Beloff, John Dunbabin, Paul McKee, Peter Pulzer, John Rowett and Michael Woods for reading and commenting on earlier drafts; and Floyd Parsons and Michael Steed for many stimulating conversations on electoral reform. But they do not necessarily accept my conclusions. I would also like to thank the staff of the Cambridge University Press.

I am very grateful to my college, Brasenose, for granting me sabbatical leave and paying the expenses of typing this book; but above all for being such a stimulating academic community.

My greatest debt, however, is to my wife for encouraging me to complete this book; and to my sons, Paul and Adam, for putting up with a father who spends so much time at the typewriter.

VERNON BOGDANOR 1981

Introduction

I

Government in Britain is pre-eminently party government. More than in any other democracy, political assumptions and conventions in Britain are geared to the idea of government by two alternating parties, each enjoying an almost complete monopoly of power and patronage. The absence of a written constitution or powerful second chamber have prevented the growth of countervailing checks upon party government; and, since the parties are not recognised in law as being corporate bodies, they largely escape legal scrutiny of their internal activities. Moreover, the electoral system and procedures for financing the parties have underwritten a two-party system which it is difficult for newcomers to challenge. The British political parties, then, have a unique position as custodians of the British Constitution.

In recent years, there has been much questioning of British constitutional arrangements. Hitherto sacrosanct doctrines such as the absolute supremacy of Parliament, collective Cabinet responsibility and the unitary state, have all come under challenge. Yet the parties themselves have largely escaped critical scrutiny. For obvious reasons, neither the government nor the opposition of the day have sought to ask how well the party system serves the nation. So the dominant institutions of the British political system have continued to monopolise the perquisites of government despite their failure to fulfil the expectations which they have aroused or to convince the electorate that they can solve the country's difficulties. Few have been willing to ask whether the party system actually serves the common good as effectively as its beneficiaries would have us believe.

That there is a conflict between popular aspirations and the party system has been a theme, if a subordinate one, in British political debate for over a hundred years. It played a particularly important part in the argument over the extension of the franchise and the coming of democracy in the nineteenth century. Concern that the aspirations of the new electorate might be frustrated rather than fulfilled by the interests of the parties was shown by writers from very different political standpoints: by John Stuart Mill, a leader of advanced radicalism, Henry Maine, the conservative jurist, and Moisei Ostrogorski, an individualist who supported no party and was a pioneer of modern political sociology.[1]

Any contemporary discussion of the party system must begin from the realisation that parties are essential to democracy, and accept the truth of Disraeli's dictum, 'without Party, Parliamentary government is impossible'. For democracy gives the majority the right to rule. But – except perhaps in a city-state – there is no way of creating a majority without establishing a political party. In every democracy in the world, political parties compete for the right to form a government. So any attack upon the party system which called for the abolition of parties would be entirely futile.

Yet if political parties are necessary in a democracy, their degree of organisation and mode of operation are not sacrosanct, but legitimate subjects for appraisal and criticism. However essential parties may be, a different approach to party government and a looser form of party organisation might well be more conducive to popular involvement in politics and to greater satisfaction with the decisions of government than is apparent in Britain today.

This question is of course a particularly important one to ask of the parties in a country such as Britain without a written constitution or any other instrument capable of limiting the scope of party government. In formal terms, the British Constitution can be summarised in eight words – what the Queen in Parliament enacts is law. But the formal approach to constitutional analysis has come increasingly to obscure the realities of British politics, and especially the dominance of party in our political arrangements. For the conventional limitations upon the power of party which prevailed in the early years of popular government, have gradually been whittled away in the twentieth century. The parties have themselves come to be the arbiters of what is constitutional and what is not. Far from guarding the processes of constitutional government, they have distorted our understanding of it.

Therefore any discussion of constitutional change which does not begin from the facts of party domination is bound to appear utopian. It is not difficult to draw up paper schemes of reform – proposals for a new Second Chamber to replace the House of Lords, proposals for a written constitution or bill of rights, proposals for a federal system of government – *et hoc genus omne*. Yet these reforms, if they were to be successful, would require the parties voluntarily to abdicate some of their powers. Like most sovereigns, they seem singularly unwilling to do so.

The central purpose of this book is to argue that there are available two weapons by which the sovereignty of the political parties can be restricted; to analyse how these weapons have been used in the historical debate over the role of the parties; and to consider how they might be used in the future. These two weapons are the referendum and proportional representation. Both, it will be argued, have a perfectly respectable place in the British political tradition, having been advocated by some of the most perceptive political thinkers this country has seen in the last hundred years.

The referendum has been used on three occasions in Britain – in 1973 to confirm the wish of the majority in Northern Ireland to remain part of the United Kingdom, to endorse Britain's membership of the European Economic Community in 1975, and to reject proposals for devolution to Scotland and Wales in 1979. It has already shown its power as a weapon in British politics. This book attempts to show how its use could be extended and how this would affect our constitutional arrangements.

Proportional representation has frequently been proposed for use in British elections, but has been employed only in elections for subordinate authorities and for university seats. It is at present used in Northern Ireland for all elections except elections to the House of Commons. Since it strikes so directly at the interests of the major political parties, they are not likely to propose it of their own free will. Its chances of adoption, therefore, probably depend upon a hung parliament such as that elected in February 1974, when the introduction of proportional representation can be made the price of allowing a party with a minority of seats in the Commons to form a government. Analysis of the operation of the British electoral system will show that the chances of another hung parliament occurring are rather greater than is popularly believed. But, of course, there can be no certainty that it will occur, and indeed the odds are probably against it.

It is, however, no longer unthinkable that these proposals might be accepted, and they are therefore worth examination to show the consequences for British institutions of their adoption. This book can be seen, therefore, as an analysis of the implications of looking at constitutional reform as an instrument of popular sovereignty. These consequences are in one sense radical in that they would involve great changes; but also conservative, in that they would bring a new authority and stability to the institutions of government in Britain.

These institutions are not merely instruments for achieving particular ends, but expressive of certain principles all the more tenaciously held for not being consciously articulated. In the past, the British electoral system reflected a sense of the importance of *locality* in politics, of the crucial nature of the link between the elector and his constituency representative; today it sustains a rigid form of party government which hampers the expression of local interests in politics; while the absence of any place for the referendum or any other instrument of direct democracy has meant that there has been, hitherto, no place for the people in the British Constitution.

For a political system to work effectively the dominant institutions in it must be congruent with contemporary social attitudes. The formalisms of the British Constitution are expressive of a society in which authority was seen to flow easily and unquestioningly from governments and political leaders. But a society in which authority resides in the electorate, and legitimacy is conferred primarily by popular election, can function successfully only if it adapts itself to the consequences, however delayed, of universal suffrage and the spread of education.

The incongruity between the principles of the constitution and the values of society is clearly displayed in the recent behaviour of the electorate. For as the political parties have become more ambitious in their claims and more exclusive in their organisation, so voters have ceased to identify with their aspirations, seeing them as narrow sects concerned as much with self-preservation as with the public good. This divergence between social attitudes and the aims of the parties has potentially serious consequences for the future of British democracy. But it also poses a challenge to those disturbed by the decline of the Westminster model of parliamentary government, once a model to be imitated, today an example to be avoided. The challenge is to show how political reform can restore the traditional virtues of the British system of government. This book is an attempt to meet such a challenge.

II

The approach adopted here is a broadly historical one. For neither constitutional principles nor political attitudes can be understood without grasping their roots in the historical experience of a society, which dominates the attitudes of the contemporary politician even when he is least aware of it. We begin therefore in Part I with an account of the struggle to introduce the referendum into British politics and the conflict which it revealed between two different conceptions of democracy. This historical analysis will enable us in Part II to appreciate the role and constitutional status of the referendum, and the scope for using it in the future.

Then we shall consider in Part III the history of the debate on the electoral system, apparently terminated in 1931, but revived by the two general elections of 1974 and by a critique casting that system as a prime cause of the country's economic decline. Part IV discusses the British electoral system and the radical alterations in its mode of operation in recent years. Part V considers various alternative electoral systems, usually classified together as forms of 'proportional representation', but in fact highly dissimilar, and productive of very different political effects. We conclude by examining the case for electoral reform as a precondition of political stability and economic progress.

III

We begin, however, with the Victorian debate. The great Reform Acts of the nineteenth century made it inevitable that Britain would become a democracy. Although the extension of the franchise stopped short of universal male suffrage – until 1918 only about 60 per cent of adult males had the vote – yet opponents of reform rightly saw the Act of 1867 as a 'leap in the dark' towards democracy. For once the principle of franchise extension was accepted, there was no logical resting-place short of 'one man, one vote': and the fourth Reform Act of 1918, which introduced universal male suffrage, raised few of the passions of earlier Acts since its inevitability was everywhere acknowledged. Even women's suffrage, once violently disputed, was easily settled when the vote was given to women over thirty in 1918, and to those over twenty-one ten years later.

Yet, however inevitable the extension of the franchise, there was no agreement on the shape which democracy should assume in Britain. For reform of the suffrage did not determine the structure of British government or the nature of the institutions through which democratic values were to be expressed. There was no consensus under the new dispensation on the roles of the electorate, the political parties and the two Houses of Parliament. Between 1867 and 1911, it was still possible to believe that Britain would retain a bicameral legislature rather than an effectively unicameral one; that the referendum would be introduced to resolve constitutional disputes; and until 1918 that proportional representation would be adopted – for it was not until then that Parliament decided, almost without being aware of it, to retain the plurality system of election.

The years between 1867 and the end of the First World War were marked by a wide-ranging debate on constitutional fundamentals – given life and force by the extension of the franchise yet focussed not on whether democracy was desirable, but on how it could be made to work successfully. It was an essentially practical debate which sought to show how the dangers of democracy could be minimised and its benefits ensured.

To the mid-Victorians, Parliament was the centre of the political universe. The supremacy of the House of Commons, claimed Gladstone in 1879, was 'the cardinal axiom' of the constitution.[2] It was therefore natural to ask how the widening of the franchise would affect it and whether parliamentary government could survive the rise of mass parties. For in stimulating party feeling, the extension of the suffrage generated a qualitative as well as a quantitative change in the working of British politics, making the Cabinet rather than the House of Commons the main initiator of legislation, and the electorate rather than the Commons the key factor in the choice of a government.

The period between 1846 and 1867 had been the golden age of

parliamentary government when the House of Commons genuinely made and unmade ministries. There were party divisions in the Commons, but no genuine party system of the kind that has dominated British politics since 1867. Instead the government was composed of a coalition of shifting groups, whose support often had to be gained afresh on each issue.

From 1867, however, aided by the vividly contrasting personalities of Gladstone and Disraeli, politics polarised and two parties – Conservative and Liberal – competed for the favours of the electorate through party programmes, admittedly of a highly generalised kind. Governments came to be formed as a result of a general election rather than parliamentary manoeuvering or coalition-building. The dominant role in the preparation of laws passed from the Commons to the Cabinet which eventually was to gain a nearly exclusive power in initiating legislation.

Under the rule of democracy, the control of government, in the view of Radicals such as Joseph Chamberlain, ought to pass from the Commons to the electorate. Parties should appeal to the voters on the basis of particular programmes which would bind their actions in government. MPs should be under an obligation to support all the items in their party programme for the electorate could be assumed to have endorsed them all. In this way the voter would gain more influence over government policy, but the role of Parliament would be further diminished.

The Whig leader, Lord Hartington, although rejecting this extreme view, nevertheless insisted that the electorate must be consulted on matters involving constitutional change; and he complained in the debate on the first Home Rule Bill in 1886 that Gladstone had failed to do this:

> Although no principle of a 'mandate' may exist, I maintain that there are certain limits which Parliament is morally bound to observe, and beyond which Parliament has morally not the right to go in its relations with the constituents. The constituencies of Great Britain are the source of the power, at all events, of this branch of Parliament: and I maintain that in the absence of an emergency that could not be foreseen, the House of Commons has no more right to initiate legislation – of which the constituencies were not informed, and, as to which if they had been so informed, there is, at all events, the very greatest doubt as to what their decision might be.[3]

The Cabinet, to amend Lowell,[4] was now to make laws not so much with the advice and consent of the Commons, as with the advice and consent of the electorate; and paradoxically, the power of the electorate was enhanced when a Liberal government was in power, since until 1911 the House of Lords, dominated by Conservative peers, could compel the abandonment of legislation, such as the second Home Rule Bill in 1893, which it believed was contrary to the wishes of the electors.

Thus the strengthening of party government had profound consequences for the development of British institutions, undermining the Whig/Liberal doctrine of parliamentary government – that Parliament was an autonomous, sovereign body free from outside interference or control. Whig/Liberal rhetoric presupposed a House of Commons composed of MPs who formed their own views without undue influence from government, party or constituency pressures. Moreover parliamentary sovereignty could guarantee rather than threaten individual liberty, because it already embodied those checks and balances necessary for good government. A Commons composed of shifting groups would be vigilant in watching the executive while the House of Lords could check a Commons majority whose pretensions outran its discretion. But could these checks and balances be maintained under a system of party government in which the government controlled the Commons and limited the powers of the Lords? Of what value was the sovereignty of Parliament if it turned out to be no more than the sovereignty of party?

Much of the debate on constitutional reform between the second and fourth Reform Acts – between 1867 and 1918 – can be seen as an attempt to define the place of party in the British Constitution and to limit the authority of party government. The debate revolved around two themes – the role of the electorate in deciding political issues, and the need for safeguards against the 'tyranny of the majority'. Paradoxically it was not always the radicals who would champion greater popular participation while conservatives pressed for safeguards. For many conservatives argued that greater popular participation would itself form a safeguard against the abuse of power since the electorate was basically hostile to change: so they championed the referendum as a weapon against the unlimited sovereignty of a potentially tyrannical House of Commons. And some radicals argued that the electoral system led to a concentration of executive power against which safeguards were needed: so they favoured proportional representation in order to ensure the representation of minorities as a counterbalance to majority tyranny.

Advocates of both these reforms were hostile to the dominance of party in British government. The referendum offered an opportunity to challenge this dominance through an appeal to the people; while proportional representation would allow minorities such as Liberal Unionists and Unionist Free Traders to retain their distinctive political position while remaining with their party. The debate on the constitution, therefore, was also a deeply political debate.

If the conflict over the referendum and proportional representation was fundamentally one about the role of party in British government, the dominance of party was confirmed by the passage of the Parliament Act in 1911, effectively undermining the possibility of introducing the referendum, and the defeat of proposals for electoral reform in the 1918 Reform

Act. That dominance continued unchallenged until political events in the 1970s reopened the debate which so agitated the Victorians and Edwardians in the years when popular government was about to come of age.

Part I

The referendum, 1890–1980

. . . look at Switzerland – where the referendum is used and always in a Conservative sense.

That's my idea of Tory Democracy, which you will see was very different from Randolph's.

A. J. Balfour

INTRODUCTION

How were the 'people' – the newly enfranchised electorate – to exercise their power: solely through representative institutions, or through the machinery of direct democracy? This was a central issue in the constitutional debates of the years between 1890 and 1912.

The first major advocate of the referendum in Britain was the great constitutional lawyer, A. V. Dicey, in 1890, and he was supported by other Liberal Unionists who sought to use it to prevent Irish Home Rule. Then in 1903 and 1904, Joseph Chamberlain proposed that the referendum be used for a different purpose, to press forward his programme of Tariff Reform against the inertia of his parliamentary colleagues. Unionists[1] began to urge that the referendum be introduced as a permanent part of the machinery of the Constitution; and during the long constitutional crisis of 1909–11, the referendum formed a central ingredient in many of the proposals put forward for a settlement.

In 1910 the Unionists formally committed themselves to the referendum and indeed fought the general election of December 1910 upon the principle that major constitutional changes should be put to the people before becoming law. At the time it seemed that the referendum had already become an accepted part of the British Constitution. St Loe Strachey, editor of the *Spectator* and one of the leading advocates on its behalf, wrote 'I never remember any proposal so wide as that for the Referendum making way so rapidly'.[2] When Arthur Balfour, the Unionist leader, came out in support of the referendum in November 1910, Dicey told Strachey, 'That it will come into existence is now morally certain. This is one of the instances where words are acts.'[3] However, it was not to be. The victory of the Liberals and their allies in the general election of December 1910 signified defeat for the advocates of the referendum, and the constitutional crisis was settled not by adopting the machinery of direct democracy, but by the Parliament Act of 1911 through which the supremacy of the House of Commons was given statutory recognition.

DICEY'S VIEWS

It is a remarkable paradox that it should have been the deeply conservative jurist Dicey who was the first to ask the question, 'Ought the referendum to be introduced into England?' in the *Contemporary Review* of April 1890. For in his classic *Introduction to the Study of the Law of the Constitution*, first published in 1885, he had attempted to codify the central doctrines of the British Constitution; and foremost amongst these doctrines was that of the sovereignty of Parliament which was 'from a legal point of view the dominant characteristic of our political institutions'.[4]

It might have been thought, therefore, that, both ideologically as a conservative, and doctrinally as a believer in the sovereignty of Parliament, Dicey would be hostile to so radical an innovation as the referendum, the effect of which might be to devalue the authority of Parliament; and yet he welcomed it. The explanation is to be found in the difficult political position in which Dicey found himself in the 1890s. He had broken with Gladstone in 1886 on the issue of Irish Home Rule, but continued to regard himself as a Liberal, seeing no reason why his allegiance should be determined by this one issue. For he believed that not only was the electorate opposed to Home Rule, but that even Liberal voters were doubtful as to its merits. Gladstone had converted the Liberals to Home Rule through force of personality, and through his command over the party machine; but he had not won over the minds of Liberals, much less their hearts. Yet, with the Liberal Party captured by Home Rulers, the swing of the electoral pendulum would be bound to bring to power a government claiming a mandate for a policy which the majority of the electorate heartily detested.

The battle over Home Rule revealed to Dicey and to other constitutionalists crucial weaknesses in the British system of government. There was, above all, 'The possibility . . . which no one can dispute of a fundamental change passing into law which the mass of the nation do not desire . . .,'[5] for one of the corollaries of the doctrine of the sovereignty of Parliament was that 'There is under the English constitution no marked or clear distinction between laws which are not fundamental or constitutional and laws which are fundamental or constitutional.'[6] A bill establishing a Home Rule Parliament in Dublin, which in other countries would require some special procedure of validation, could in Britain be passed by the Commons with the same ease as a bill to regulate hours of work in factories. Britain alone amongst representative democracies lacked any guarantee of constitutional protection of a kind which countries with written constitutions seemed to enjoy.

Until the extension of the franchise, however, this had been more of a theoretical lack than a felt defect. For the parliamentary structure contained a built-in check preventing the hasty enactment of fundamental change in the shape of the House of Lords, whose function it was to veto ill-considered legislation passed by a transitory majority in the Commons.

The sovereignty of Parliament was by no means the same thing as the sovereignty of the House of Commons, and 'influences . . . which have lost their power have until recent times, in practice though not in law, maintained a distinction between laws which affect the Constitution and laws which deal with matters of everyday life'.[7]

With the coming of popular government, however, these influences counteracting the power of the Commons were inevitably weakened. A government returned after a general election would naturally claim that it enjoyed a mandate from the electorate, and the Lords would be enjoined not to interfere with its work. The intensification of party loyalties meant that the supremacy of the Commons would become merely a cloak for the authority of government: for power would lie not with MPs but with the party leadership and organisation. This was a feature of British government which classical writers such as Mill and Bagehot had gravely underestimated, and it cast doubt on many of their conclusions. Writing to Dicey towards the end of his life, his old friend James Bryce commented:

> The tendency to groups is a deadly bacillus in modern legislatures. When one re-reads Mill's 'Representative Government' are you not struck by the fact that he did not anticipate the development things have taken and the discredit into which legislatures have fallen?[8]

The dominance of party had so altered the House of Commons that, already by 1890, it had 'ceased to be a body of men to whom the electors confide full authority to legislate in accordance with the wisdom or the interests of members of Parliament. It is really a body of persons elected for the purpose of carrying out the policy of the predominant party'.[9] The increasing importance of party might seem no more than an inevitable accompaniment of the coming of popular government were the House of Commons genuinely representative of the electorate: for then the Member of Parliament, although no longer a Burkean representative, would have become an agent of the people. But the very machinery of party which undermined the traditional role of the House of Commons also ensured that the Commons now represented only a distorted conception of the popular will, because of the rise of the party caucus and the development of wide-ranging political programmes. This served to undermine the authority of the elector. In theory, admittedly, the elector might appear supreme, since the parties in courting his vote and presenting their programmes would seem to be tacitly accepting that no major changes could take place without the consent of the electorate. In practice, however, the voter was able to offer a judgment only on the general political colour of the government; he could not, except in very rare cases, make his views felt on particular issues.

The judge who should direct a jury that they could not properly give a verdict upon a most difficult case, unless they at the same time gave a verdict on twenty others as difficult, would not be allowed to remain a day longer upon the Bench. But the behaviour which would argue madness in a judge when asking for the verdict of a jury, is considered the wisdom or astuteness of politicians when appealing to the verdict of the country.[10]

Because governments claimed that they enjoyed a mandate from the electorate, they felt justified in carrying out major changes, even though these changes were in reality contrary to the wishes of the bulk of their party supporters, let alone the electorate as a whole. Thus not only did British government come to operate without any constitutional check on its actions, there was not even a guarantee that its policies would represent popular wishes. For the very party organisations necessary for the effective working of representative government tended to frustrate its purpose by giving power to unrepresentative oligarchies.

The conclusion which Dicey drew from his analysis was the urgent need for some form of constitutional protection such as was available to other countries, some power which could act as a countervailing force to the dominance of party. To prescribe a written constitution with 'guarantees' of fundamental rights was, however, anathema to him for it would interrupt the flow of British constitutional development by substituting something rigid and artificial for institutions which were adaptable and elastic.

The great advantage of the referendum for Dicey lay in its being a *democratic* check upon the excesses of popular government. It was therefore an instrument which suited the spirit of the age. The referendum offered to the electorate a veto over bills passed by Parliament; and just as the monarch had, until the eighteenth century, enjoyed such a veto, so now this right would pass to the electorate which would become in effect a third chamber, an illustration of the process through which 'the prerogatives of the Crown' would be transformed 'into the privileges of the people'.[11] Opponents of the referendum who believed that it would undermine the traditional role of Parliament were, in Dicey's view, lacking in a sense of reality. They treated parliamentary government as it ought to have been, not as it actually was. Parliament's role had already been undermined by the growth of party, and if the legislature was no longer composed of Burkean representatives, then it was foolish to argue against the referendum on the grounds that it weakened the standing of Parliament or the individual MP. On the contrary, knowledge that the electorate would have the right to pronounce upon a bill might encourage MPs to seek improvements in legislation so that it became more acceptable to the electorate. If this happened, it would lead to an increase and not a decrease in the influence of the MP, and of Parliament. Indeed, claimed Dicey, 'it is conceivable (wild though the idea appears) that the power of reasoning might become a force of some slight moment again in practical politics'.[12]

Sir Henry Maine, in his book *Popular Government*, published in 1885, had argued that an appeal from Parliament to the people was one from knowledge to ignorance, but this too was implausible provided that the role of the electorate was restricted to voting on a bill already passed by Parliament. Voters would have no right themselves to initiate legislation; they could therefore only act as a check upon government, and not as originators of policy. The referendum might even have an educative role to play since it encouraged the elector to decide public issues upon the weight of the argument, and not on the basis of party loyalties – it enabled him to distinguish men from measures.

While, therefore, popular government might well not be a particularly desirable form of government, arguments such as those of Maine were now irrelevant; they showed why popular government should be avoided; they did not show how to deal with its excesses once it had arrived: and political arrangements which worked perfectly well under a limited franchise might be wholly unsuited to a new dispensation. 'Personally', declared Dicey,

> I think that I should have preferred real Parliamentary government as it existed up to 1868. But I have not the remotest doubt that under the present condition of things sham Parliamentary government means a very vicious form of government by party, and from this I believe the referendum may partially save us.[13]

Dicey's espousal of the referendum displayed many of the themes to be prominent in later discussion. The referendum was advocated less to encourage popular participation than to secure constitutional protection. It supplied 'the best, if not the only possible, check upon ill-considered alterations in the fundamental institutions of the country', and it was 'the only check on the predominance of party which is at the same time democratic and conservative'.[14] Its motive force stemmed less from a theoretical belief in the sovereignty of the people than from distrust of representative institutions, and especially the party system. The referendum would be a powerful weapon against the wire-pullers in local constituencies, for it denied the fundamental premiss of the Radicals that victory in a general election yielded a mandate for specific legislation. It was 'the one available check on the recklessness of Party leaders', and would give 'formal acknowledgment of the doctrine which lies at the basis of English democracy – that a law depends at bottom for its enactment on the consent of the nation as represented by the electors'.[15] That Parliament ought to reflect the will of the people was for Dicey the central constitutional principle lying behind the rule that what the Queen in Parliament enacted was law; and so the referendum was 'an emphatic assertion of the principle that the nation stands above parties'.[16]

In the 1890s, however, Dicey's arguments made little practical headway; for Home Rule could be defeated without the aid of the referendum. It was true that, as Dicey had feared, the Liberals were returned to office in the general election of 1892, but they were dependent for their parliamentary majority upon the support of the Irish Nationalists; and this deprived the Liberal government of its moral authority with regard to Home Rule. In the event a Home Rule Bill was passed by the Commons, but massively rejected in the Lords by a vote of 419 to 41. Gladstone's Cabinet colleagues would not allow him to dissolve Parliament on this issue, and Home Rule was abandoned, to remain in abeyance for nearly twenty years.

THE REFERENDUM AND TARIFF REFORM

The next instance of support for the referendum came, most unusually, from a politician who sought to use it to hasten action, rather than veto it – Joseph Chamberlain. For in launching his campaign for Tariff Reform in 1903, Chamberlain too found himself muzzled by the ties of party. The Unionists contained a strong minority Free Trade faction, and the Unionist leader, Arthur Balfour, mindful of the need to hold the Party together, claimed that he lacked a mandate to introduce Tariff Reform. He refused to go any further than advocating 'retaliation' as a compromise policy which he hoped might reconcile conflicting views in the Party. Chamberlain, believing that public opinion was on his side and could be mobilised against a timid party leadership, asked in November 1903 why it was

> that we have never adopted the principle of the Referendum. . . . It is the only way in which the decision of great national questions can be separated from all the complicated issues of party government. At a General Election the voter is influenced partly by his desire to see his own party in office, and partly by his views on a number of special questions, many of them purely local or even personal. . . . If, in the case of a new policy, not necessarily political, it were possible to eliminate all side issues, we might have a national verdict which all sections would accept, and which would be given without reference to the perennial struggle between the 'outs' and 'ins' which is at present the chief occupation of political life.[17]

'This party system of ours', Chamberlain declared at Gainsborough in February 1905, was 'very good at times . . . but in times of crisis like this it is utterly out of place.'[18]

Balfour's government, however, refused to initiate a referendum, and the result of the general election of 1906 seemed to show that public opinion was hostile to Tariff Reform; indeed many Unionists held the Tariff Reformers responsible for the Liberal landslide. Implicitly accepting this estimate, the Tariff Reformers turned against the referendum which, paradoxically, came to be championed by the Free Traders as a means of assuring the electorate that it could vote for a Unionist administration without being committed to Tariff Reform; and after 1906 the referendum was to be the weapon of the Unionist Free Traders against the 'whole-hoggers', as the full-blooded Tariff Reformers came to be known.

THE DOCTRINE OF THE MANDATE[19]

It was during the long constitutional crisis caused by the House of Lords' rejection of Lloyd George's 'People's Budget' in 1909 that the referendum was most intensively advocated and discussed. Its supporters were mainly, although by no means exclusively, Unionists, and they sought to use it for a number of different and conflicting purposes which were not always clearly distinguished.

Unionist advocacy of the referendum stemmed from the doctrine of the specific mandate, the notion put forward by Lord Salisbury and other Unionist leaders that laws were morally acceptable only if they enjoyed the specific approval of the electorate. The originator of the doctrine was Disraeli, and the claim was first made when, in 1868, he objected to Gladstone raising the issue of the disestablishment of the Irish Church in the Commons without having first brought it before the country. Disraeli denied the 'moral competence' of Parliament

> to do that without an appeal to the nation . . . You cannot come, on a sudden, and without the country being the least informed of your intention, to a decision that will alter the character of England and her institutions. . . . Technically, no doubt, Parliament has power to do so. But, Sir, there is a moral exercise of power as well as a technical, and when you touch the principles on which the most ancient and influential institutions are founded, it is most wise that you should hold your hand unless you have assured yourselves of such an amount of popular sympathy and support as will make your legislation permanent and beneficial.[20]

The disestablishment of the Irish Church was, Disraeli told the Queen, 'too grave a question to be decided upon without the opinion of the nation being taken'.[21]

Gladstone found this doctrine 'most extraordinary', 'ultra-democratic . . . anarchical . . .',[22] but his victory in the general election of 1868 gave him authority to legislate. Lord Salisbury urged the Lords to accept the disestablishment of the Irish Church, since 'when the House of Commons is at one with the nation'[23] the Lords should give way. The implication, of course, was that where a measure had *not* been put before the electorate, the Lords would be perfectly justified in rejecting it; and this was indeed Salisbury's view:

> there is a class of cases small in number, and varying in kind, in which the nation must be called into council and must decide the policy of the Government. It may

be that the House of Commons in determining the opinion of the nation is wrong; and if there are grounds for entertaining that belief, it is always open to this House, and indeed it is the duty of this House, to insist that the nation shall be consulted. . . . We must decide . . . whether the House of Commons does or does not represent the full, the deliberate, the sustained convictions of the body of the nation.[24]

It was this doctrine which was to form the basis of the Conservative Party's defence of the constitutional role of the Lords until 1911.

Lord Derby, however, did not share Salisbury's view that Gladstone's bill disestablishing the Irish Church should be meekly accepted by the Lords; for it was only the general principle of disestablishment, and not the bill itself, which had been before the country in the general election. 'The Bill now before your Lordships', Derby claimed, 'was never before the country . . . Indeed . . . it would seem that many of its provisions were studiously kept back.'[25] Derby's view was not that the electorate should be enabled to pronounce on legislation before it was introduced into Parliament, but that it was entitled to ratify legislation *after* a bill altering the 'fundamental law' of the country had been passed: and it was in this form that the doctrine of the specific mandate came to be held by the Conservatives.

For the argument in its original form as adumbrated by Disraeli could always be met simply by the Liberals notifying the electorate of the 'fundamental' change in question by putting it into their election programme; they could then claim, if they won the election, that this change had been endorsed by the voters. So the Conservatives were unwilling to concede that a general election yielded a mandate to introduce legislation into the Commons. Indeed it was the Liberals themselves who adopted this doctrine. They claimed that, provided an item had been part of the election programme, endorsement by the electorate should of itself be sufficient to disarm parliamentary opposition: as the Radical Henry Labouchere put it,

The Democratic creed was that there ought to be very frequent elections – say, once every three years; that certain measures ought to be submitted to the people at those elections; that there should be a *plébiscite* with regard to them; and that if the people made up their minds that they should pass, the Ministry representing the majority, having received an imperative mandate to carry them through, discussion was therefore useless.[26]

Thus, the Liberals were able to claim a mandate for the whole of their programme, although many of the individual items would have been rejected by the electorate in referendums.

The Conservatives, then, were on shaky ground if they accepted the implications of Disraeli's approach, by agreeing that a general election gave the victorious party a mandate to introduce the legislation prefigured in its election programme; they were happier with Derby's contention that 'fundamental' change required ratification by means of a general election before it could become law. The Conservatives, moreover, had an instrument to hand to force acceptance of this doctrine – the House of Lords, which could ensure the reference of 'fundamental' changes to the electorate; thus the doctrine of the specific mandate could be used to justify the pretensions of the Lords in forcing a dissolution of parliament. This was indeed the justification of the action of the Lords in 1893 in rejecting the second Home Rule Bill. Believing that there was no majority in the country for Home Rule, the Lords challenged Gladstone to dissolve and to prove them wrong. This challenge, however, was one which Gladstone's Liberal colleagues, implicitly accepting the Lords' estimate of the views of the electorate, preferred not to take up; and by refusing to dissolve they seemed to confirm the constitutional propriety of the Lords' action.

The development of the doctrine of the specific mandate reflected an important shift in the attitude of those Conservatives who had formerly been hostile to democracy. Amongst mid-Victorian critics of democracy, Lord Salisbury had been pre-eminent both for the force of his convictions and the vitriolic way in which these convictions were expressed. To place supreme power in the hands of the people was, in his view, to give it to the ignorant, the emotional and the propertyless, and it would herald the end of civilised government. But, having lost the battle to defeat the 1867 Reform Act, Salisbury was forced to come to terms with the advent of popular government, and he came to believe that the people were in reality sounder at heart than their representatives. It was the voters rather than their institutions, so easily perverted by 'That organiser of decay, the Radical agitator',[27] who would provide the bulwark against radicalism and the pretensions of the Left.

This belief had been the hallmark of 'Tory Democracy' which had long resisted the Whig identification of the wishes of the people with the decisions of the House of Commons. The Commons, according to Disraeli in his *Vindication of the English Constitution*, published in 1835, was merely an estate of the realm, the most important estate of the realm perhaps, but nothing more. Those whom society had invested with legislative functions were trustees and not masters:

> There was a time when our kings affected to rule by divine right. It cost our fathers dear to rout out that fatal superstition. But all their heroic labours will prove worse than fruitless, if the divine right of kings is to be succeeded by the divine right of the House of Commons.[28]

Disraeli's romantic conception of an alliance between Crown and People against a predatory Whig Parliament was easily transmuted in later Conservative thought to a scepticism over the pretensions of representative institutions, and a willingness to allow the voice of the electorate to be heard in the consideration of legislation.

Nevertheless, Salisbury's doctrine of the specific mandate was by no means logically watertight. It was as much a partisan ploy as a serious constitutional doctrine. For, since the House of Lords was dominated by the Conservatives, the right to force a dissolution in compliance with the doctrine was in practice a right to be enjoyed only against governments of the Left, against Liberal governments. In Sir Charles Dilke's words, 'The claim of Lord Salisbury to force us to "consult the country" is a claim for annual Parliaments when we are in office, and septennial Parliaments when they are in office.'[29]

Moreover, the doctrine of the specific mandate in the form in which it was adopted by the Conservatives was very unclear: for even if a Liberal government were to accept a challenge laid down by the Lords, dissolve parliament and secure an election victory, the Liberals could never be justified in claiming that they had won the election *because of*, rather than *in spite of* the contentious legislation in question. It would hardly ever be possible to show that the electorate had unequivocally supported a specific item of legislation. For Salisbury, this was part of the charm of the doctrine:

> The plan which I prefer is frankly to acknowledge that the nation is Master, though the House of Commons is not, and to yield our own opinion only when the judgment of the nation has been challenged at the polls and decidedly expressed. This Doctrine, it seems to me, has the advantage of being: (1) Theoretically sound, (2) popular, (3) safe against agitation, and (4) so rarely applicable as practically to place little fetter upon our independence.[30]

The specific mandate doctrine did not immediately lead the Conservatives to advocate the referendum, as perhaps it should have done. For, as advocated by Dicey, the referendum was a device to allow the Conservatives' opponents, divided by Home Rule and by much else, to hold together in government despite these divisions. It could not be in the interests of the Conservatives to encourage that. The purpose of the specific mandate doctrine was not to increase the cohesion of the Liberal Party, but to justify the right of the Conservatives, via the House of Lords, to force a dissolution. Thus the referendum began as a doctrine not of the Conservatives, but of the Liberal Unionists, and it came later to be espoused primarily by the Unionist Free Traders, a minority within the Unionist Party; while the Unionist leadership, when it eventually came to advocate the referendum, did so much more hesitantly and for a different purpose. The referendum was a doctrine for politicians at odds with their party: the specific mandate was a doctrine for Conservatives anxious to turn out a Liberal government.

THE REFERENDUM AND THE CONSTITUTIONAL CONFERENCE

It was the practical employment of the doctrine of the specific mandate which, in 1909, precipitated a constitutional crisis lasting until August 1911 when the powers of the House of Lords were restricted by statute through the Parliament Act. In 1909, the Unionists resisted the traditional constitutional principle that the House of Lords had no right to reject a money bill, by bringing into play a moral principle more suited in their view to the age of popular government – the principle that changes of the magnitude proposed in Lloyd George's Budget should not become law until the electorate had been given the opportunity to pronounce upon them. Lord Lansdowne, the Unionist leader in the Lords, moved *not* the rejection of the Budget but rather its referral to the people via a general election. His motion declared that the Lords would not be 'justified in giving its consent to this Bill, which contains provisions of a dangerous and unprecedented character, until it has been submitted to the judgment of the country'. In the draft of the motion, in Arthur Balfour's papers, rejection of the Budget has been explicitly altered to referral by substituting the words 'until it has' in the motion for the words 'and has not' in an earlier draft.[31]

The Liberals met this challenge by restricting the power of the Lords to reject legislation; through the Parliament Act of 1911, they converted the absolute veto of the Lords into a two-year suspensory veto on all bills except money bills, over which the Lords were to lose their legislative veto entirely. But, before introducing the Parliament Bill into the Commons, the Liberals sought a compromise which might produce an agreed settlement. The death of Edward VII in May 1910 and the accession of a new and inexperienced monarch was made the occasion for a 'truce of God', and Liberals and Unionists came together in a Constitutional Conference which met from June to November 1910. The two parties were represented by their leaders in the Commons and the Lords, Asquith and Crewe for the Liberals, and Balfour and Lansdowne for the Unionists, together with the Chancellor of the Exchequer, Lloyd George and the Chief Secretary for Ireland, Augustine Birrell, and Austen Chamberlain and Lord Cawdor for the Unionists.

At this conference, the main Unionist contribution to the resolution of the constitutional crisis was to recommend the use of the referendum as part of the regular machinery of government. But the Unionists were not clear as to the proper function of the referendum nor did they agree upon specific proposals. Both at the conference and subsequently until the Parliament Act was passed they put forward a number of different proposals, and the difficulties involved in disentangling them have confused both contemporary observers and historians.

The basic problem which the conference had to resolve was how a disagreement between the two Houses was to be settled. Two methods were proposed. The first was the referendum, championed by Balfour and Lansdowne and by Birrell, the junior member of the Liberal delegation. This method would allow the Commons to retain its supremacy in cases of dispute with the Lords, provided that the Commons could secure the support of the electorate: and the government, which would have to initiate the referendum, would retain the option of seeking a compromise with the Lords or dropping legislation where it did not believe that popular approval would be forthcoming. This method would also offer to the Unionists a check upon the untrammelled power of the Commons to replace the absolute veto of the Second Chamber. But, not surprisingly, Asquith, Lloyd George and Crewe objected to a settlement which meant that in practice only Liberal bills would be referred; and Austen Chamberlain was hostile to the introduction of a weapon which could be used by the Unionist Free Traders to block Tariff Reform. So use of the referendum to resolve deadlocks between the two Houses did not command sufficient support to secure inter-party agreement, and the Unionists dropped the proposal; although in April 1911, in the first ever debate on the referendum in the Commons, George Cave, on behalf of the Unionist opposition, moved an amendment to the Parliament Bill providing for a referendum on a non-financial bill three times rejected by the House of Lords.[32] This too, given the large Unionist majority in the Lords, would have meant a one-sided use of the referendum and the Liberal Government could not accept it.

The alternative method of resolving deadlocks was by a joint sitting of representatives from the two chambers, and agreement was reached surprisingly easily on this proposal, although the precise representation of each House at such joint sittings was to remain a matter of contention. The Unionists, however, were unwilling to accept that this method be used to resolve *all* disagreements between the two Houses. For, thinking of Home Rule, they were unwilling to admit that even the most sweeping Liberal victory in a general election could possibly yield a mandate for so radical a change.

They insisted, therefore, that a special category of 'constitutional' legislation should be distinguished for which some safeguard over and above that of joint sittings must be found; and it was on this issue that the Constitutional Conference ultimately foundered. The Liberals could not agree that Home Rule, the constitutional proposal which the Unionists had in mind, should be submitted to a referendum. For the Irish Nationalist Party, upon whom the Liberals depended for their parliamentary majority, had made their support conditional upon the placing of Home Rule on the statute book, and would not allow the introduction of a new type of veto in the form of a referendum to interfere with this process.

At the Constitutional Conference, Asquith declared himself unwilling to draw any distinction between 'ordinary' and 'constitutional' legislation. He

> stated the difficulties – difficulty of defining 'constitutional questions' where there was no written constitution, difficulty of selecting a tribunal to decide on disputed cases, danger of producing a deadlock over nearly the whole field of legislation by the width of our definition.[33]

The Liberals were prepared to concede that some special procedure should be adopted for the passage of the coming Home Rule Bill, which both Asquith and Lloyd George saw 'as the real crux of the situation', but they were prepared to do this only on an ad hoc basis. They were not willing to agree that this special procedure, whatever it might be, should be made applicable also to future Home Rule bills; nor were they prepared to introduce any permanent procedure for a specified class of legislation labelled 'constitutional', a proposal which to Lloyd George meant 'bringing in the judicature to settle what was and what was not organic. He regarded the position and power of the Supreme Court in America as wholly alien to the spirit of our constitution.'[34]

The magnitude of the task facing the Constitutional Conference was truly daunting: it was attempting 'nothing less than to convert the immemorial unwritten into a written constitution';[35] and, given the irreconcilable nature of the division over Irish Home Rule, it is hardly surprising that it broke up without reaching agreement. The conference had, however, exposed the dilemmas inherent in the Conservative Party's espousal of the referendum: how was the distinction between 'constitutional' and 'ordinary' legislation to be drawn if the referendum was to be confined to 'constitutional' issues; and why should it be only Liberal legislation which would run the risk of being referred by a solidly Conservative and partisan House of Lords? If the referendum was to be made more generally acceptable, therefore, the Unionist would have to show either that the House of Lords could be reconstituted so as to eliminate the permanent Conservative majority (Lord Lansdowne was to attempt this, unsuccessfully, in his House of Lords Reconstruction Bill in 1911), or they had to show that the referendum was capable of being used fairly and impartially between the parties without wholesale reconstruction of the Lords. This was the path taken by Balfour when in November 1910 he pledged that the issue of Tariff Reform would be put to referendum by a future Conservative government.

BALFOUR'S PLEDGE

The Liberals' response to the breakdown of the Constitutional Conference was to secure guarantees from George V that, if they could win another election, the monarch would agree to the creation of enough peers to overcome Conservative opposition to the Parliament Bill. Armed with these guarantees, the government dissolved Parliament and called a second general election for December 1910. On 29 November, four days before the voters went to the polls, Arthur Balfour, speaking at the Albert Hall, promised that a future Unionist government would not introduce Tariff Reform without putting the issue to the people, and urged the Liberals to do the same with Irish Home Rule. This was an attempt to secure Free Trade support for the Unionists in the general election of December 1910, and to divert attention from the issue of Peers versus the People. It also had the 'inestimable quality', in Beatrice Webb's view, of delivering him 'from the domination of a political sect that has got hold of the caucus. . . . It is the last move in his duel with Chamberlain; it is a final checkmate to tariff reform.'[36]

The Unionist proposal, put forward at the Constitutional Conference, that the referendum should be used only when the two Houses disagreed would mean that in practice only Liberal measures would be put to referendum. Balfour's Tariff Reform pledge, however, promised a referendum even when the two Houses did agree, thus giving the electorate the power to alter an agreed decision of Parliament. This would mean that the referendum could be used to veto Unionist as well as Liberal measures. Balfour's hope was that this would make the referendum more credible as part of the normal working machinery of government.

The Unionists did not, however, succeed in winning the December 1910 general election, and Balfour's pledge was repudiated by Bonar Law, his successor as Conservative leader, in 1912.

LORD BALFOUR OF BURLEIGH'S BILL

The next attempt made by Unionists to show that the referendum could be introduced under conditions which would be fair to both parties was undertaken by Lord Balfour of Burleigh who introduced his Reference to the People Bill in the House of Lords in March 1911. Balfour of Burleigh was a staunch Free Trader who had resigned from Balfour's government in 1903 because the Prime Minister had refused to disavow Joseph Chamberlain's Protectionist programme. He had watched with dismay Chamberlain's capture of the party machine which had made it almost impossible for a Unionist Free Trader to be adopted as a Conservative candidate, and therefore had a strong motive for wishing to see a counterbalance to the power of party in British politics.

Balfour of Burleigh's Bill provided for the use of the referendum in two situations: the first was, as in the Cave Amendment, in the case of deadlock between the two Houses; the second would occur when 200 members of the House of Commons petitioned the Crown for a bill to be referred. The purpose of this second provision was, of course, to disarm Liberal criticism by ensuring that Unionist as well as Liberal legislation would be put to referendum. The figure of 200 was designed to deter calls for a referendum by a small minority of MPs, but it would ensure that all government legislation would be potentially subject to the referendum unless, as in 1906, the main opposition party numbered less than 200 in a House of over 700 members. The opposition would not, Balfour of Burleigh believed, seek to use the referendum in a frivolous way since it would be humiliated if defeated upon a referendum which it had itself requested. Nor would use of the referendum necessarily be frequent; the government of the day, before introducing its legislation, would have to consider carefully whether it would survive an appeal to the people, and it would not introduce legislation which would be unable to meet this challenge. The referendum, therefore, would act as a deterrent only to unpopular measures.

Balfour of Burleigh's Bill would have allowed the referral to the electorate of any measure without restriction of subject. It did not require any distinction to be drawn between 'constitutional' and 'ordinary' bills, which would 'have this crowning disadvantage, that it would necessitate the creation of some tribunal to decide whether or not any particular Bill came within the category'.[37] It therefore avoided difficulties which Asquith and Lloyd George had noticed at the Constitutional Conference.

But what Balfour of Burleigh was proposing involved a radical transformation of the British Constitution; in the words of Lord Crewe, 'a more abrupt departure, a wider deflection from the Constitutional path on which we have marched in this country for the last 600 years, than almost any other measure which could be proposed'.[38] For the British Constitution, as it was developing during the first decade of the century, was coming to be one in which an omnicompetent government, sustained by the Commons, could be checked only in a general election. Under Balfour of Burleigh's proposal, on the other hand, there would be a new constitutional firmament comprising three elements – Commons, Lords and electorate, any two of which could check the other. It would be a revolutionary change whose consequences were so wide as to be incalculable.

It is not surprising, then, that Balfour of Burleigh's Bill failed to make headway in the Lords. It was opposed not only by the Liberals, but also by the Unionist leadership, frightened of its implications and fearful of the opposition of Tariff Reformers – who realised that Balfour of Burleigh's Bill would give 200 backbenchers the right of initiating a referendum on the Tariff even after a Unionist government committed to Tariff Reform had been returned at a general election. During the debate on Balfour of Burleigh's Bill, Lord Cromer, a prominent Unionist Free Trader, was quite explicit about the link between the referendum and the rejection of Tariff Reform. With the referendum,

> the country would then have to choose between a Liberal Government purged of Home Rule and a Unionist Government purged of Tariff Reform. My Lords, from the point of view of a Unionist Free Trader, nothing could be better.[39]

Balfour of Burleigh told St Loe Strachey, another Unionist Free Trader, who had been busy behind the scenes promoting the Bill (and who in 1924 was to write a book *The Referendum* commending the principles behind it),

> It is quite clear that the Tariff Reform interest was stirred up into active opposition. . . . I am confident that private pressure was brought upon the Front Opposition Bench to abstain from saying anything in support of the Bill. This was partly on account of its supposed Free Trade origin and partly from genuine dislike of some of its provisions.[40]

The result of this pressure was that Balfour of Burleigh was persuaded to withdraw his Bill.

Reflecting upon the experience, Strachey came to the conclusion that the referendum was unlikely to be secured by the method which he and Balfour of Burleigh had pursued. It was unlikely to be brought into existence as the result of a general measure, but would probably be the result of an ad hoc decision. 'I have always felt', he wrote to Lansdowne,

> that it is very unlikely we shall get this (i.e. as a general measure), because I cannot help noticing that we have never introduced reform in that way. The natural way it seems to me for the Referendum to come would be to have it applied at first occasionally and ad hoc to particular Bills, and for it then to gradually grow into a custom of the constitution. Therefore as one who believes intensely in the Referendum I feel we can only get it through what I admit is the awkward plan of mixing it up with a particular measure.[41]

Strachey's prediction was a prescient one, as the introduction of the referendum in the 1970s was to show.

LORD LANSDOWNE'S PROPOSAL

The 'particular measure' which seemed an obvious candidate for 'mixing up' with the referendum was, of course, the Parliament Bill being prepared by the Liberal Government which would transform the Lords' absolute veto into a suspensory veto. Strachey had hoped to persuade the Lords to embarrass the Liberals by passing the Parliament Bill subject to referendum, but Lansdowne refused to countenance this. Lansdowne was sympathetic to the use of the referendum in the case of deadlock between the two Houses, but the Parliament Bill should be the subject of a general election which, in his view, would perform the same function as a referendum. Despairing at Lansdowne's failure to grasp the argument for the specific mandate, Strachey pointed out to him that a general election had certain defects as a referendal instrument. There could be no guarantee that the general election would be restricted to this one issue: and, under the existing electoral law, the distribution of MPs following a general election did not seem to bear any precise relationship to the distribution of votes: indeed it was possible for a minority of voters to return a majority of MPs. So the result of the general election could not possibly provide a mandate for any particular line of policy – that in fact was the whole case for the referendum. In Strachey's view, therefore, Lansdowne was 'imperilling our cause by admitting in any shape or form that a general election can be regarded as a referendum'.[42] The validity of Strachey's contention was borne out by the result of the general election of December 1910 which the Liberals claimed gave them a mandate to proceed with the Parliament Bill, a claim which the Unionists were of course unwilling to grant.

The Unionists therefore had to develop in some haste an alternative policy to that embodied in the Parliament Bill. They decided at last to propose officially that the referendum be made part of the regular machinery of government, despite the fact that the result of the general election had made this proposal irrelevant. The referendum had to serve the *raison d'être* of Unionism by ensuring that the Liberals would be unable to carry Irish Home Rule without being required to secure popular endorsement. But, if the Unionist leadership was to avoid antagonising the Tariff Reform interest, the referendum could not be made applicable to financial legislation. The particular shape taken by the referendum proposal was therefore determined by these essentially political requirements.

The Unionists reverted to the distinction between 'ordinary' and 'constitutional' legislation which they had attempted to draw at the abortive Constitutional Conference. They now sought to be more specific about which legislation was to be regarded as 'constitutional' and which 'ordinary'. In an amendment to the Parliament Bill, supported by Balfour, the Unionists proposed that the following categories of legislation be excluded from its operation, that is from the suspensory veto, until after a referendum:[43]

A Bill which

(a) affects the existence of the Crown or the Protestant Succession thereto; or

(b) establishes a National Parliament, or Assembly, or a National Council in Ireland, Scotland, England or Wales, with legislative powers therein; or
(c) affects the constitution or powers of either House of Parliament or the relations of the two Houses one to the other

would require validation by referendum in cases of disagreement between the two Houses. Later, a fourth category, the franchise or the distribution of seats, was added to this list.

Bills falling within these categories could be deemed to be 'constitutional' because they involved changes in the machinery by which laws were made, rather than simply changes in the laws themselves. These changes in machinery required, so the Unionists argued, some special protection over and above that which the Parliament Act would provide.

For the government, Winston Churchill, the Home Secretary, argued that these categories were not really as precise as they seemed. In reality, whether a particular bill did or did not fall under one of the specifications would be a matter for interpretation.

> Although they appear fairly definite on paper [Churchill argued], I think there is no doubt whatever that disputes and questions would arise in connection with almost every one of the categories he has placed on the Paper, which would require for their solution the intervention of a judicial body of some kind or other.[44]

The Unionists attempted to meet this objection when a similar amendment was proposed in the Lords. Lansdowne proposed that whether a bill was 'constitutional' or not could be decided by a new 'Joint Committee' which it was proposed to establish, consisting of the Lord Chancellor, the Speaker of the Commons, the Chairman of Committees in the Lords, the Chairman of Ways and Means in the Commons, a Lord of Appeal, other peers of Parliament who had held high judicial office, together with appointees of the Speaker, making a total of fifteen members in all.[45]

This was of course a crude and desperate attempt to patch up a proposal whose implications had not been clearly explored. It did not require great penetration to see that the 'Joint Committee' would be in effect a third Chamber of Parliament able to override the government of the day and ignore the verdict of a general election. Given that the appointees from the Lords to the Committee would be predominantly Unionist, it would require only a small Unionist contingent from the Commons for the Committee to be able to act as an arm of the Unionist Party in constitutional disputes. Thus the Committee would acquire some of the functions of a Supreme Court without being properly equipped by virtue of its composition to play such a judicial role.

Furthermore the Unionist proposal involved a one-sided use of the referendum. At least under Balfour of Burleigh's Bill, the referendum might be expected to operate fairly between the main political parties. The

Unionist proposal, however, meant that in effect only Liberal measures which were held to be 'constitutional' would be referred to the electorate. There was no inducement for the Liberals to accept a new check upon their party programme when the whole point of the Parliament Bill was to remove an existing check.

THE REFERENDUM AND ITS FUNCTIONS

The issue of the referendum, then, was made to serve a number of very disparate purposes during the constitutional crisis of 1910–11. It was proposed by the Unionists with no less than four different aims in mind.

The first was as a new method of resolving deadlocks between the two Houses, an *alternative* to the Parliament Bill. The Unionists would accept the Liberal case that the Lords should not be able to force a dissolution, provided that they would be allowed to force a referendum instead. The Liberals, however, were in the process of removing one check upon reforming governments – the absolute veto of the Lords: they had no intention of allowing the Unionists to establish another in the form of the referendum.

The second function which the referendum might have served for the Unionists was as a *supplement* to the Parliament Act, so that certain measures of a 'constitutional' kind could be exempted from its working and reference to the electorate would be obligatory. This proposal, as we have seen, involved constitutional complexities of a daunting kind, and seemed to require the construction of a 'rigid' constitution of the American type, with a Supreme Court; it was hardly an issue to be decided upon by means of an amendment to the Parliament Bill on behalf of a party which had lost the last three general elections.

But behind the constitutional debate, there lay the crux of the political conflict – Irish Home Rule. The Unionists hoped to use the referendum to prevent the passage of Home Rule without some further appeal to the people. The Parliament Act ensured that no appeal to the people via a general election need take place, so long as Home Rule was presented by the end of the second session of Parliament; therefore the appeal to the people had to take the form of a referendum. But the Parliament Act was also part of the price which the Liberals were paying to the Irish Nationalists for their parliamentary support; and the Nationalists made it clear that the removal of the Lords' veto must not be followed by the introduction of a new popular veto against Home Rule. So that conception of the referendum also fell victim to the political realities.

The third use of the referendum was one intended to assist in securing a Unionist electoral victory by disengaging the party from the incubus of Tariff Reform. J. L. Garvin, the editor of the *Observer*, although himself an ardent Tariff Reformer, pressed Balfour to make his Albert Hall pledge, arguing that the key to victory in the general election of December 1910 lay in the abandonment of Tariff Reform. Was it worthwhile to take the risk of jeopardising the House of Lords, the Constitution and the Union with Ireland, all for the sake of Chamberlain's 'Great Policy'?

Balfour's referendum proposal, however, not only alienated the powerful Tariff Reform wing of the party, thereby contributing to the attacks on his leadership which were to gain momentum after the election defeat; but the transparently tactical nature of his approach discredited the use of the referendum as an instrument of government. Even on its own terms, moreover, the idea of a referendum on Tariff Reform was not without problems. For Balfour's pledge did not make clear whether a Unionist government would institute a referendum *before* negotiating with the colonies on preference or *after* negotiations had been completed, to ask the electorate to ratify the agreement which had been reached. In fact Balfour was on the horns of a dilemma: the first alternative would have infuriated the Tariff Reformers still further, while the second would have infuriated the colonial negotiators. The idea of a referendum on the tariff was not, therefore, very convincing, and Balfour's commitment served only to embarrass his party.

The most wide-ranging proposal for the use of the referendum as a regular part of the machinery of government had come from Balfour of Burleigh. His bill attempted to demonstrate that the referendum could be used fairly as between the two great parties of the state; and that it would fulfil an important constitutional need by providing a necessary check upon the power of party government.

The paradox was, however, that to secure this constitutional stability, it would be necessary to implement a constitutional revolution; and it is hardly surprising that the bill proposing such a revolution, introduced by a backbench peer whose highest political office had been Secretary for Scotland, should make little headway.

Here also there were deep political antagonisms which shaped what could seem like a purely constitutional issue. Balfour of Burleigh's Bill was an attempt to reorientate the Constitution so that it gave more weight to moderate opinion rather than that of the activists who, in his view, dominated the two parties. It is no coincidence that many of the most eager protagonists of the referendum – Balfour of Burleigh himself, St Loe Strachey, Dicey and Lord Hugh Cecil – were Unionist Free Traders. They faced the dilemma in 1910 that whichever party they supported in the general elections, radical change – either Home Rule or Tariff Reform – would result, although they believed that there was a moderate consensus amongst the electorate which wanted neither. Introduction of the referendum would enable them to continue supporting the Unionists without jeopardising their Free Trade beliefs. Strachey told Lansdowne what an immense relief it was for him

to be back again whole-heartedly with my party, for I never admitted that I had left the Unionist Party, though I felt obliged in 1906 to vote against it. The adoption of the Referendum has lifted a great weight off my mind. Curiously enough the Referendum will have the effect, not of injuring the party system in the good sense, but of helping it.[46]

But, by the same token, the party activists were lukewarm about the referendum, and strong enough to prevent its adoption. For Tariff Reformers such as Chamberlain, the forces of moderation and consensus were also the forces of negativism, responsible for Britain's industrial decline and unable to reverse it. The Tariff Reformers were in politics to secure radical change, not to entrench the status quo; and as Dicey noticed, 'every party which wishes to force its own will upon the nation detests this particular reform'[47] (i.e. the referendum). Since the Unionist Free Traders had already lost the battle for control of the Unionist Party, it was unlikely that they would be able to win upon the new ground on which they had chosen to fight. The Tariff Reformers refused to countenance the introduction of the referendum except for the very limited uses which Lansdowne proposed for it. The referendum might perhaps have been acceptable to a traditionalist and conservative Unionist Party in 1911; but then a traditionalist and conservative Unionist Party would not have taken the radical step of rejecting the Liberal Budget of 1909, and thus triggering off the constitutional crisis.

The Unionists, therefore, were unable to secure a consensus within the party on the proper use of the referendum; and their advocacy frequently gave the impression of political opportunism rather than a considered response to the constitutional crisis. For this reason, Unionist proposals failed to arouse a widespread response in the country, and they did not succeed in convincing the electorate – nor perhaps even themselves – of the value of the referendum.

CONFLICTING CONCEPTIONS OF DEMOCRACY

The years 1909–11 seemed to many to be a turning point in Britain's constitutional evolution, marked as they were by a bitter struggle between the Liberal Government and its Unionist opponents over the proper role of the House of Lords. But the conflict was about more than the Second Chamber. It embraced also two different conceptions of the working of democracy: and the resolution of the conflict not only confirmed the subordinate status of the Lords, it also ensured that the role of the people in government would be negative.

For, however much the approach of the Unionists was one of expediency, there was a real constitutional issue at stake to which they had drawn attention; and the consequences for the development of British institutions of a Unionist victory in the constitutional crisis could have been far-reaching and profound.

How were representative institutions to be made properly accountable in an age of popular government? This was the basic issue which divided the parties, and the crisis was as much a conflict between different conceptions of democracy as it was a battle between the Peers and the People.

'We all of us start', claimed Asquith in the Second Reading debate on the Parliament Bill,

> from one common point – the assumption which lies at the root of representative government that the House of Commons, itself a product of popular election, is, under normal conditions, a trustworthy organ and mouthpiece of the popular will.[48]

But it was precisely this assumption which Unionists denied. That the Commons represented the popular will was for them not an assumption, but something which required proof.

> . . . I draw the widest possible distinction [Salisbury had argued] between the opinions of the House of Commons and the opinions of the Nation. . . . that the House of Commons is the expression of the opinion of the Nation is a constitutional fiction which it is convenient for practical purposes to respect.[49]

Because they could not appreciate the force of the Unionist position, the Liberals saw it as *merely* tactical, which it was not.

The Liberals' identification of 'representative government' with the supremacy of a House of Commons chosen by the plurality method of election was not, however, wholly plausible. Indeed, the position adopted by the Liberals had no less of tactics in it than that of the Unionists. For the Liberals sought to claim that a general election gave them a mandate to implement the whole of their programme, even though there was no reason to believe that the voters had given their support to all of the policies in the programme. Foremost amongst the unpopular policies was Home Rule, which would have stood little chance under a referendal system of the kind proposed by the Unionists whereby specific mandates were required for particular items of policy.

The Liberal view, then, begged the question of whether a verdict in favour of a particular party in a general election was also a verdict in favour of all the items in that party's programme. It also begged the question of whether the House of Commons was genuinely representative. Indeed, many of the arguments used in favour of the referendum could also be used to support proportional representation; and a number of

Unionist advocates of the referendum – such as Balfour of Burleigh, Strachey and Lord Hugh Cecil – were also members of the Proportional Representation Society.

The Unionists, however, came too late to the referendum to be able to hope for success. Admittedly, some Unionists had toyed with it before 1910, but the proposal had not been treated as a matter of urgency, since it was believed that the House of Lords would better serve the interests of the party. As one Liberal peer noticed, the referendum before 1910 played the same role for the Unionists, as God had done for Falstaff:

> When Falstaff thought he was dying he said
> 'God! God! God!' and Mrs Quickly saw
> there was no need to think of God yet.[50]

The referendum was a necessity only when the absolute veto of the Lords was dying, but not before. Had it been worked out in advance as part of a programme of reform aimed at preserving popular influence in the age of the party machine, the referendum might have received the benefit of a more serious and dispassionate appraisal. It would have appeared as a genuine instrument of constitutional reform, and not as the tactical device of an electorally discredited party.

THE REFERENDUM, 1911–1945

The Parliament Act of 1911 decided the question against advocates of the referendum, and it ceased to be a major issue in constitutional debate until, in the 1970s, the Common Market came to divide the parties as Home Rule and Tariff Reform had done earlier. The referendum was, however, proposed on a number of occasions in the intervening years in an attempt to paper over political differences.

During the controversy over women's suffrage in the first two decades of the century, the anti-suffragists seriously considered whether they ought to call for a referendum on the issue. Lord Curzon, a leader of the anti-suffragists, composed a memorandum in February 1913, entitled 'Woman Suffrage and the Referendum' in which he debated this question. His conclusion, however, was that a referendum would be unlikely to end the controversy. If it was to be confined to men, and produced a majority hostile to women's suffrage, this would not bind the suffragists; while if women were allowed to vote on the issue, men might not accept the result.[51]

Nevertheless, Curzon did not entirely discount the possibility of a referendum. It might be necessary if women's suffrage passed the House of Commons when, through the operation of the Parliament Act, it would become law after three sessions if rejected by the Lords. At that stage the referendum would at least allow the issue to be referred to the electorate; and, during the passage of the fourth Reform Bill granting women over thirty the vote, 53 peers signed a memorial to *The Times* calling for a referendum on women's suffrage. In the event, however, the Bill passed comparatively smoothly through both Houses, and the demand for a referendum was not taken very seriously.

The next proposal to hold a referendum was made by Stanley Baldwin, leader of the Conservative Opposition, in 1930 as an attempt to secure a compromise on the issue of Protection. For, after their election defeat in 1929, the Conservatives were once again in danger of being split on Tariff Reform: as party leader Baldwin found his personal position under threat from the 'Empire Free Traders' under the leadership of Lord Beaverbrook, and for the sake of party unity, Baldwin acceded in March 1930 to a proposal by Beaverbrook that a referendum be held before a Conservative government introduced Protection.

Baldwin's promise was as full of ambiguity as Balfour's Albert Hall pledge had been. Did it mean that a future Conservative government would in fact campaign for Protection in the referendum? At what stage in the negotiations with the countries of the Empire would the referendum be introduced? Baldwin's purpose in proposing the referendum was to kill the Empire Free Trade movement, a movement which through its grass roots support in the Conservative Party was capable of removing him from the leadership. Beaverbrook, on the other hand, believed mistakenly that Empire Free Trade was now to become the official policy of the Conservative Party. Disillusioned, he complained in a speech at Hastings in May 1930: 'The Central Office appears to me to be using the referendum, not as a spear with which to fight for Empire Free Trade but as a shield behind which to shelter itself.'[52]

In the event the referendum pledge was abandoned in October 1930. It did not succeed in preserving party unity, and it was only the political ineptitude of the press lords and the hesitancy of the heir apparent, Neville Chamberlain, which enabled Baldwin to hold on to the Tory leadership.

Between November 1934 and June 1935, an unofficial, nation-wide, postal ballot was organised by the League of Nations Union – the so-called 'peace ballot' – designed to test the state of public opinion on matters such as support for the League, disarmament and sanctions against aggression. The ballot secured a response from 11.6 million voters, 38.2 per cent of the eligible electorate. It was, however, in no sense a scientific test of opinion, and the response was heavily weighted in favour of supporters of the League. The result of the ballot was widely held to have influenced the National Government's foreign policy, but its influence has almost certainly been exaggerated. Strictly speaking it was not a referendum, since it did not call upon the electorate to approve or reject a measure which had already been endorsed by the government, but more like an initiative, an attempt by a pressure group to press a particular line of policy upon a supposedly unwilling government. But it showed that such a method was hardly suited to securing clear decisions on fluid and complex issues of foreign policy.

Ten years later, the referendum was again to be proposed in a rather unexpected context. For, in May 1945, Winston Churchill sent a letter to the leaders of the Liberal and Labour parties suggesting that a referendum should be held to determine whether the wartime Coalition should be continued and 'the life of this Parliament should be further prolonged' until the end of the Japanese War. This proposal was rejected by the two Opposition parties. The Labour Party Conference, which was in session at the time, turned it down by a large majority, and Attlee replied in the following terms:

> I could not consent to the introduction into our national life of a device so alien to all our traditions as the referendum, which has only too often been the instrument of Nazism and Fascism. Hitler's practices in the field of referenda and plebiscites can hardly have endeared these expedients to the British heart.

Sir Archibald Sinclair, the Liberal leader, replied in more moderate if no less negative terms. The referendum, he claimed,

> would be an innovation in constitutional practice which has more than once been considered in times of political crisis and rejected for reasons which cannot lightly be set aside.

THE DECLINE OF THE REFERENDUM

The referendum had been advocated as a defensive weapon to prevent party fragmentation, whenever political differences arose which could not be accommodated within the party system.

Before 1914, the issue of Tariff Reform imposed a unique strain upon the Unionists. The Unionist Free Traders, with a small number of exceptions, were unwilling to desert their party or join the Liberals, since many of them – men such as Lord Hugh Cecil and Lord Balfour of Burleigh – were deeply opposed to Home Rule and to other Liberal proposals such as Welsh Disestablishment and House of Lords reform. The referendum, as we have seen, offered them a life-belt by which they could remain within the Unionist party while retaining their Free Trade convictions; and if they were right that Tariff Reform was unpopular with the electorate, it would allow voters to elect a Unionist government, safe in the assumption that they would be consulted again before a Tariff could be introduced.

The Unionist Free Traders did not, however, fully succeed in persuading the party to adopt the referendum as official policy, because the Tariff

Reformers were strong enough to resist it. The Tariff Reformers felt that party unity was best secured by driving the Unionist Free Traders out of the Unionist party, and, through their control over local Unionist constituency associations, were able to ensure that Free Traders were not adopted as Unionist candidates. For the referendum to have been made a permanent and central part of Unionist policy before the First World War, the balance of forces within the Unionist Party between the two factions would have had to be rather more equal than in fact it was.

Home Rule had been an equally divisive issue in pre-First World War politics. But in 1886 Gladstone and the Home Rulers succeeded in capturing the National Liberal Federation, and, after that, adherence to Home Rule became an essential test of loyalty for Liberal candidates. Liberal Unionists, therefore, were left with little option but to form a separate party. Had the referendum been recognised at that time as an appropriate constitutional weapon, they could have remained within the Liberal Party, and it would have been left to the electorate to decide between the two factions.

Before 1914, therefore, the two party machines were strong enough to prevent dissenters from seriously threatening their dominance. Dicey had argued that it was this very strength of the party machines which made the case for the introduction of the referendum so overwhelming. But, paradoxically, it was just because they were so strong that the referendum stood no chance of acceptance. The tighter the party system, the less need there was to accommodate differences of opinion, and the more the battle became one for control of the party machine, rather than a compromise between mutually contending factions.

After the First World War, the Labour Party came to replace the Liberals as one of the two great parties in the State. It was, officially at least, committed to the doctrine of socialism, and for many years the struggle between the Labour and Conservative parties was thought of by the party leaders as one between advocates of two opposed economic systems. Until the 1960s, politics was polarised around this cleavage, and other issues were subordinated to it. One of the premisses of socialism was that the policies required to secure it formed a total package the ingredients of which could not be separated and presented seriatim for inspection by the electorate. It was for this reason that most socialists were opposed to the introduction of the referendum. Ramsay MacDonald represented the feelings of the Labour Party when he claimed that the various policies of the party 'all fitted into one set of general progressive ideas'.[53] Socialism was not merely a set of disparate causes tied together – it was an organic creed whose components were not separable from each other. From 1922 onwards, therefore, the policies of one of the two major parties seemed interdependent and based upon an ideologically coherent set of principles. It was not until this ideological coherence seemed to be breaking down, under the impact of issues such as the Common Market, that the referendum again came to be seen as a useful weapon. Indeed the referendums on whether Britain should remain a member of the European Community, and on devolution to Scotland and Wales, were held because these issues divided the Labour Party in such a way that neither the Whips nor the party machine could resolve them in the manner that Home Rule and Tariff Reform had been resolved. In each case, the effect of the referendum was to enable the Labour Party to preserve its unity on what appeared to many of its MPs as subordinate issues, and thus to prevent a split of the kind which had so disrupted the Liberals in 1886. The referendum, as Strachey had predicted, enabled the party system to continue, but on a more flexible basis.

THE REFERENDUM AND THE EEC

In 1971, Edward Heath, as Prime Minister of a Conservative government, secured agreement amongst the other members of the EEC on the terms of British entry. His attempt to secure parliamentary acceptance of these terms revealed that the issue was one which could break up Britain's party system.

Home Rule had divided only the Liberal Party, and Tariff Reform only the Conservatives. The Common Market divided both major parties. The Conservatives seemed to be united on the issue, since their leader was so deeply committed to entry, and Heath let it be known that if the Commons rejected entry, his government would resign. But a number of Conservative MPs remained unreconciled, and these represented a substantial section of Conservative opinion in the country. Until 1974, Conservative opposition to the EEC on 'patriotic' grounds was led by Enoch Powell who, for a period following his utterances on immigration in 1968, found himself the most popular politician in the country. But other influential Conservatives were also sceptical of the benefits of entry. Speaking two days before the 1975 referendum, Edward Du Cann, the Chairman of the 1922 Committee, and one of the most powerful backbenchers in the Commons, said:

> Official Conservative policy it may be to remain a signatory of the Treaty of Rome, but the Conservative Party is divided too. The divisions may show much less than the split in the Labour party, which is now taking personal and bitter forms, but it is real none the less.
>
> It is muted for one good reason. The Conservative Party is naturally loyal to its leaders, past and present, and wishes to support them, or at least not to be seen to oppose them, whenever possible.
>
> Were this not so, I have no doubt that at least as many Conservative Party

members would be publicly seen to be against our remaining members of the EEC as are in favour. Perhaps there might even be a majority for withdrawal, for membership of the EEC is bound to offend against much of our history, and the consequent attitude of the Conservative Party.[54]

The Labour Party was more openly divided. The parliamentary leadership and much of the Right-wing of the party were, until 1970, broadly sympathetic to the EEC. The Left and the extra-parliamentary organs of the party, however, were strongly opposed to entering what it regarded as a 'capitalist' institution, while a number of Right-wingers led by Douglas Jay were hostile on pragmatic economic grounds.

It could not be denied, therefore, that there was a substantial body of opinion in the country which opposed entry. Yet in the general election of 1970, this body of opinion had no way of making its voice heard. For all three parties were officially committed to entry provided that suitable terms could be negotiated. The electorate, it appeared, would have no voice in what seemed to many the most important constitutional issue of the century, involving as it did the permanent transfer of legislative powers, including the power to tax, away from Westminister.

It was accepted by many pro-Marketeers that the success of Britain's participation in the Community could well depend upon the strength of popular support for entry. Edward Heath, who was strongly opposed to a referendum which he saw as an anti-EEC tactic, said, in Paris on 5 May 1970, that the 'full-hearted consent of the parliaments and peoples' of the new member countries would be necessary if enlargement of the Community was to be a success. But he did *not* say, as was frequently to be alleged, that the full-hearted consent of Parliament and people *in Britain* would be necessary, and at a press conference on 2 June 1970, he made it clear that in his view Britain's representative institutions were perfectly adequate instruments for securing the consent of the people to the Common Market.

I always said that you could not possibly take this country into the Common Market if the majority of the people were against it, but this is handled through the Parliamentary system.

The Conservative manifesto did not, however, propose to 'take this country into the Common Market', but stated 'Our sole commitment is to negotiate; no more, no less.'

Heath's remarks did not make it clear how 'the Parliamentary system' would necessarily reflect the state of public opinion on the Common Market. Indeed, if the opinion polls are to be believed, he succeeded in doing in 1972 what he had earlier declared to be impossible by taking Britain into the Common Market when a 'majority of the people were against it'. There was no constitutional mechanism, other than the referendum, which could prevent him from doing so.

THE LABOUR PARTY'S COMMITMENT TO THE REFERENDUM

Although the 1975 referendum came about as a result of a commitment made by the Labour Party, it was the Liberals who at their Assembly in 1969 were the first of the political parties to urge that a referendum be held on the EEC issue. They did so, although supporting Britain's membership of the EEC, because they believed that, given the deep divisions in the country on the issue, the referendum offered the only means by which these divisions could be resolved. For a vote in the Commons would not be accepted as final and morally binding by opponents of the EEC, and therefore was not capable of settling the question.

In the Labour Party, the demand for a referendum was first raised by Douglas Jay in August 1970, when he argued that 'where the constitution and the powers of Parliament itself were being altered, there was unique justification for a referendum *or* election'.[55] Jay, a leading anti-Marketeer, naturally hoped that the electorate would return a negative verdict on the EEC; but the case for a referendum was backed by Tony Benn, then still favourable towards the EEC, as part of a general programme for increasing popular participation in government. Until 1972, however, they were unable to secure the support of Labour's National Executive or Shadow Cabinet.

The argument was carried further by the publication of Philip Goodhart's book *Referendum* in 1971. Goodhart was a respected Conservative backbencher whose sympathies lay broadly with the pro-Marketeers; nevertheless he found it intolerable that the voice of the electorate was not to be heard on an issue of such fundamental importance. In his book he argued that the referendum, far from being an alien device suited only to Continental countries but irrelevant to Britain's problems, had a perfectly respectable place in Britain's political tradition, having been advocated by Conservative leaders such as Balfour, Baldwin and Winston Churchill. Further, he showed that referendums, far from being the plaything of dictators and demagogues, had been used by almost all democracies at some time or other without in any way weakening their parliamentary institutions. He demonstrated, therefore, that two of the central arguments against using the referendum in Britain were entirely without substance.

The introduction of the referendum into British politics, however, owed little to these arguments, but arose from seemingly fortuitous circumstances. It was the internal situation in the Labour Party rather than the force of the constitutional agreements which led to the EEC referendum. Indeed, the process by which it came to be adopted offers an excellent illustration of the unplanned way in which constitutional change occurs in Britain.

During 1970 and 1971, the Labour Party had firmly set its face against the referendum. In the general election campaign of 1970, Harold Wilson hotly denied that he would alter his position if the polls swung against the EEC. 'I'm not going to trim to win votes on a question like that . . . I shall not change my attitude on that.'[56] Tony Benn was unable to find a seconder in the National Executive Committee when he proposed a referendum in 1971; and the Labour Party Conference in that year rejected it by a majority of over 2 to 1.

On 14 March 1972, however, the Conservative anti-Marketeer Neil Marten put forward an amendment to the European Communities Bill providing for a referendum on the EEC, and this forced the Labour Party to make a definite decision on what course of action it should adopt. Accordingly, on 15 March, the Shadow Cabinet decided not to support the Marten Amendment. On the 16th, however, President Pompidou, for domestic political reasons, announced that a referendum would be held in France on whether Britain and the other countries seeking entry into the EEC should be admitted. Not only was Britain the only country of the four then seeking admission to the EEC (Britain, Denmark, Ireland and Norway) which would not be holding a referendum, but it now appeared that the French electorate would be offered the right denied to the British of determining whether there was 'full-hearted consent' for British entry.

The Labour Party's National Executive Committee met on 22 March, and, under the impact of the Pompidou decision, voted 13 to 11 in favour of a motion moved by Benn calling for a referendum, at a meeting at which Wilson, Roy Jenkins, the Deputy Leader, and James Callaghan, the Shadow Foreign Secretary, were absent. Two days later, Heath announced that, with the introduction of direct rule in Northern Ireland, a series of regular plebiscites on the border would be held; and on 29 March, the Shadow Cabinet approved by 8 votes to 6 (with two members, Denis Healey and Willie Ross absent) the referendum proposal. Wilson and Edward Short, soon to be Jenkins's successor as Deputy Leader, changed their 'No' vote of 15 March to a 'Yes' vote on the 29th. With the Parliamentary Labour Party also accepting the referendum, it had become official party policy.

The intention of the referendum commitment was to ensure the unity of the Labour Party, although the immediate effect was divisive. The Party's Deputy Leader Roy Jenkins resigned, together with two other members of the Shadow Cabinet, George Thomson and Harold Lever, and four junior spokesmen, David Owen, Dick Taverne, Dickson Mabon and Lord Chalfont. In his resignation letter to Harold Wilson, Roy Jenkins denied that the referendum would prove a unifying device – 'It would', he claimed, 'in my view be incomparably more damaging than any differences between us in the House of Commons.'[57] But this view was not in the long run borne out, and it is difficult to see how the Labour Party could have avoided being committed to withdrawal from the EEC if the leadership had not been prepared to accept the referendum. Nor could the Labour Government elected in March 1974 have been held together without the twin devices of the referendum and the suspension of collective responsibility on the Common Market issue.

Nevertheless, it would be wrong to attribute the EEC referendum solely to the internal difficulties of the Labour Party. For adoption of the referendum was also in harmony with feeling in the country that some form of popular endorsement of the EEC was necessary if the decision to enter was to attain legitimacy. Indeed, from February 1971 opinion polls had regularly shown large majorities in favour of a referendum on it.[58] Thus the Labour Party's commitment may have contributed to their two election victories in 1974: certainly it defused what could have been a deep populist resentment against politicians who were denying to the electorate the right to decide so central an issue.

THE 1975 REFERENDUM

The Labour Party fought the general election of February 1974 on the policy of renegotiating the terms of EEC membership accepted by the Conservatives; these renegotiated terms would then be presented to the electorate for approval either through a general election or a referendum. There having been two general elections in 1974, it was obviously unrealistic to hold a third; and therefore when the negotiations were nearly completed, in January 1975, Harold Wilson announced that the government proposed to hold a referendum, and to suspend the convention of collective responsibility on the EEC issue for the duration of the campaign. Seven Cabinet ministers, including Michael Foot and Tony Benn, were to take advantage of this provision.

The referendum itself was held on 5 June 1975. A total of 64.5 per cent of the electorate voted; and of those voting 67.2 per cent voted Yes, and 32.8 per cent No. The result was as follows:

Total electorate	40,456,877
Total voting	25,903,194
Spoilt papers	54,540
Yes	17,378,581
No	8,470,073
Majority	8,908,508

This was a convincing 'Yes' majority, and it was spread surprisingly evenly across different parts of the country, varying in mainland Britain between 55 and 76 per cent. In Northern Ireland the 'Yes' vote was only 52 per cent; but the Western Isles and Shetland were the only counting areas to yield a 'No' majority.

The result was regarded everywhere as an unequivocal endorsement of the EEC. 'It means', claimed Harold Wilson, 'that 14 years of national argument are over.'[59] David Watt, writing in the *Financial Times* declared that 'The Common Market issue is settled. By their unambiguous vote – the most overwhelming expression of popular will, certainly since 1931 . . . Secession is now politically inconceivable in this generation.'[60] And Tony Benn commented:

> I have just been in receipt of a very big message from the British people. I read it loud and clear . . . By an overwhelming majority the British people have voted to stay in and I am sure that everybody would want to accept that. That has been the principle of all of us who have advocated the Referendum.[61]

Nor did the referendum seem to have produced any harmful effects upon Parliament or indeed any other British institution. The divisions in the Labour Government seemed to heal rapidly, and it was able to turn its attention to the country's economic problems; whereas, according to Shirley Williams, 'The Government would have broken up if it had not been decided to hold a referendum.'[62]

Both the 'Yes' and the 'No' campaigns in the referendum cut across party lines: each campaign formed an 'umbrella' organisation to which public money was channelled. In the 'Yes' camp, members of the three main parties were compelled to work together, and found it, possibly to their surprise, an enjoyable experience. Amongst the 'Noes' patriotic Conservatives found themselves allied to trade unionists and to the Left wing of the Labour Party. Many of those who participated in the campaign, moreover, seemed not to have been previously involved in political activity. In their study of the referendum, David Butler and Uwe Kitzinger noticed that 'new personnel have been drawn into local political life, some of them already casting about for new causes in which to organize party co-operation, and also that certain personal bridges and some greater mutual understanding was built up across party barriers'. In the campaign 'several hundred thousand private individuals were prepared to give time, money and effort publicly to witness to their convictions'; and this was evidence of 'a certain public spirit at the grass roots that could also prove important for the future health of British democracy'. The urge to participate in political affairs was hardly being satisfied by the existing party organisations, and the referendum seemed to open up the possibility of a new style of politics based upon shifting coalitions formed to campaign on specific issues.

Within the umbrella organisations, there was inevitably some jockeying for position, and despite complaints of Communist or Trotskyist infiltration in local 'No' groups, many seemed to have found the experience an educative one.

Almost every group seemed to have come to 'the realisation how easy it was, with a little effort, to find common ground on a whole range of issues' that the other side was 'human (almost)' or that – as in Sussex – they could no longer 'regard each other as people with horns and tails'.

Some Conservatives participating in the 'No' campaign may well have gained greater understanding and sympathy for the role of the trade unions: one academic claimed that

I, for one, am more sympathetic now to the Labour Party and to organised trades unionism than I was before. Only someone as blinkered as Edward Heath could provoke into opposition people who are a good deal more loyal and patriotic than he is.

A lady from Norfolk is quoted as saying:

I have learnt one thing myself – that is that not all Trade Unionists are selfish left-wing extremists but are in many cases more patriotic than many a Tory and certainly as hard working as many employers! This is a minor revolution in my own philosophy.[63]

On the 'Yes' side, co-operation was even more pronounced, and it gave rise to a feeling in the country that more co-operation between politicians in different parties would be beneficial to the body politic. In the light of the consensus in favour of the EEC, many of the everyday party squabbles seemed rather unimportant. There seemed little to divide such leading supporters of the EEC as Roy Jenkins, William Whitelaw, Shirley Williams, David Steel and Edward Heath. Mrs Williams said during the campaign that she had never 'believed a coalition to be possible except in war. But I feel there is a need to be more sensible – not always to go in for the most slam-bang kind of politics.'[64] But the referendum in fact had little effect upon either the style of party politics or the working of British institutions.

If the result of the referendum was a victory for the 'moderates', it was a defeat for the 'extremists' and especially for Enoch Powell and Tony Benn, with whom the anti-Common Market cause had increasingly become identified. The claim of the Left wing of the Labour Party to 'speak for the working class' had been 'exploded in full sight',[65] and it was seen that the TUC, which had voted 2 to 1 in favour of withdrawal, did not represent the views of the organised working class either. In addition, the extra-parliamentary machinery of the Labour Party – Conference and the National Executive Committee – were seen to be less representative of

Labour Party supporters than the parliamentary leadership, since it was almost certain that a majority of Labour supporters had voted 'Yes'.[66] Moreover the fairly even spread of the 'Yes' vote across the whole of the United Kingdom seemed to show that fears of the break-up of the kingdom might be exaggerated. Scotland and Wales had both voted 'Yes', ignoring the advice of their respective nationalist parties; while Ulster ignored the advice of the United Ulster Unionists and their most prominent leader Enoch Powell by voting 'Yes' also.

It was, then, not difficult to understand how the referendum could appear as 'the most exhilarating event in British politics since the war', and 'a tonic for Britain and a tonic for Europe'.[67]

Yet a more detached analysis would have shown that such optimism was misplaced. For it can be seen in retrospect that the success of the 1975 referendum was due in large part to fortuitous circumstances, which would not be repeated in the referendum on Scottish devolution; and that the large majority voting for EEC membership was no indication that the British electorate had finally committed itself to the EEC.

The 1975 referendum resulted in a clear and indisputable outcome, thereby yielding the first condition for a successful referendum. Moreover, the result was the 'right' one from the point of view of the government of the day. The government was fortunate also in having the advantage of Opposition support; for Conservative hostility to the EEC was muted so as not to give offence to the party leadership or rub salt into the wounds of the recently deposed leader, Edward Heath.

If, however, the referendum had yielded a 'No' majority, there would have been a convulsion in British politics. Two Cabinet ministers – Roy Jenkins and Shirley Williams – had indicated that they would resign in such an eventuality, and Shirley Williams announced that she would leave active politics entirely. The Labour Left would have been given a powerful boost, and the authority of Harold Wilson and James Callaghan correspondingly reduced. The government would have been forced to the humiliating expedient of preparing legislation to take Britain out of the EEC, despite the fact that the majority of the Cabinet had strongly recommended remaining in the EEC. This would have involved breaking an international treaty obligation for a cause in which the majority of the Cabinet and the Commons did not believe.

Most embarrassing of all perhaps would have been a small 'No' majority on a low turnout. Would the government have been prepared to follow a policy which it believed harmful to British interests if the result of the referendum had been, say, 30 per cent of the electorate No, 29 per cent Yes? When proposing the referendum, Edward Short had indicated that 'The Government will be bound by its result, but Parliament, of course, cannot be bound by it.'[68] This was sound constitutional doctrine, but with a 30 per cent No, 29 per cent Yes result, would the Commons, containing a large majority of pro-Marketeers, have accepted a government proposal to withdraw from the EEC? If they had done so, it would have meant voting against their consciences, and taking a step they believed to be harmful to the country. If they had not, they could be accused of flouting the will of the people, and would lay themselves open to a populist campaign against the unrepresentativeness of Parliament. In either case the dilemma facing MPs would have been an unenviable one.

It was fortunate also that the referendum produced a fairly even 'Yes' vote across the country. If, as at one time seemed likely, there had been a 'Yes' vote in the United Kingdom as a whole but a 'No' majority in Scotland, the referendum would have given a powerful boost to the Scottish Nationalist Party, and it might have proved impossible to prevent serious conflict between Scotland and the rest of the United Kingdom. Indeed, if the government had clung to its original intention of having a single national count, rather than one based on counties, the SNP would undoubtedly have claimed that the overall 'Yes' majority masked a 'No' majority in Scotland. In the political climate of the mid-1970s, with support for the SNP growing until, in spring 1977, the polls showed it to be the most popular party in Scotland, that too could have had catastrophic results for the unity of the kingdom.

Six years after the referendum, it can be seen that the result was not the ringing endorsement of the EEC that it appeared to be at the time. Indeed, Butler and Kitzinger had offered a prescient warning, when they said of the verdict, that it was 'unequivocal, but it was also unenthusiastic. Support for membership was wide but it did not run deep.'[69]

In fact the referendum result had less to do with the supposed merits of the EEC than with other factors. The first of these was the general feeling that, whatever the merits or demerits of entry in 1972, Britain's economic position was now so precarious that to leave the Community would be to court disaster. Sir Christopher Soames summed up this mood in his warning that 'This is no time for Britain to consider leaving a Christmas club, let alone the Common Market.'[70] Remaining in the Common Market appealed to those forces of conservatism and passivity which so often influence election results in Britain, and frequently influence the results of referendums in countries where they form a regular part of the machinery of government. It was this conservatism and passivity which determined the result, and not an active desire for 'moderation' in politics or for coalition government. That is the main reason why the political alignments forged during the campaign proved to be so short-lived.

These attitudes were reinforced by the fact that the political leaders most respected by the electorate advocated remaining in the EEC. The anti-Marketeers had believed that they would be likely to win the referendum, but the 'No' majority in the opinion polls began to fall as soon as the government recommended acceptance of the renegotiated terms. Thirty-two per cent of those intending to vote 'Yes' believed that Britain had been wrong to enter the EEC – but 53 per cent of those polled believed that a 'No' verdict in the referendum would lead to an immediate political and economic crisis.[71] The 'leadership effect', whereby the electorate took its cues from those political leaders whom it trusted, was observed by Humphrey Taylor who, as head of the Opinion Research Centre, conducted polls for the pro-Marketeers. He argued that the lead of pro-Marketeers in the campaign was large but fragile. Many voters were weakly committed to the EEC and potentially fickle in their allegiance. He noticed 'the enormous importance of the leadership effect. One strong card in our hands now is that the major public figures advocating EEC membership are relatively popular while those advocating leaving the EEC are relatively unpopular.' A private poll conducted for the Britain in Europe campaign showed that in a list of the twenty best-known politicians, the thirteen pro-Marketeers each attracted a high 'respect and like' rating, while the anti-Marketeers in general received a negative rating, with the maximum dislike being aroused by Tony Benn, Ian Paisley and Enoch Powell.

This meant that the referendum campaign gradually came to be identified as a struggle of 'moderates' against 'extremists', and in such a struggle there could not be much doubt where the allegiance of the British electorate would lie. 'We must focus attention', Taylor argued, 'on Paisley, Clive Jenkins, Jack Jones and Scanlon.' This meant that the 'moderate' case for leaving the Common Market, which could have been put by politicians such as Douglas Jay and Neil Marten, was submerged amidst fears of 'extremism', of a Britain dominated by politicians who profoundly frightened the electorate. The main hope of the anti-Marketeers would have been to develop a populist campaign against the 'Establishment', but this was not possible for ministers such as Tony Benn and Michael Foot who were already part of the government and dependent upon the Prime Minister; nor for the Conservative anti-Marketeers who would have to rebuild their bridges with the party leadership as soon as the referendum was over.

Humphrey Taylor admitted sadly that the pro-Marketeers had 'not managed to generate much enthusiasm or to appeal successfully to more idealistic motives'.[72] Six years after the referendum, a large number of Labour MPs, perhaps the majority, would like to see Britain leave the EEC, and in 1980, the Labour Party Conference voted for withdrawal without a further referendum; while, after Margaret Thatcher's further renegotiation of Britain's budget contribution in 1979–80, the possibility of Britain's withdrawal is no longer the great unmentionable which it used to be for many Conservatives who now realise that in becoming the 'European' party it has lost part of its natural 'patriotic' constituency. Public opinion is again hostile, as it was before 1975. It is, therefore, by no means beyond the bounds of possibility to imagine a government taking Britain out of the EEC at some time in the future.

Thus the 1975 referendum did not, as many then imagined, settle the issue of British membership. It did not even defuse the issue for very long. For in the immediate aftermath of the referendum, there came the debate over direct elections to the European Assembly, and this allowed the anti-Marketeers to continue the argument in another form; while in the autumn of 1978 James Callaghan raised the issue of Britain's excessive budgetary contribution to the EEC in such a manner as to offer comfort to the anti-Marketeers in the Labour Party. Clearly, the one lesson which could not be drawn from the referendum result was that the British electorate had decided to make a permanent and binding commitment to remain with the EEC.

THE REFERENDUM AND DEVOLUTION

The Labour Government had been insistent that the referendum on whether Britain should remain within the EEC was a unique and unrepeatable event. In January 1975, Harold Wilson, Edward Heath and Edward Short all agreed that the referendum was 'unique', and the preface to the White Paper *Referendum on UK Membership of the European Community* declared, 'The referendum is to be held because of the *unique* nature of the issue . . .'[73] When the referendum was over, a Conservative backbencher, Sir John Eden, asked Wilson

> Will he keep to his determination not to repeat the constitutional experiment of the Referendum?

and the Prime Minister replied,

> I certainly give the Right Honourable Member . . . the assurance he seeks.[74]

The nature of the uniqueness of the EEC issue was explained by Gerry Fowler, a junior minister in the Labour government:

> I have made absolutely clear that in my view and that of the Government, the constitutional significance of our membership of the EEC is of a quite different order from any other issue. It is not just that it is more important; it is of a different order. There is, and there can be, no issue that is on all fours with it. That is why we say that this issue is the sole exception, and there can be no other exception to the principle that we normally operate through parliamentary democracy.[75]

The defect of this argument, however, had been exposed by Roy Jenkins when he resigned from Labour's Shadow Cabinet in 1972. He repudiated the claim that the referendum on the EEC would be unique:

> Who can possibly say that? Once the principle of the referendum has been introduced into British politics it will not rest with any one party to put a convenient limit to its use.[76]

Within just 18 months of the EEC referendum, the Labour Government was forced as a result of backbench pressure to concede referendums on devolution in Scotland and Wales to secure passage of its legislation through Parliament. The devolution referendums, like the EEC referendum, were proposed to avoid a split in the Labour Party; but whereas the EEC referendum had been proposed by the party leadership, the devolution referendums were forced on the Labour Government by dissident backbenchers anxious to defeat a major item of government legislation without driving the government out of office or condemning it to loss of face.[77]

In its October 1974 election manifesto, the Labour Party had committed itself to the establishment of directly elected assemblies in Scotland and Wales. In Scotland, devolution was an attempt to undercut the SNP by offering a moderate alternative which reconciled Scottish autonomy in domestic affairs with her continued membership of the United Kingdom. Welsh devolution was a response to pressure from the Labour Party in Wales which had sought an elected Welsh Council since 1965. The attitude of the Labour Party in Wales made it politically difficult to propose an assembly for Scotland without offering Wales one also. Fearing, however, that a number of Welsh Labour MPs were opposed to the party's commitment, the government introduced its proposals in 1976 in a bill covering both countries – the Scotland and Wales Bill. This had the effect of preventing the Welsh dissidents from voting against Welsh devolution unless they also wished to destroy the Scottish Assembly and since, at that time, it was widely thought that setting up a Scottish Assembly was the only way of containing the SNP, this would not be a popular option.

The referendum was an instrument which would enable the Welsh dissidents to defeat the government's stratagem. They could vote for the Scotland and Wales Bill in Parliament, but then campaign against it in the referendum in Wales. Thus the Labour Government would secure its legislation, Scotland could have her assembly – it was at this stage thought unlikely that Scotland would fail to endorse devolution – and Wales could honourably reject it.

Thus the referendum was proposed by Labour backbenchers intent on killing Welsh devolution. They asked the obvious question. If it was right to hold a referendum on the EEC, should one not also be held on devolution which was equally a major constitutional issue, and a policy which, if not irreversible in theory, would be nearly so in practice. The EEC referendum had created a precedent for the Welsh dissidents by making the device available to them. Had there been no referendum on the EEC, it would probably not have occurred to the anti-devolutionists to suggest one: certainly they would not have been successful in pressing what would have appeared as a radical constitutional innovation.

The Labour Party in Wales attempted to distinguish devolution from the EEC by claiming that devolution, unlike EEC membership, was a manifesto commitment. On the EEC, Labour's commitment had been to hold a referendum. But

> On devolution, Labour's manifesto commitment is to go ahead with its policy, just as it was with the Industry Act, the Community Land Act, the Nationalisation of Aircraft and Shipbuilding, and all the other policy commitments in the manifesto.

The Welsh Labour Party then went on to draw the obvious implication:

> The question of a referendum involves issues much wider than devolution. The introduction of Government by referendum would be a complete reversal of our whole system of Government. Once this principle was accepted, then any party could call at any time for a referendum on any controversial proposal. Those who advocate a referendum must accept the full implications of this change, and must be aware that any radical changes proposed by a Labour Government – whether extensions of public ownership or abolition of the 11-plus – would have to overcome this new hurdle before being carried out. In effect, Clause 4 of the Party Constitution would have to be rewritten 'To secure for the workers by hand or brain the full fruits of their industry' etc. – SUBJECT TO REFERENDUM.[78]

The Welsh Labour Party, echoing Radical arguments at the end of the nineteenth century, was claiming that victory in a general election gave the winning party a mandate to carry out all the items in its programme. The presumption was that they had all been endorsed by the electorate. But the devastating defeat of the Wales Act in the 1979 referendum was to show that this presumption was without foundation.

On the Second Reading of the Scotland and Wales Bill in December 1976, the Prime Minister, James Callaghan, announced that the government had not yet made up its mind whether to hold a referendum. But his hand was forced by an amendment put down by Leo Abse, MP for Pontypool, inviting MPs not to approve the Second Reading unless a referendum clause was added to the Bill. This had attracted 80 signatures by the time the Second Reading debate began, and offered a threat to the safe passage of the Bill.

The government, therefore, conceded a referendum, and a referendum clause itself was finally introduced on 10 February 1977 amidst scenes of procedural chaos rarely seen in the Commons. Backbenchers on both sides of the House bitterly objected to the tactical manoeuvre by which the proposal for a referendum was being introduced as a new clause on an already published bill in order to overcome opposition to it. Was this not establishing a precedent which could be used on any bill when a government found itself in difficulties; and if so, did not this represent a wholly unwarrantable increase in the power of the executive?

The referendum would achieve its effect by allowing opponents of the Bill to vote for it in Parliament – thereby, in the view of many MPs, who found it an unedifying spectacle, making a mockery of parliamentary responsibility. 'It is', said Malcolm Rifkind, one of the few Conservative supporters of devolution, 'a unique constitutional matter that this Parliament is likely to put on the statute book a Bill in which it does not believe.'[79] Speaking at Bexhill on 25 November 1977, Enoch Powell called it

> an event without precedent in the long history of Parliament . . . that members openly and publicly declaring themselves opposed to the legislation and bringing forward in debate what seemed to them cogent reasons why it must prove disastrous, voted nevertheless for the legislation and for a guillotine, with the express intention that after the minimum of debate the Bill should be submitted to a referendum of the electorate, in which they would hope and strive to secure its rejection.

Objection was also taken to the fact that the referendums were to be restricted to the electorate in Scotland and Wales, and that the English electorate was not to be allowed to pronounce upon devolution. For many MPs held that devolution to Scotland and Wales would affect not only the government of Scotland and Wales, but also the rights and material interests of English voters and taxpayers.[80]

Despite the appearance of expediency, however, there was a case to be made for the Government's approach. If part of the argument for devolution was, in the eyes of many, popular pressure in Scotland and Wales, then it was perfectly reasonable to make support for the Bill conditional upon popular approval. An important part of the case for devolution was that it met a powerful demand in Scotland and Wales. The referendum was a means of testing that case. Furthermore, if devolution was to fail, it was better for it to be rejected by the Scots and Welsh themselves, rather than by the House of Commons, for if the Commons rejected it, the nationalists would score a propaganda victory and claim that the demands of the Scottish and Welsh people were being frustrated by an 'English' parliament. Defeat in a referendum on the other hand would, in the view of those hostile to devolution, kill the issue for good.

So also, a referendum on devolution to Scotland and Wales held in the United Kingdom as a whole would frustrate the very purpose for which it was being proposed. For an intolerable situation would be created if Scotland and/or Wales voted in favour of the Bill, but was overruled by an

English majority. No doubt in strict constitutional logic, the English had as much right to vote on devolution as the Scots and Welsh; but the Commons, which after all contained a majority of English MPs, was clearly sensible in waiving that right in the interests of good relations between the different parts of the kingdom, relations which would be spoilt if the public and clearly expressed wishes of Scotland and Wales were overridden by England. English voters, then, through their MPs, could be regarded as having voluntarily agreed not to exercise their right to vote in a referendum. One MP quoted Shakespeare:

> O! it is excellent
> To have a giant's strength, but it is tyrannous
> To use it like a giant.[81]

The concession of the referendum was not, however, sufficient to secure passage of the Scotland and Wales Bill; and after the government failed in its attempt to guillotine the Bill, it had to be abandoned. But it was reintroduced in the 1977–8 session in the form of two bills, one for Scotland and one for Wales. After a stormy parliamentary passage, both bills secured Royal Assent in the summer of 1978 and they were referred to the electorate in Scotland and Wales for approval or rejection on 1 March 1979.

THE DEVOLUTION REFERENDUM IN WALES

During the referendum campaign in Wales, the electorate was left in no doubt that the referendum had been secured by the opponents of devolution, and pressed by them on an unwilling government. This put supporters of devolution at a considerable disadvantage; for they were made to appear lacking in confidence in their case, and unwilling to allow it to be put to a popular vote. Opponents of devolution such as Neil Kinnock had claimed that the referendum had 'been wrung out of those whose enthusiasm for devolution was only exceeded by their determination not to allow the people of Wales to make a real decision through the ballot box on their future'.[82] Opponents of devolution could argue that, had it not been for them, the electorate would never have had the chance to make its voice heard at all.

In Wales, the referendum resulted in a devastating defeat for devolution. The turnout was 58.3 per cent and, of those voting, only 20.3 per cent supported the implementation of the Wales Act, while 79.7 per cent supported repeal. In terms of the electorate as a whole, only 11.8 per cent could be found to endorse the Wales Act, while 46.5 per cent voted No.

This result constituted a powerful refutation of the theory according to which support for a political party in a general election also constitutes support for the particular policies outlined in its manifesto. The Wales Act was supported by three of the four political parties in Wales – Labour, the Liberals and Plaid Cymru – which had recommended devolution in their October 1974 manifestoes and had gained 75.8 per cent of the Welsh vote in the general election of October 1974 and 65.6 per cent of the Welsh vote in that of 1979. The only party opposing it was the Conservative Party which had received only 23.9 per cent of the vote in October 1974 and 32.3 per cent of the vote in 1979. Yet it was clearly shown that the parties supporting the Wales Act did not, on this issue, represent the views of their supporters. The referendum ensured that the views of the electorate were given effect, and that a major constitutional change would not occur unless supported by a popular consensus.

THE 40 PER CENT RULE[83]

In Scotland, a crucial role in the devolution campaign and in the eventual repeal of the Scotland Act was played by a provision inserted into the Scotland Act (and also the Wales Act), against the wishes of the government, requiring 40 per cent of the electorate to vote 'Yes' to ensure that the act came into force.

This provision resulted from an amendment by a Labour backbench MP, George Cunningham, and it has some claim to be regarded as the most significant backbench initiative in British politics since the war. It also represented a constitutional innovation in that it entrenched the status quo – the unitary state – by requiring a qualified majority to overturn it. The implication, of course, is that certain changes require something more than bare majority support if they are to secure legitimacy, and so the 40 per cent rule may form a precedent of considerable significance for the future.

When the devolution legislation was reintroduced in the 1977–8 session of Parliament, it was, as we have seen, divided into two bills, one for Scotland and one for Wales. Labour opponents of devolution, realising that the government could not afford a second legislative defeat, sought an alternative method of inflicting damage upon the Scotland Bill without actually preventing its passage through Parliament. They attempted to do this by stiffening the conditions required in the referendum for the Act to be brought into force.

In the original version of the Scotland Bill as presented to Parliament, the relevant clause, 82 (2), read:

> If it appears to the Secretary of State having regard to the answers given in a referendum and all other circumstances, that this Act should not be brought into effect he may lay before Parliament the draft of an Order in Council providing for its repeal.

This left open the possibility that, if there was a very narrow 'Yes' majority on a low turnout, the Secretary of State might regard that as sufficient to bring the act into force, although Parliament would wish to repeal it. For, it could be argued, Parliament's support for the Scotland Act was conditional not merely upon there being a bare majority for devolution, but upon there being a powerful demand for it.

On 25 January 1978 – Burns' Night – therefore, George Cunningham, an expatriate Scot who was Labour MP for Islington South and Finsbury, introduced an amendment which required an Order for the repeal of the Scotland Act to be laid before Parliament unless there were a 40 per cent 'Yes' vote in the referendum. To the Government's surprise this amendment was carried by 166 to 151 votes, and three weeks later an attempt to delete it on the Report Stage of the Bill failed by 298 votes to 243.

The Cunningham Amendment, which became Section 85 (2) of the Scotland Act, provided:

> If it appears to the Secretary of State that less than 40 per cent of the persons entitled to vote in the referendum have voted 'yes' he shall lay before Parliament the draft of an Order-in-Council for the repeal of this Act.

An equivalent provision was inserted into the Wales Bill.

This seemingly straightforward provision concealed two complex and difficult problems. The first was how the number 'entitled to vote' for the purposes of the section should be determined; the second was the nature of the hurdle imposed by the amendment.

The only clear way of determining who is 'entitled to vote' in a British election or referendum is to consult the electoral register. However the register can record only those entitled to vote at a particular moment in time, and it is already out of date by the time it is published. The register used in the devolution referendums came into force on 16 February 1979, two weeks before they were held, and it was based on a qualifying date of 10 October 1978. Between October and February, however, some of those on the electoral register would die, or be committed to prison and so be legally disqualified from voting. The electoral register is estimated, for these reasons, to become 0.75 per cent out of date each month after the qualifying date. Thus one illogicality of the 40 per cent rule was that in practice the possible turnout would depend upon the age of the register. The devolution referendums were in fact held on a new register; had they been held in, say, October 1978, the practicable turnout would have been considerably lower.

Moreover, the register itself is unlikely to be completely accurate. A 1967 Home Office survey made in England and Wales[84] showed that there were 4 per cent of omissions. The 1971 Census, however, 'showed that the electoral register contained 98.8 per cent of the census names which, with allowance for aliens, is pretty close'.[85] So if 4 per cent of the electorate were missing from the electoral register, which was still accurate in terms of total numbers, there must be further errors and duplications.

In addition to deficiencies in the register, there were many electors who were properly registered, but would for practical purposes be unable to vote. The *Scotsman* estimated that on any given day in Scotland there would be 51,500 hospital patients including 39,000 of voting age – the vast majority of whom would not have applied for postal or proxy votes, many having entered hospital within the fortnight preceding 1 March and being too late to do so; they would effectively be disfranchised. Another 100,000 people of voting age were seriously disabled, and a further 150,000 would be too ill to vote, although legally qualified. More would be debarred from voting by home removals. It was estimated that 68,000 electors would have to travel from another local authority area in order to vote; and clearly few of them would do so.[86]

The electoral register was not designed with a rule such as that proposed by the Cunningham Amendment in mind. For, as the Electoral Registration Officer for the Lothian Region explained:

> . . . I made it my business not to lose sight of the purpose of the register. It is a *register of electors*, and my task in preparing it is to ensure, as far as I reasonably can, that all those entitled to the franchise are included in it. . . . Accordingly, insofar as the register may contain names that ought not to have been included, this is the result of deliberate policy.[87]

On 20 February 1979, nine days before the referendum, Bruce Millan, the Secretary of State for Scotland, announced that he was bound by the terms of the Cunningham Amendment to make a discount only for those not *entitled* to vote; he would be acting illegally if he also made a discount for those *unable* to vote. Moreover, he could make a discount for those not legally entitled to vote only where there was an authoritative estimate of the size of the category.

He proposed to do so for the following four categories in Scotland.

Voters reaching 18 years after 1 March – these voters would be on the electoral register but legally disqualified from voting until reaching the age of 18	49,802
Voters who had died between the time when the register was compiled and 1 March	26,400
Double-registered students and student nurses	11,800
Convicted felons	2,000
	90,002

This discount amounted to 2.3 per cent of the February 1979 electoral register, and reduced the requirement for a 40 per cent 'Yes' vote in Scotland from 1,534,846 to 1,498,845.

Millan was, however, unable to take account of the following categories:

Errors in register (say 6%)	228,550
Hospital patients	39,000
Seriously disabled	100,000
Ill at home	150,000
Removals	68,000
	585,550

Note: These figures comprise my own view of the maximum possible number of deductions, taking into account all those in practice unable to vote. The figures are obtained from Butler and O'Muirchear-taigh in *The Economist*, 19 Feb. 1979; and the *Scotsman*, 12 Feb. 1979.

If we subtract from this figure the 52,000 valid postal ballots cast in the referendum, we obtain a figure of 533,550. Adding Millan's deductions, we obtain a total of 623,552. The target for a 40 per cent 'Yes' vote would then be not 1,498,845 but 1,285,422, only 54,485 more than the actual 'Yes' vote in the referendum, whereas on Millan's figure, the 'Yes' vote was 267,906 short.

It is clear, then, that the 40 per cent rule placed upon the electoral register a burden which it was ill-equipped to bear, and that the requirement of a qualified majority cannot be completely fair unless the efficiency of the register is improved.

In the Scottish referendum, supporters of devolution could legitimately claim that they were handicapped to the extent of over 200,000 votes, the difference between the 1,498,845 announced by Millan and the figure of 1,285,422 which would result from taking into account all possible deductions. In different circumstances, this could have seriously compromised the legitimacy of the result.

What kind of hurdle did the Cunningham Amendment impose? By using the proportion of the electorate rather than the proportion of voters as the criterion for implementing the Scotland Act, it subtly combined two different requirements, the first being that a minimum percentage of the electorate should turn out to vote, and the second that there should be a decisive majority in favour of devolution for the Scotland Act to come into force. For the lower the turnout, the higher the majority would need to be to secure implementation of the Scotland Act. On a turnout of 80 per cent, precisely 50 per cent of the voters would need to vote 'Yes'; if the turnout was 70 per cent, there would need to be a 57 per cent 'Yes' vote; and with a 60 per cent turnout, a 67 per cent 'Yes' vote would be required.

However, the failure of the Scotland Act to meet this test in the referendum would not necessarily mean that the act would be repealed, for the referendum was an advisory, and not a mandatory one. The relevant provision only required the Secretary of State to 'lay before Parliament the draft of an Order-in-Council for the repeal of this Act', and it is certainly possible to imagine circumstances in which Parliament would decide that the draft Order should be voted down. If, for example, there was a 36 per cent 'Yes' vote and a 25 per cent 'No' vote, Parliament would hardly have refused to allow devolution to go ahead. So the 40 per cent provision, as George Cunningham appreciated, did not 'decide whether devolution takes place or not, but only whether the matter goes back before Parliament in the event of an inconclusive referendum result'.[88] The outcome of the referendum would determine not whether the Scotland Act came into force, but whether or not the draft repeal Order needed to be laid.

When the referendum Orders came to be debated in the Commons, Leon Brittan, a Conservative spokesman on devolution, argued that there would need to be not a 40 per cent 'Yes' vote but a 'clear majority' for the Scotland Act to come into force; and in the debate on the Welsh Order, the following revealing exchange took place:

Gwynfor Evans (Plaid Cymru): What is a sufficient vote? Let us suppose that 35 per cent were in favour of the Assembly and 25 per cent were against it. Would that be a sufficient vote?

Donald Anderson (Labour, anti-devolution): Yes.

Gwynfor Evans: I wonder whether the House would interpret it in that way. I am sure that the Conservative Opposition would not so interpret it.

Nicholas Edwards (Conservative, Shadow Secretary for State for Wales): We would.[89]

The Cunningham Amendment, therefore, gave to Parliament the discretion to decide whether a 'Yes' majority which failed to meet the 40 per cent requirement was sufficient to allow devolution to be implemented. Parliament would decide for itself whether the Act should be repealed; and no doubt such a decision would be based to a large extent upon the balance between the 'Yes' and 'No' votes. The advisory nature of the referendum made it a flexible instrument enabling Parliament to make the final decision if the 40 per cent requirement was not met.

But the 40 per cent test also indicated to the Scottish electorate how Parliament intended to use its discretion, and gave a warning that a bare majority of votes cast would not be sufficient to ensure the setting up of the Scottish Assembly. It therefore prevented the Assembly being established by a bare majority on a low turnout. With a large majority – say 10 per cent – then a 35 per cent 'Yes' vote might have been acceptable; with a narrow 'Yes' majority, a high turnout would be necessary to surmount the 40 per cent hurdle.

THE DEVOLUTION REFERENDUM IN SCOTLAND

Polls taken in Scotland since 1974 had seemed to show that opinion was divided fairly evenly amongst a number of different constitutional options. Roughly 20 per cent favoured the status quo, and 20 per cent independence, but the 60 per cent who declared themselves in favour of devolution were divided between those favouring an assembly indirectly elected via the local authorities, an assembly on the lines proposed by the government, and an assembly giving Scotland complete control of all her domestic affairs. But, despite this division of opinion, there seemed little doubt until shortly before the referendum itself that there would be a large 'Yes' majority for the Scotland Act. Indeed an opinion poll conducted by System Three for the *Glasgow Herald* in January 1979 indicated that 52 per cent of respondents intended to vote 'Yes' and only 29 per cent 'No'. Gradually during the campaign, however, the 'Yes' lead was whittled down, until the final result on 1 March was as follows: on a turnout of 62.9 per cent

Yes	1,230,937	51.6 per cent of those voting	32.9 per cent of the electorate
No	1,153,502	48.4 per cent of those voting	30.8 per cent of the electorate

In Scotland, as in Wales, the Labour Party was deeply divided, and the Conservatives were the only party officially to oppose the legislation. But they were careful to argue that they were campaigning not against devolution as such, but against the Scotland Act. In this way they sought to ensure that only those favouring the specific scheme proposed by the Labour Government would be found in the 'Yes' camp, while others could vote 'No' and yet retain their commitment to devolution.

The close result of the devolution referendum in Scotland posed a dreadful dilemma for James Callaghan who was dependent upon SNP votes for his majority in the Commons. According to Sir Harold Wilson:

> There had been some hope in the Cabinet that having laid the repeal order, their own supporters would vote the other way and keep devolution alive. But strenuous inquiries by the Government Whips revealed that some forty or so Government back-benchers would join the Conservatives in killing devolution.[90]

The credibility of devolution had been destroyed by the result of the referendum. Its advocates had argued for it on the ground that there was a surge of popular demand for it in Scotland, but the result of the referendum had entirely undermined this argument.

It is possible that, if the Cunningham Amendment had not been passed, the narrow 'Yes' majority would have been sufficient for the Scotland Act to have been put into force: but two MPs who had supported devolution implied that, even without the 40 per cent rule, the Scotland Act could not have been implemented. Donald Dewar claimed that 'The 40 per cent was never the difficulty. It was the closeness in the popular vote that was a shock to the supporters of the cause,' while Malcolm Rifkind, a Conservative, said 'There has been considerable discussion in this debate on the 40 per cent rule that was written into the Act, but I think that there are few hon. Members who would doubt that, even if that rule had never been introduced into the Act, given the result of the referendum, we would still be here today and still about to come to a very similar decision.'[91] Rifkind instanced not only the small total 'Yes' vote, and the narrow gap between the 'Yes' and 'No' votes, but the fact that the 'Yes' majority was so uneven. Only the regions in the central belt of Scotland – Strathclyde, Central, Lothian and Fife – together with the Highlands and the Western Isles – showed a 'Yes' majority. The other outlying areas – Border, Dumfries and Galloway, Grampian, Tayside, Orkney and Shetland – had all voted 'No', reflecting the fears of those in the rural parts of Scotland that they would be consistently outvoted in the Assembly by the Labour machine in the industrial areas. The 'Yes' majority in Strathclyde alone – 87,920 – was in fact larger than the overall 'Yes' majority of 77,435.

The 40 per cent rule, whether or not it changed the significance of the result, may also have altered the terms on which the referendum campaign was fought: for it may have seemed to many voters as if an abstention was equivalent to a 'No' vote. In the absence of the Cunningham Amendment, therefore, a sufficient number of the abstainers might well have voted 'No' so as to ensure a 'No' majority. This was certainly claimed by the opponents of devolution, and Teddy Taylor, then Shadow Secretary of State for Scotland, declared that the 40 per cent rule (which he had supported) 'may have kept us from achieving an outright majority'.[92]

In the event, however, it was not the referendum which killed devolution in Scotland, but the result of the general election which followed shortly afterwards on 3 May 1979. The Callaghan Government was defeated by one vote, since it could no longer command the support of the SNP, in a no-confidence motion on 28 March, and the SNP hoped to be able to capitalise upon the fact that a 'Yes' majority, albeit a narrow one, in the referendum was being thwarted by an English-dominated Parliament. Thus the defeat of devolution led directly to the fall of the Labour Government.

During the election campaign, one of the SNP's main slogans was 'Voters can choose to save Scotland Act', and Mrs Margo Macdonald, a leader of the party, claimed that 'A vote for the Scottish National Party would be a vote to rescue and amend the Scotland Act.'[93] But, unfortunately for the SNP, devolution played hardly any role at all in the election campaign. A *Glasgow Herald* poll found only 3 per cent who were prepared to regard it as a key issue, as compared with 47 per cent who felt that the cost of living was the main issue, while 28 per cent mentioned jobs and employment. The 1979 general election was fought not on self-government for Scotland, but on more familiar economic questions; and it was perhaps not surprising that the SNP's campaign failed, its representation in the Commons falling from 11 seats to 2.

On the other hand, if the SNP had increased its parliamentary representation, the new government would have been compelled to take devolution seriously. Thus the Scottish electorate could still have rescued the Scotland Act if it had really wished to do so; the Scots were offered a second opportunity to circumvent the 40 per cent hurdle. The fact that they did not take it showed that, for the time being at least, Scots accepted that the narrow majority in the referendum offered no mandate for fundamental constitutional change. This is confirmed by the evidence of an ORC poll reported in the *Scotsman* on 26 April 1979. According to this poll, only 26 per cent believed that the Scottish Assembly should now be set up, but 33 per cent thought that although the 'Yes' side had won, the Scotland Act should not be implemented: while 30 per cent of those polled actually believed that the 'No' side had won the referendum. Scottish opinion seemed to accept the legitimacy of a rule passed by the United Kingdom Parliament as opposed to the legitimacy of a decision made by the majority of Scottish voters.[94]

Thus the legitimacy of the 40 per cent provision was broadly accepted by both pro- and anti-devolutionists (with the exception of course of the SNP). It was widely regarded as having saved Parliament from the considerable embarrassment of either allowing the Scotland Act to come into force on a narrow 'Yes' majority, or rejecting it without having informed the Scottish electorate of its intentions beforehand; and on 20 June 1979, the new Conservative Government repealed the Scotland Act, facing only token opposition from the Labour Party.

It is, however, possible that, at some time in the future, the SNP's campaign on the iniquity of the 40 per cent rule will bear fruit, and the Scottish electorate may come to accept the view that it was cheated. The 40 per cent rule provides convenient material for the growth of a powerful nationalist myth to the effect that an extra hurdle was erected by those who knew that devolution could not be defeated on a straight vote. If the failure of devolution were to lead in the long run to a polarisation of opinion in Scotland, the way would be clear for a party which claimed that there was no middle path between the status quo and full self-government. It would be a terrible irony if the SNP proved to be the eventual beneficiary of the Cunningham Amendment; but it would not be the first time that history had played such tricks.

Dicey, as we have seen, regarded the referendum as a method of validating constitutional laws and as offering the electorate the only means available under the British Constitution for distinguishing them from ordinary laws which required no such validation.

To impose the 40 per cent test is to go further in drawing this distinction. For the implication of the Cunningham Amendment is that the powers of Parliament ought not to be devolved unless it is clear beyond all possible doubt that this is desired by the electorate.

In proposing the repeal of the Scotland Act, George Younger, the Secretary of State for Scotland, suggested that 'it would be improper to promote any further version of a Scottish Assembly with legislative and executive powers without holding another referendum'.[95] George Gardiner, a Conservative backbench opponent of devolution, went further and claimed that

> it will be difficult for a future Government to refuse a referendum on any significant constitutional proposals that they bring forward. . . . Moreover . . . I hope that when that happens, it will be judged relevant also to retain the 40 per cent hurdle . . . that rule has set a precedent that cannot lightly be ignored by any future Government proposing constitutional changes.[96]

It is difficult to avoid the conclusion that the Cunningham Amendment sets an extremely persuasive precedent for any future devolution legislation making it risky for any government to propose devolution unless it has the assurance of a massive demand for it. But, more generally, it may be that whenever a referendum comes to be held in the future the defenders of the status quo will insist that a 40 per cent requirement be inserted so as to ensure the genuinely 'full-hearted consent' of the voters. It will be a difficult demand to resist, for whenever there is less than the support of 40 per cent of the electorate for any change proposed in a referendum, the opponents of change might contest the verdict; and to that extent, the result of the referendum would lack legitimacy.

Whether or not one regards a qualified majority as a desirable requirement will depend upon the importance one ascribes to turnout in a referendum. In France, in the referendum of October 1946 which approved the Constitution of the Fourth Republic, 36 per cent of the electorate voted 'Yes', 31 per cent 'No', and the rest abstained. De Gaulle was to claim that the institutions of the Fourth Republic lacked legitimacy because they had been approved by default: 'One third of the French people had resigned itself to it, one third had rejected it, one third had ignored it.'[97] As President of the Fifth Republic, de Gaulle always insisted that a narrow majority in a referendum would not be sufficient for him to be able to continue his work – he would not accept a majority which was 'faible, médiocre ou aléatoire'.[98]

However, the Fourth Republic did not collapse because it lacked legitimacy, but for quite other reasons, primarily its inability to sustain a government strong enough to solve its colonial problems. If governments had been more successful, then the Fourth Republic would have survived however narrow the majority by which it had been born.

Whatever the constitutional rules, the legitimacy of political institutions will depend upon the degree of acceptance which they receive from the people. It is perfectly possible for institutions which enjoy little public support when they come into existence to succeed in winning public support through working effectively; while conversely a large victory in a referendum is no guarantee of popular acceptability in the long run, as the EEC referendum shows. So the 40 per cent rule can be no guarantee of the legitimacy of a referendum result, although it may make some contribution towards it.

It is difficult, therefore, to come to any final judgment on the value of a qualified majority in the referendum. So much is bound to depend upon the issue involved, the particular circumstances, and the flexibility with which constitutional requirements are interpreted by Government and Parliament. In 1979, both Government and Parliament were prepared to interpret the 40 per cent rule flexibly; they were not proposing to deny Scotland her Assembly if there was a clear majority in favour of it, whether or not that majority succeeded in clearing the 40 per cent hurdle.

One may contrast this flexibility which an unwritten constitution permits with the formalism of a written constitution. Before the revision of the Danish Constitution in 1953, a mandatory 45 per cent 'Yes' vote was required for constitutional laws to be brought into force (the revision of 1953 lowered the requirement to 40 per cent). In a referendum in 1939 on the abolition of the Second Chamber agreed by the main political parties, 966,277 voters (equal to 44.5 per cent of the electorate) voted 'Yes' while only 85,717 (equal to 3.9 per cent of the electorate) voted 'No'. Since the 45 per cent requirement was mandatory, however, it was not possible for the reform to be implemented. It is to be hoped that British politicians will avoid the introduction of rigid and binding rules in referendums, but continue to display flexibility in interpreting what are bound to be contentious provisions.

The 40 per cent rule stands as a graphic illustration of how even within an unwritten constitution, a barrier to fundamental change can be constructed; and the Conservative Party in a policy pamphlet, *The Referendum and the Constitution*,[99] has recommended that it be adopted for all 'constitutional' matters, except that where the question to be referred was the independence of Northern Ireland, Scotland or Wales, a 50 per cent affirmative vote should be required.

To what extent did the devolution referendums finally settle the question of self-government for Scotland and Wales? In Wales, where the Wales Act was rejected by a vote of 4 to 1, it might appear that the vote finally settled the issue. But it seemed from polls taken by BBC Wales on 8 and 28 February (the referendum being on 1 March), that an Assembly as proposed by the government was less popular than either a legislative assembly of the type proposed for Scotland, or complete self-government (although there was a firm majority in Wales against devolution of any kind). Moreover the agitation in 1980 over using the fourth television channel in Wales for Welsh-speaking programmes shows that the forces which gave rise to the demand for devolution are by no means dead; and it is perfectly possible that the growth of unemployment and the economic recession in Wales will again lead to demands for some kind of political autonomy.

The effects of the inconclusive Scottish referendum are far more difficult to appraise. It is not yet possible to tell whether or not it settled 'the Scottish Question'. If the SNP were again to make electoral gains, it is perfectly possible that the 40 per cent rule will be seen as a trick designed to rob Scotland of the Assembly for which a majority had voted. The introduction of the referendum, and indeed the whole debate on devolution, was marked by such a high degree of confusion and cynicism that it would not be difficult to indulge in the politics of myth-making about the result.

One cannot, however, blame the referendum if such a development were to occur. Given the fairly even division of opinion in Scotland concerning the merits of the Scotland Act, no test of opinion could be expected to yield a definite decision. But, if the referendum did not *settle* the issue, it at least *defused* it. For, it showed that, contrary to the claims of the SNP, the Scots were not straining at the leash to establish their own Assembly. It therefore succeeded in isolating extremists by showing that they did not command popular support.

Moreover, the referendum was the *only* instrument which could have succeeded in defusing the Scottish Question. For if the Scotland Act had been defeated in Parliament, the issue would have been kept alive since the SNP would have been able to say that Parliament was ignoring the will of the Scottish people. In the absence of a clear-cut result which might have settled the issue, the referendum decided it in favour of those who sought to defuse it, as against those who sought to keep it alive.

THE REFERENDUM IN NORTHERN IRELAND

We have seen that where one side is unwilling to accept the result of a referendum and can claim some degree of popular support, its natural response will be to dispute the terms of the referendum. This may well happen in Scotland. It has certainly happened in Northern Ireland, and it constitutes the main reason why the border poll held in Northern Ireland in 1973 proved incapable of making more than a marginal dent in the Ulster problem.

The border poll was held to reassure Northern Ireland that the prorogation of Stormont – her local Parliament – in 1972 did not alter her constitutional status. For, when Eire elected to become an independent republic outside the Commonwealth in 1948, Parliament had passed the Ireland Act in 1949, section 1 (2) of which affirmed that Northern Ireland would not cease to be a part of the United Kingdom without the consent of the Parliament of Northern Ireland.

In the absence of a Parliament in Northern Ireland, the British government had to find some alternative means of ascertaining the will of the people of Northern Ireland, and Heath as Prime Minister promised that 'a system of regular plebiscites'[100] would be held for this purpose. So far only one plebiscite has been held in Northern Ireland – the border poll of 1973.

Advocates of the border poll hoped that it would 'take the border out of politics'. Northern Ireland politics, the argument ran, had been so bedevilled by the dispute about the border that the province had been polarised into a Protestant Unionist party and various Republican parties supported by the Catholics. If the issue of the border was to be decided by a plebiscite, rather than through the competitive party battle, then it was hoped that the parties would evolve on the British model, and forget sectarian conflicts.

The difficulty was, however, that in the view of the Catholic population, and of the politicians and parties supporting Irish unity, Ireland as a whole, rather than Northern Ireland, was the unit within which the referendum ought to be held. For the Republicans, Northern Ireland had been carved out of Ireland without regard to the homogeneity of its population or to the history of Ulster as a unit – for Northern Ireland comprised only six of the nine counties of historic Ulster, the largest possible area within which, according to the Unionists in 1920, they could be sure of maintaining a permanent Protestant majority.

In the view of the opponents of the border poll, the plebiscite was nothing more than a propaganda exercise. It was hardly needed to discover the opinion of the majority in Northern Ireland; as long as the majority was Protestant, it was inconceivable that the province would opt to join the Republic; and the result of the plebiscite was predetermined by the way in which the boundary was drawn between the North and the South in 1920. The solution of the Northern Ireland problem, however, depended not upon displaying again the obvious fact that there was a Protestant majority in the North, but in working out a satisfactory and permanent relationship between Great Britain, Northern Ireland and the Irish Republic; and it is by no means clear how the border poll could be expected to contribute to that aim.

Two questions were asked in the border poll – 'Do you want Northern Ireland to remain a part of the United Kingdom?' and 'Do you want Northern Ireland to be joined with the Irish Republic outside the United Kingdom?' But some suggested that this was by no means exclusive of the possibilities, even if the option of independence for Northern Ireland were ruled out.

When the Border Poll Bill was debated in the Commons, Merlyn Rees, the Shadow Secretary of State for Northern Ireland, proposed that a third question be asked – 'Do you want eventually to live in a united Ireland brought about by free consent of the peoples of Northern Ireland and of the Republic of Ireland?'[101] For it was the aim of the leading opposition party in Northern Ireland – the Social Democratic and Labour Party (SDLP) – to secure a united Ireland through such free consent, although it was prepared to accept the status quo until then. It could thus answer 'Yes' to both of the questions actually asked in the poll – 'Yes' to membership of the UK in the short term, but 'Yes' also to membership of the Irish Republic in the long term.

Some might hold that other constitutional options were available – for example that Northern Ireland be governed as a condominium or as part of a confederation of the British Isles. Yet clearly the border poll would be unsuitable for elucidating the degree of detail and subtlety of argument needed to determine Northern Ireland's constitutional future. In such a situation, the referendum is a very blunt instrument indeed.

In the event, the SDLP and the other parties supported by the Catholic minority advised electors to boycott the poll, since, according to an SDLP statement, 'neither of the two questions posed represented the point of view held by most anti-Unionists in Northern Ireland'. This made the poll 'an empty exercise'.

The result of the poll was as follows:

Turnout: 58.6%	
For remaining within the United Kingdom	591,820
(57.4% of the electorate)	
For joining with the Irish Republic	6,463
(0.6% of the electorate)	

The poll may have assisted British politicians and diplomats who wished to emphasise to the representatives of other countries that the majority in Northern Ireland did genuinely wish to remain a part of the United Kingdom, and that Britain was not holding down the population of Ulster by force. It did nothing, however, to 'take the border out of politics' or to resolve the political problems facing Northern Ireland; nor did it assist the growth of non-sectarian parties in the divided province. If the poll is to be held periodically, it may indeed intensify the issue of the border by highlighting it each time the referendum approaches.

In 1980, there was a suggestion that a further referendum be held in Northern Ireland on the Conservative Government's devolution proposals. The government had decided that it would establish a directly elected assembly in Northern Ireland, provided that agreement could be reached on a structure whereby the two communities – Protestant and Catholic – would share power. In face of intransigence from politicians on both sides, some argued that the government should attempt to reach out beyond the politicians to the people so as to elicit their consent to the new proposals.

A referendum, however, would have to be held separately amongst each of the two communities; for clearly the minority Catholic community would not regard itself as bound by a majority composed exclusively of Protestants. But it would be difficult, and a remarkable departure from British practice, to hold an official referendum amongst two separate electorates.

Moreover, there would be no point in holding a referendum unless the politicians had *already* agreed a basis for settlement. For the 1973 border poll showed that the electorate of Northern Ireland would follow the advice of the politicians; the Protestants voted solidly for the link with Britain, while the Catholics did as their leaders asked and boycotted the poll. There is little reason to believe that a different outcome is likely in a referendum on devolution. Protestants who in 1973 saw power-sharing as a lesser evil are now more conscious of their strength, having, by means of direct action, destroyed the power-sharing arrangements in 1974; this gave them a new determination not to allow avowed republicans into a Northern Ireland cabinet. The Catholic community, on the other hand, having been offered power-sharing in 1973, will not now be willing to settle for anything less. The government, therefore, failed to secure agreement, and the initiative was dropped without a referendum being held. Were there to be any change in the outlook of either of the two communities, it would be fanciful to suppose that a referendum would be needed to register it; just as, if there were ever to be a swing of opinion in the province so that a majority came to favour union with the Republic, no referendum would be required to exhibit the fact.

Neither of the two communities in Northern Ireland is willing to recognise as legitimate a constitutional solution to which it is opposed, whether or not it is favoured by a majority. Therefore, the referendum can do little to assist in solving the Irish problem, which remains a good illustration of Maine's dictum that 'democracies are quite paralysed by the plea of Nationality. There is no more effective way of attacking them than by admitting the right of the majority to govern, but denying that the majority so entitled is the particular majority which claims the right.'[102]

CONCLUSION

The referendum, then, has become an established part of the British Constitution, introduced not through deliberate intent but as a result of the vicissitudes of party politics. 'It is singular', said Dicey, 'and not perhaps very fortunate that in accordance with English habits, a reform good in itself, should be proposed by men who probably do not believe in it, and who want to meet a party difficulty. Still I hail it with satisfaction.' For, 'I am quite certain that, once established, the Referendum would never be got rid of by anything short of a revolution.'[103]

Because the referendum was introduced in such an unplanned way, however, there has been singularly little discussion as to its precise constitutional status: nor has there been any attempt to determine its proper scope. In Part II, therefore, we attempt to resolve these issues and to show how the referendum can be used to mitigate some of the evils arising from party government.

Part II

The referendum and the constitution

The full and complete definition of a citizen is confined to those who participate in the governing power.

ARISTOTLE

THE REFERENDUM AS A WEAPON OF ENTRENCHMENT

The referendum is generally seen as an instrument of popular sovereignty, an institutional expression of the doctrine that political authority derives from the people. Yet, as the history of the debate in Britain shows, the urge towards popular participation or self-government has not played a very important part in its advocacy. On the contrary, since first proposed by Dicey, the referendum has been suggested primarily as a means of checking disagreeable legislation – whether Home Rule, Tariff Reform, reform of the Lords, entry into the EEC or devolution. It has been, in the words of Beaverbrook, 'not a spear but a shield', an adjunct to representative government and not a replacement for it.

As advocated and employed in Britain, the referendum has been seen as an instrument through which the electorate can check the work of government. Parliament remains the source of political authority, but it becomes subject to the restraint of the people. The electorate, somewhat like the pre-1911 House of Lords, is given the right of veto; its power is restricted to offering a verdict on measures to which Parliament has already assented. The electorate is put in the position of being asked to give a Third Reading vote on a particular proposal or bill. It cannot itself initiate proposals for Parliament to vote on; nor, so far, has it been asked for its opinion upon a proposal or legislative measure before it has been presented to Parliament.

It is clear that the referendum, as hitherto used in Britain, must be a conservative device; for it provides an extra check against government, an additional protection to that given by Parliament. If the popular verdict approves of what Parliament has done, then the measure in question can be put into effect, as would have been the case without the referendum; if, on the other hand, the electors reject the work of Parliament, then the measure must be dropped. Thus the role of the electorate is essentially negative. The referendum is an instrument of protection and not of change.

Insofar as the referendum is confined to a vote on a measure which has passed through Parliament, some of the extreme fears which its use has aroused must appear unfounded. It is, for example, sometimes suggested that the referendums on the EEC and devolution make it more likely that there will in future be referendums on subjects such as capital punishment or the repatriation of immigrants, the implication being that the electorate, in contrast to Parliament, would reach illiberal and unjust decisions on such issues. But such a suggestion ignores the fact that referendums on those topics would be possible only if Parliament had already agreed to pass the necessary legislation. If MPs were unwilling to support such legislation, it could not be submitted to referendum; if they were willing to support it, the referendum would offer the possibility of preventing its implementation. For it can be a check on illiberal as well as liberal legislation.

Use of the referendum as a check or veto might seem peculiarly appropriate for Britain which, almost alone among democracies, lacks a constitution imposing limits upon the power of government. A government, elected perhaps by less than 40 per cent of the popular vote, can make radical changes against the wishes of the majority – or even before the majority's views have been heard or allowed to crystallise.

The British electoral system, by exaggerating the size of parliamentary majorities, generally allows one party to govern without its being required to consider the views of other parties. Its legislation may derive from commitments in the manifesto imposed by party militants, or as a result of bargaining with key pressure groups, rather than from the considered views of its electoral supporters. Yet party loyalty is generally sufficient to ensure that this legislation is carried in Parliament. In this way, Parliament can implement legislation unwanted by the electorate.

The referendum can offer to Britain a form of security, which in other countries is given by a written constitution, against such changes. It does this by in effect entrenching particular parts of the constitution against parliamentary majorities.

If, for example, a referendum is thought to be required before directly elected Assemblies can be established in Scotland or Wales, then the unitary state is entrenched to the extent that any government is deterred from proposing devolution by the knowledge that a referendum is needed to validate it: the degree of entrenchment is of course greater if a qualifying majority, for example 40 per cent of the registered electorate, is also required.

A government can use the referendum to entrench parts of the Constitution against changes proposed by its opponents. It could for example entrench the House of Lords against radical demands for abolition by passing an act declaring that such legislation should require a referendum before taking effect.

It might be objected that a future government could ignore this provision and abolish the Lords without holding a referendum. But this objection, although it seems plausible at first sight, is not valid, since the obloquy which would be incurred by a government attempting to deprive the electorate of its right to be appealed to, would make it hesitate before resorting to so drastic an act. It is extremely difficult in a democracy to take away a right of this kind, and if a government were to attempt to do so, it would at once concede that its proposals did not enjoy the support of the electorate.

The referendum, therefore, is a method of securing entrenchment, and it may well be the only means by which, in a country such as Britain without a rigid constitution, entrenchment is possible. If so, it is an important way of securing constitutional protection by placing an issue beyond the reach of a government with a majority in the Commons.

To the extent that the referendum is an entrenching device, it acts as a deterrent to government, a disincentive to legislate in the particular area which it protects. In most of the democracies which employ the referendum, it is used sparingly rather than frequently. But its efficacy is not to be measured simply by looking at the number of times it is used. To evaluate the referendum fully, we need to look not only at the legislation actually put to the electorate for endorsement, but also at the legislation which might have been passed if provision for the referendum did not exist.

It then becomes clear that by ensuring that legislation cannot be passed against the will of the electorate, the referendum can be an instrument for securing consensus. This can be illustrated from the experience of Denmark. There is in the Danish constitution provision for one-third of the members of the Folketing (Parliament) to call for a referendum on any item of government legislation; to succeed, the legislation as well as securing a majority of supporters over opponents, must also secure the support of at least 30 per cent of the electorate. The government can therefore be defeated simply by the electorate staying at home. This provision has been employed only once since it was adopted in 1953, on four land laws proposed by the Social Democratic government in 1963. These laws were all defeated comfortably. Thus a government, however large a majority it may enjoy, is prevented from carrying legislation which arouses the active disapproval of the electorate. In such a situation the referendum serves to encourage the politics of agreement, for if all-party agreement can be secured in Parliament, then, as the contrasting examples of the EEC and devolution show, the chances of success in a referendum are greater. It is no coincidence that in Denmark the provision in the 1953 Constitution allowing government legislation to be put to referendum was a quid pro quo exacted by the Right in exchange for the abolition of the Second Chamber. For the referendum performs a similar function to that which might be performed by a good Second Chamber, that of encouraging the search for consensus; and, as we have seen, it was first advocated by Conservatives in Britain when it became clear that the House of Lords would not be allowed to preserve its absolute veto upon government legislation, its right to force a dissolution, an appeal to the people. For that, too, was a referendal function.

By performing the function of entrenchment, then, the referendum limits the power of an otherwise omnicompetent government. It does so by disjoining legislative and executive powers. The government of the day retains to the full its executive powers, but its legislative powers are limited by the rights of the electorate in those areas where there is provision for referendum. In this way the referendum helps to secure a partial separation of powers analogous to that enjoyed by many countries with written constitutions. It can, therefore, play a powerful constitutional role, provided only that a clear place can be found for it within the British system of government. To find out what that place should be, however, is no easy task.

WHEN SHOULD THE REFERENDUM BE USED?

Serious difficulties arise in the attempt to translate the referendum into a practical instrument of government precisely because Britain lacks a written constitution and therefore an authoritative source prescribing rules for the use of referendums. In the case of most countries which provide for the use of referendums, a written constitution will isolate when a referendum is needed to secure legislative validation; and the constitution will prescribe a mechanism through which the referendum is brought into play. In Britain, however, there is no such constitutional mechanism. How, then, is one to distinguish between those laws which should be submitted to the electorate to receive legislative validation, and those which are not to be so submitted? And what is to be the mechanism by which the referendum is to be put into effect? These questions seem first to have been raised by Asquith in a speech in November 1891;[1] and Dicey was asked by his friend James Bryce in 1911

> (1) What is to be the authority to decide when a Bill should be referred?
> (2) How can 'constitutional changes' be defined in a country that has no [rigid] constitution?[2]

In 1975, the Labour Government avoided this problem by claiming that the referendum on Britain's membership of the EEC was a unique occasion which would never be repeated. After the devolution referendums, however, it is clear that the problem cannot be evaded in this way.

If the referendum is to be restricted to certain types of issues, then it seems natural to suggest that it be restricted to 'constitutional' issues; and at various times, attempts have been made to define by enumeration which issues are to count as constitutional. As we have seen, the Conservatives in

1911 defined as 'constitutional' and therefore requiring a referendum any bill affecting the existence of the Crown or the Protestant succession, the creation of a national legislature or Parliament within the United Kingdom or the constitution or powers of one of the Houses of Parliament, or their relations with each other.

More recently, a Conservative Party Committee has proposed the introduction of a 'Constitution (Fundamental Provisions) Bill' requiring a referendum to be held to protect:

(a) The existence of the Second Chamber;
(b) the unity of the realm;
(c) the Crown;
(d) the Bill of Rights;
(e) the electoral system.[3]

There are, however, a number of difficulties with this approach. The first is that it may include issues which are hardly of major importance, while excluding more fundamental issues. It is doubtful, for example, whether the prerogative or even the Protestant succession requires entrenchment through referendum. On the other hand, some might argue that legislation affecting the respective rights and duties of central and local government is 'constitutional' and that existing relationships should not be altered without a referendum. Others might claim that the relationship between trade unions and government is a 'constitutional' matter, such that any proposals to make changes in the rights or powers of the trade unions should be subject to a referendum.

The problem is that in Britain constitutional issues can easily arise out of seemingly non-constitutional legislation. For example, it could be argued that the 1976 Education Act (now repealed), requiring local authorities to have regard to the need to avoid selection in secondary education, proposed a fundamental alteration in the balance between central government and local authorities in education. Many would claim that the 1980 Local Government Act, providing for a much closer scrutiny by Whitehall of the spending needs of individual local authorities, raises vital constitutional issues. In the absence of a written constitution, there is no way in which such claims can be authoritatively refuted.

The point is not only that there is legitimate disagreement about such matters, but that this disagreement will naturally mirror existing political differences. Ulster Unionists, for example, would probably like to see the Protestant succession entrenched, while many others would regard such an approach as archaic. Conservatives would like to see the existence of the Second Chamber entrenched, while those on the Left might prefer to entrench the pre-1979 structure of trade union law.

It is difficult to see how an authoritative list of 'constitutional' issues can be drawn up which commands the allegiance of those of diverse political viewpoints. A list drawn up by a government of one political colour would seem merely partisan, and would not be accepted as legitimate by its opponents. Instead of defining and delimiting what is to count as 'constitutional', it would offer a standing invitation to the next government to alter the list. So the enumeration of constitutional issues could not, in the British context, disguise the fundamentally political nature of the decision to be taken. The attempt to codify rules is inevitably prescriptive; it cannot be neutral between different political viewpoints.

Moreover, even if it were possible to enumerate an agreed list of 'constitutional' issues, this would still require the introduction of some authority to decide whether or not a given piece of legislation in fact lay within the class of constitutional legislation. Clearly, the government of the day could not be the judge in its own cause; and to give such a power to the Speaker would probably involve him too greatly in party political issues. What would be needed, as Liberal critics of referendum proposals at the beginning of the century appreciated, would be the creation of some judicial-type tribunal which could give an authoritative ruling on what was constitutional and what was ordinary legislation.

It seems, then, that the attempt to enumerate those matters which are constitutional and therefore to be submitted to referendum, leads only to an impasse. It cannot solve the problem of delimiting authoritatively those occasions when the referendum can properly be used. Nor is it consistent with the process of constitutional development in Britain which is sceptical of the use of a priori rules, and relies upon a spirit of flexibility and adaptiveness to meet political exigencies.

That the character of British government means that the use of the referendum could not be restricted was apparent to St Loe Strachey. Writing to Balfour of Burleigh in March 1911, he said:

> I have had a characteristic letter from Rosebery in which he says: '. . . I am strongly for Referendum as you know, but not as our daily bread: only for rare and exceptional occasions . . .'
>
> You will see that he is at the stage we were at when we started, namely of trying by artificial means to keep the Referendum within narrow limits. I am sure that if he went through the same practical process as we did he would come to the same conclusion, namely, that in the attempt to create artificial restrictions we should only get a cure which would be worse than the disease. That is inevitable if you do not have a fixed constitution and a Supreme Court already in existence. The trouble of it is that no one will own that as we have an elastic constitution we must have an elastic Referendum until they have been through what we went through in the matter of racking our brains.[4]

It is not possible within a flexible structure such as the British Constitution to prescribe in advance limitations upon the subjects which can be put to referendum. As Strachey noticed, 'we must have an elastic Referendum' in that Parliament decides what matters are referred (and also the size of the majority required for validation). Just as Parliament can legally do anything, so also it can call a referendum on any matter as it sees fit and decide for itself what majority is required.

In reality, of course, the power of Parliament is today generally a euphemism for the power of government; and the constitutional principle that Parliament can call a referendum on any issue it thinks fit translates all too easily into giving the government an unfettered discretion to call a referendum. But this could offer governments an immense accretion of power, for it would seem that they could always, as with the devolution bills, overcome opposition in the Commons by calling for a referendum. The possibility for manipulation would become considerable, and the referendum could easily be used in a 'Gaullist' manner to buttress the government against its critics.

Thus, it would seem that in Britain, the absence of a written constitution means that the referendum, far from acting as a check upon government, could serve to increase its power. If the calling of a referendum is to be at the discretion of the government of the day, how can such a power be limited or curbed?

There is a counter to this line of argument. For it is extremely unlikely that governments would eagerly resort to the referendum when faced with parliamentary difficulties or difficulties within their own party which prevent them from carrying their legislation. No government will wish to advertise its disagreements, but will appreciate that the appearance of MPs from the governing party on opposed platforms in a referendum campaign will do little to enhance its credibility.

Moreover, no government can ever be sure that it will win a referendum. To call for a referendum, therefore, may be to risk its prestige unnecessarily. The outcome of the EEC referendum proved a fortunate one for the government of the day; but things could easily have been otherwise. For, as the devolution referendums were to show, public opinion can change dramatically during the course of the referendum campaign, and the electorate can decide to use the referendum as an opportunity to show its displeasure at the general direction of government policy. Indeed the devolution referendums led directly to the fall of the Callaghan Government, just as the referendum in France in 1969 led directly to the fall of President de Gaulle.

Nor would it be plausible for governments to make a regular practice of tacking on a referendum clause in committee to an already published bill as the Labour Government did with the Scotland and Wales Bill in 1977. For, although that particular clause was passed, its many inconsistencies and illogicalities were drastically exposed; and the procedural shambles following the introduction of the clause was a major factor in the failure of the government to secure its guillotine motion shortly afterwards.

It is highly improbable, therefore, that governments would attempt to add a referendum clause to a bill whenever there was backbench opposition to it. Much more likely would be the use of the referendum, as in the past, on occasions when the party system is unable to provide clear or coherent solutions to major problems. On such occasions, the government may propose a referendum but it will do so unwillingly, as a last resort rather than a first expedient. The announcement of a referendum will be a sign not of the strength of the government, but of its weakness.

Backbenchers may, as with devolution, insist upon the introduction of a referendum clause as a condition for supporting a particular bill. In such circumstances, the referendum can prove an important addition to backbench power, enabling MPs to propose a popular veto on legislation without endangering the survival of the government which in general they support. As it develops pragmatically in Britain, therefore, the referendum may become a weapon for backbenchers against government. Far from undermining the rights of Parliament, it would strengthen those rights against the government of the day. For the availability of the referendum will have a deterrent effect upon governments, rendering them unwilling to put forward legislation which is strongly opposed by backbenchers and unpopular in the country. Backbenchers will have available to them the possibility of preventing contentious legislation reaching the statute book without compelling the government to resign.

So far, the referendums which have been held in the UK (excluding local referendums) have all been concerned with the legitimacy of transferring the powers of Parliament, either by excluding an area from the United Kingdom (Northern Ireland Border Poll), by the transfer of powers to the European Community (EEC referendum), or by limiting the power of Parliament to legislate for Scotland and Wales (devolution referendums). Such a transfer of power is generally irreversible in practice. It may seem, therefore, as if Parliament has decided that a referendum should be held on any proposal to transfer its powers to another body. It would be difficult to assert that a referendum was constitutionally necessary in such circumstances, but there are at the very least persuasive precedents, amounting perhaps to a constitutional convention, for requiring a referendum, and it would be very difficult for a government proposing a significant transfer of Parliament's power to avoid holding one.

There is also a clear rationale for such a requirement. For proposals to transfer the powers of Parliament deal with the machinery by which laws are made, the framework within which legislation is conducted. The electorate, it might be said, entrust their MPs as agents with legislative power; but they give them no authority to transfer this power. Such authority, it is natural to suggest, can be obtained only through a specific mandate, that is, a referendum. The idea that power is entrusted to the nation's representatives only for specific purposes reflects one of the central principles of liberal constitutionalism, and has its origins in Locke. 'The Legislative', he claims, 'cannot transfer the power of making laws to any other hands. For it being but a delegated power from the People, they who have it cannot pass it to others.'[5] There is thus a clear and principled justification for requiring a referendum to be called whenever it is proposed to transfer the powers of Parliament.

It is possible therefore to discover a rationale for the use of the referendum as it has developed so far in Britain without laying down a priori rules for its use, or being committed to an overall constitutional settlement involving a written constitution or a reformed House of Lords. Indeed the pragmatic introduction of the referendum is much more in accordance with the British approach to constitutional matters than a new constitutional settlement would be.

IS THE REFERENDUM COMPATIBLE WITH THE BRITISH CONSTITUTION?

Analysis of the constitutional effects of the referendum in Britain has mainly dwelt upon the alleged conflict between use of the referendum and the principle of the sovereignty of Parliament. Insofar as it conflicts with this principle, then, so it is sometimes argued, the referendum is not compatible with the British Constitution.

A traditionalist objection of this kind can easily be answered at a number of different levels. At a purely formalistic level, if it is held that Parliament is sovereign and able to do anything, then clearly if it so wishes it can call for a referendum. What it cannot do, if the theory of parliamentary sovereignty is correct, is to allow itself to be *bound* by such a referendum. The referendum therefore must be advisory only. Now all four referendums so far held in Britain have been advisory; and in the EEC referendum, Edward Short was eager to stress that 'The Government will be bound by its result, but Parliament, of course, cannot be bound.'[6] Thus a majority vote in favour of withdrawal from the Community would not have been binding upon Parliament.

Of course, such a formalistic answer is hardly convincing, and indeed Short added, 'Although one would not expect honourable Members to go against the wishes of the people, they will remain free to do so.'[7] For although in theory Parliament cannot be bound by a referendum result, in practice, provided that the result is clear-cut and there has been an adequate turnout, then it would be almost impossible for either Parliament or government to ignore it. It is only if the result is a very close one – as in the Scottish devolution referendum – or the turnout is very low, that Parliament really retains its discretion. So, whatever the position in constitutional theory, there can be no doubt that politically the result of a referendum will almost invariably limit the options of government and Parliament.

But in any case the formalistic approach to the British Constitution is inadequate because it does not ask what purpose is served by constitutional principles and conventions. The classical writers on the British Constitution did not regard it as a set of rules suspended in a formalistic limbo, and lacking any connection with political reality. Instead they saw an intimate connection between constitutional rules and actual political conditions. For Dicey, the purpose of constitutional principles in a representative system was to allow the electorate to influence the working of government; and the principle of the sovereignty of Parliament, therefore, ought to reflect that of the sovereignty of the people. Under representative government, 'the difference between the will of the sovereign [i.e. Parliament] and the will of the nation was terminated',[8] and the 'ethics' of the Constitution comprised 'rules meant to ensure the ultimate supremacy of the true political sovereign, or, in other words, of the electoral body'.[9] Indeed, Dicey saw the purpose of constitutional conventions as being 'to secure that Parliament or the Cabinet . . . shall in the long run give effect to the will of that power which in modern England is the true political sovereign of the state – the majority of the electorate'.[10] 'Our modern code of constitutional morality secures, though in a roundabout way, what is called abroad the "sovereignty of the people".'[11]

If the purpose of conventions is to secure the political sovereignty of the electorate, then the electorate has a *right* to be consulted on major issues of policy. In his *Introduction to the Study of the Law of the Constitution*, first published in 1885, Dicey did not mention the referendum in the British context, for he hoped that the right of the electorate could be secured without it. The Commons, because it was based on popular election, had an interest in conforming to popular wishes, and the House of Lords was able to veto legislation which was not in accord with those wishes. He came to see, however, that the growth of party and the imposition of limits upon the power of the Lords meant that the purposes of constitutional conventions could be circumvented, and that legislation of major or 'constitutional' importance could be passed perfectly easily by Parliament even though it was quite contrary to the wishes of the electorate. It was to prevent this happening that, as we have seen, he advocated the referendum.

At this point, Dicey consciously parted company with the Whig view of the Constitution according to which Parliament was the centre of the political universe. Continued adherence to this conception in an era of disciplined parties seemed to Dicey mere constitutional formalism such as would frustrate the very objectives of limited and moderate government which he, as a Whig, had championed. Balfour of Burleigh argued in Diceyan terms when introducing his Reference to the People Bill:

> Let me turn aside for a moment to consider what is the theory of the Constitution under which we live. I think I am right in saying that the theory is that the will of the people shall prevail. If all cannot meet and discuss matters of public interest they are to do it through their chosen representatives.[12]

Balfour of Burleigh further claimed that Tacitus' aphorism, 'On smaller things, the chief men deliberate; on greater matters *all* the people',

> contains the very essence of the whole of our Constitutional theory. Our Constitution was never intended to deprive the people as a whole of real power in managing their own affairs, and all through our Constitutional history you find there has been a system of checks and balances solely with the idea of securing that the people shall not be taken by surprise, and have the real power taken away from them. . . .
>
> The whole value in these days of our representative system is bound up with the fact that it ought to be a real and true reflex of the people whose business it is supposed to transact.[13]

It was not, however, to be expected that such a doctrine would appeal to the Liberal government of the day, and opposing theories of the Constitution are piquantly contrasted in the following exchange between the Unionist, Lord Selborne, and Lord Morley, the Liberal leader of the House of Commons.

> Selborne: I think I shall be carrying all noble Lords opposite with me when I say that we are agreed that the sovereign power of government in this country resides in the Crown and in the people.
> Morley: Crown and Parliament.
> Selborne: In the Crown and the people.
> Morley: Crown and Parliament.[14]

Whether the referendum was 'unconstitutional' or not seemed to depend upon little more than one's political predilections. Dicey himself had dismissed the issue by saying '. . . unconstitutional. This word has no terrors for me; it means no more than unusual.'[15] Since the referendum involved a redistribution of political power away from 'extremists', from those advocating Home Rule, Tariff Reform, or other measures of political radicalism, it was natural that protagonists of these causes should have opposed them; since it meant a redistribution of power towards the 'moderates' – those Liberals who opposed Home Rule and those Conservatives who opposed the Tariff – it is not surprising that these were the groups which tended to favour the referendum. Conformity to pre-ordained constitutional rules was hardly relevant.

THE REFERENDUM AND THE ROLE OF THE MP

A further argument claiming to show that the referendum is incompatible with the British Constitution suggests that it is an attack on parliamentary government because it undermines the independence and judgment of the MP. It is, according to this view, the MP who, as a representative, must make up his mind on the issues of the day, and not the electorate; and authority for this claim is frequently derived from Burke's Speech to the Electors of Bristol in which he said of the role of the MP:

> But his unbiassed opinion, his mature judgment, his enlightened conscience, he ought not to sacrifice to you. . . . Your representative owes you, not his industry only, but his judgment; and he betrays, instead of serving you, if he sacrifices it to your opinion.[16]

It is, however, difficult to understand the relevance of this conception of the MP's task to the conditions of the last quarter of the twentieth century. Burke was, after all, writing well before the coming of universal suffrage, and before the Commons could be regarded as representative of the people as a whole. In Burke's time, rotten boroughs and nomination boroughs still returned members to Parliament, and there were constituencies which were no more than a mound – Old Sarum – or had fallen into the sea – Dunwich. 'Mr Canning was an eloquent man,' it was said, 'but even he could not pretend that a tree stump was the people.'

Most important of all, Burke was writing long before the advent of organised and disciplined political parties, dominated by professional politicians, and concerned to use Parliament for the advancement of their political creed. MPs today are elected as representatives of a political party; they are expected by their supporters and leaders to sustain that party in office; and indeed it would hardly be possible for a political party to campaign on a particular programme if it did not have some reasonable assurance of being able to carry it out in the event of gaining a majority in the Commons.

It is therefore beside the point to ask whether the referendum interferes with the independence and judgment of the MP. A system in which the referendum is available may be worse than one in which the MP acts as a Burkean representative. That, however, is hardly relevant. The real question to ask is whether a system in which the referendum is available is worse than one in which MPs are in fact unable to prevent the passage of major legislation they oppose other than by bringing down a government which they support. 'The Referendum', said Richard Body, an anti-Common Market Conservative, in the Commons in November 1974,

> is profoundly distasteful to those who pretend to trust the people. They are driven . . . to every sort of excuse for opposing it. . . . Their most delightful plea is that it

would injure the self-respect of the gentlemen who hope to dominate a gagged and boss-driven House of Commons.[17]

It is therefore absurd to argue that the use of the referendum is incompatible with the role of Parliament or the position of the individual MP. Indeed, as we have seen, the referendum may improve the position of the individual MP by providing him with an additional and powerful weapon to use against governments. 'I know', argued one peer in 1911,

> that some of your Lordships think that the Referendum would diminish the authority of the representatives of the people. That is not the case. It enlarges their responsibility. It makes them responsible, not merely to the Party caucus, as they are in this country, but to the people at large. It also has another good result. It renders Ministers more open to reason, and more open to compromise.[18]

The knowledge that the electorate will be able to pronounce upon legislation, far from weakening the Commons might strengthen it, since MPs who favour a particular bill will do their best to ensure that it is put to the people in an attractive and convincing form; and the government will have an incentive to accept reasonable amendments if they increase the likelihood of the legislation gaining public endorsement. It is possible, for example, that if the Labour Government had known, during 1974 and 1975 when it was formulating its policy on devolution, that the Scotland and Wales bills would be put to the country, then better legislation might have resulted. If this view is correct, then the referendum can serve to buttress the position of the individual MP and therefore the role of Parliament.

Nor did the ordinary elector regard the introduction of the referendum as a profound attack upon his representative institutions. Opinion poll evidence showed that the majority of the electorate was eager to be given the opportunity of expressing its opinion on the EEC and on devolution. The referendums held on these issues, despite incidental difficulties, increased popular satisfaction rather then diminishing it.

> The mass of the politically comatose electorate, far from being outraged at the supposed violation of the constitutional citadel, accept the holding of a referendum phlegmatically, not expecting it to change significantly the way they are governed. Whereas seasoned professors of politics rush, like old ladies gathering their skirts after hearing some impropriety, to the columns of journals and newspapers to complain of the violence that is being done to the 'British system of government'.[19]

The referendum is not an attack upon representative government, but an instrument to remedy its defects. Its especial purpose is to weaken the domination of party. The referendum is incompatible not with the British Constitution but with an over-rigid party system. It will be advocated by those who desire to loosen the authority of party, but rejected by those content with the present system of party government. 'It is certain that no man, who is really satisfied with the working of our party system, will ever look with favour on an institution which aims at correcting the vices of party government.'[20] The demand for the referendum arises out of distrust of the efficacy of representative institutions, but more particularly from dislike of the rigidity of the party machine. From the standpoint of the electorate, it increases the influence of those not deeply pledged to the doctrines of the main political parties: the referendum, because it gives an equal value to every vote, yields due weight in deciding political issues to that important segment of political opinion which is not merely *party* opinion.

THE REFERENDUM AND THE PARTIES

Evaluation of the referendum, then, should focus not on its supposed incompatibility with the British Constitution, but on its consequences for party government. There is little likelihood of referendums being held with great frequency in Britain. Britain will not become another Switzerland, nor even follow in the footsteps of Australia which has held 39 referendums this century. But it is possible that the referendum may be called into play again simply because the party system is less capable of handling contentious issues than it was. For the Common Market and devolution are by no means the only issues which cut across party lines. We have seen that from the 1920s to the end of the 1960s, the referendum was in abeyance. This was partly because the House of Lords, the natural 'trigger' for a referendum, that is, the body which might have insisted that a particular measure be put to referendum, had lost its power to insist that issues be put to the people; but more important was the fact that the party conflict during those years corresponded to a greater extent than it does now to the real divisions in the electorate.

In recent years, however, much of the division of opinion in British politics has been within the parties rather than between them; just as, at the beginning of the century, when the referendum lay in the forefront of political debate, questions such as Home Rule and Tariff Reform divided opinion within the parties, rather than between them. Today, issues such as support for free collective bargaining or incomes policy, or attitudes towards the EEC, also divide the parties. To this extent, it will be even less easy to claim that a vote for a party is also a vote for the particular line of policy recommended by the faction which happens, perhaps temporarily, to lead the party. In any case, the policies can change with such rapidity that the notion of general elections yielding a mandate becomes drained of all content. For example, a vote for the Conservatives in 1970 must be interpreted as a mandate for free collective bargaining, yet by February 1974, it was the Labour Party which stood for free collective bargaining, while the Conservatives had adopted a rigorous statutory incomes policy. Between 1974 and 1979, the parties changed sides again, and in the general election of 1979 it was Labour which argued the need for an incomes policy, while the Conservatives were once more the party of free collective bargaining. There was no way in which the electorate could prevent such U-turns by the parties. The argument that party government allows for the clear and consistent development of public policy can hardly be sustained in the light of these and similar examples.

It thus becomes natural to see electoral support for a party as indicating nothing more than a very broad agreement with the general objectives of the party, something which does not preclude strong disagreement on individual items of policy. Voters do not, as perhaps they once did, regard the parties as ideologically coherent bodies; and they find them less and less worthy of their support or approbation. Nor do voters any longer feel tied so exclusively to one political party, and this has led, in recent years, to considerable electoral volatility as they become tempted to express disapproval through abstention, or to experiment with 'unsound' alternatives such as Liberals or Nationalists. If Britain does not return to the 1950s model of a contented two-party system, this will increase the scope for further use of the referendum, which in such a climate can appear a valuable device for resolving political issues.

If the electoral system came to be reformed, the referendum would still be necessary, even though the danger of unrepresentative legislation would be less. For under proportional representation, coalition government would probably result; and the business of government would have to be conducted by a process of bargaining between different parties and groups. There may, however, be some issues which are not amenable to settlement in this way, issues involving such major principles that they require direct endorsement from the electorate through a referendum; or they may be issues which cannot be solved through the process of interparty negotiation and must be put to referendum to avoid a split in a governing coalition – as, for example, in the referendum in Sweden on nuclear power held in 1979. Within a reformed electoral system, the referendum could help to ensure that the electorate was not ignored by the party negotiators.

THE REFERENDUM AS AN EDUCATIVE DEVICE

We have already seen that many of the conventional arguments brought into play against the referendum hold little weight. So long as the referendum remains an instrument of veto and not of initiative, the dangers of demagogy and extremism are likely to be remote. Nor need the referendum necessarily increase the power of government or permit the manipulation of public opinion. Moreover, it can be used without involving the upheaval of a written constitution or a judicial-type tribunal of interpretation.

We have also shown that one of the central arguments in favour of the further use of the referendum lies in a desire to loosen the ties of party; and that those most dissatisfied with the workings of the party system are the most likely to advocate the referendum.

But this does not exhaust the case that can be made for its use as part of the machinery of British government. For a loosening of the party system is by no means the only benefit to be expected from the referendum, which could also improve the quality of the citizen's relationship to government.

In a democracy it is important that the citizen identify himself with the public good, with the interests of the nation as a whole. The referendum brings the voter directly into contact with these interests; it requires him to pay attention to public issues if he is to be able to cast his vote intelligently, and it may encourage him to take an interest in the activities of Parliament. The voter may ask himself not – what is the good of my party, nor perhaps even what is for my own personal good, but rather – what is for the good of the country. It may, therefore, have a profoundly educative effect upon the electorate.

It could be argued that the devolution referendums, for example, exerted such an effect; for many voters seem to have made up their minds how to vote upon the basis of a careful appraisal of the legislation offered to them, ignoring party cues and the interests of the parties which they supported. It is plausible to believe that one main reason for the rejection of devolution was that the Scotland and Wales Acts seemed so patently inadequate to many voters who might, in principle, have been in favour of devolution. Such a result must act as a deterrent to the introduction of bad legislation; and it will be an incentive for governments in the future to ensure that legislation which is to be put to the people can be more easily defended. The EEC referendum, it can be argued, encouraged a sense of social unity by enabling some political activists to reach out across party lines and establish contact with those holding similar opinions on the EEC but widely differing opinions on other political issues. Through the anecdotal evidence quoted by Butler and Kitzinger we have seen what effect this had upon some of the participants. The EEC referendum seemed to bring out a sense of public spirit which had barely been tapped by the main political parties. If this public spirit could be properly stimulated, it would do a great deal to overcome popular alienation from politics.

For one of the central factors in such alienation is the feeling held by many voters that they are utterly unable to influence the decisions of politicians and bureaucrats. In their minority report of the Royal Commission on the Constitution (Kilbrandon Commission), Lord Crowther-Hunt and Professor Peacock drew attention to a 'pervading sense of powerlessness' in the country, and an 'erosion . . . of the extent to which we as a people govern ourselves'.[21] If the referendum encouraged popular interest in political issues, it could play an important part in counteracting these phenomena and therefore improve the working of democracy.

This argument forms an important supplement to the argument for the referendum as a veto, an entrenching device. For, as we have seen, the case for the veto is broadly a conservative one, based upon a distrust of the efficacy of representative institutions, and, in particular, of political parties. But the case for the referendum based upon its educative nature and the need to encourage participation relies upon arguments of an entirely different type. For they reflect not a conservative scepticism towards representative institutions, nor a belief that the source of authority lies with government, but a view that authority derives from the electorate itself.

This argument, however, needs to be carefully qualified. For it is by no means the case that electors welcome frequent referendums. Turnout at referendums is generally lower than in general elections, and where referendums are held frequently, it falls very markedly. In Switzerland there has been a turnout of over 50 per cent in only 6 of the 34 referendums between March 1976 and May 1978.

Almost all countries other than Switzerland which employ referendums use them infrequently,[22] and it seems plausible to argue that the referendum is most likely to exert an educative effect if not used regularly. It should be confined to major issues which cannot be solved by the machinery of party but require the endorsement of the electorate if the final decision is to acquire legitimacy. This, of course, is an important limitation upon the effectiveness of the referendum as an instrument for loosening the party system.

THE INITIATIVE

The referendum ensures that governments cannot pass legislation unwanted by the majority; it repairs a government's sins of commission. But it can do nothing to ensure that governments actually pass legislation which the majority wish to see put into effect. It does nothing to repair the government's sins of omission. For that, the initiative would be needed.

The initiative is a weapon of direct democracy whereby the electorate itself can trigger off a referendum. It can take two forms. The *popular veto* allows a certain number of electors to petition for a referendum on legislation already passed by parliament; this is the form which the initiative takes in Italy and Switzerland. But in Switzerland there is, in addition, provision for the *popular initiative* allowing a specified number of electors to secure a referendum on whether a legislative proposal of their own shall come into effect through a direct vote of the people.

It might be thought that acceptance of the referendum would inevitably lead to the introduction of the initiative also. But there is no necessary political connection. For while many democracies employ the referendum, only two – Switzerland and Italy – use the initiative also; and in Italy, where there is provision for the popular veto but not for the popular initiative, it has been used only three times since 1945. The initiative in both its forms is also used in a number of American states, mostly west of the Mississippi. Nevertheless, the experience of most democracies shows that use of the referendum does not lead to irresistible demands for further instalments of direct democracy.

Some of the leading advocates of the referendum have been extremely hostile to the initiative. St Loe Strachey, for example, claimed that it was 'an encouragement to crude legislative schemes'.[23] He believed that while it might suit a small community such as a Swiss canton or one of the less populous American states, it could not work in a complex modern community with a vast number of laws already on the statute book which would have to be brought into harmony with initiative proposals. But more recently, Professor Finer has argued powerfully for it. In his view a referendum held at the discretion of Parliament – what he calls an optional referendum –

> would not help the people to set their own agenda or to express their own view on what *they* themselves regarded as impertinently unrepresentative measures. On the contrary, it would reinforce the two-party system, confirm its closed nature, merely calling in the public as an ancillary, or, to change the metaphor, inviting it to become its own executioner.[24]

He proposes that Britain adopt the popular veto, with half a million signatures being required to secure a referendum on government legislation; and the popular initiative with one million signatures being required to secure a referendum on a legislative proposal deriving from the electorate.

In communities where the initiative is employed, it is generally used with caution and moderation. It has not led to a flood of legislative proposals, nor to frivolous or unrealistic laws being placed upon the statute book. In Switzerland, the home of the referendum and the initiative, the popular veto has been used 95 times in the years between 1848 and 1978, but it was successful in overturning government legislation only 34 times. The popular initiative has been used only 73 times during the same period, but was successful in placing laws on the statute book only seven times. In Italy, the popular veto has been used only three times, although the threat of using it has persuaded governments to alter the law so as to forestall humiliation at the hands of the electorate. For example, the Italian parliament in 1978 rapidly approved an abortion law so as to pre-empt a threat by the Radical Party to collect signatures for a referendum on the issue. As Finer comments, 'it is fair to say that without this initiative no such legislation would have been passed given the opposition of the Roman Catholic Church. The incident provides an instance of how the device can break the parties' monopoly of issue definition'.[25]

The popular veto is also used in 24 American states and the initiative in 22, mainly western, states; indeed, 17 out of the 24 states west of the Mississippi employ the initiative, while only five of the 26 states east of the Mississippi make provision for it. This reflects, of course, the impact of the Progressive movement in the United States at the beginning of the century, for whom the initiative was part of a much wider package of democratic reforms designed to prevent corruption by controlling the special interests which dominated state legislatures.

Although the initiative has been used in the American states over 1,000 times since 1898, as many as one-third of the initiatives have taken place in only two states, Oregon and California. They are employed over a wide range of issues from the legalisation of dog race betting to the regulation of nuclear power plants. The initiative has not been used recklessly or frivolously, and the electorate has displayed considerable caution in passing popular legislation. In California, for example, there have been, between 1912 and 1978, 171 initiatives, but less than 30 per cent of them have been approved. This itself is an inducement to caution on the part of would-be legislators to think carefully before spending money and time on a proposal which has little chance of success. One student of the initiative process in California has commented: 'California's well educated voters [seem] far more able to cope with intricate initiatives than had been presumed by political scientists. . . . The easy assertions about the apathy, indifference and susceptible nature of voters can at least be questioned by the Californian experience.'[26]

Another criticism frequently made of the initiative is that it gives too much weight to powerful interest groups who can influence the result through injecting large sums of money into the campaign. To secure the requisite number of signatures for an initiative clearly involves a considerable amount of organisational work, and at a later stage much effort is needed to get out the vote. It is natural to suppose that this organisational work will be undertaken by powerful lobbyists who wish to secure legislation in their own interests; and in the American states, companies have attempted to secure initiatives to reduce property taxation, and estate agents have attempted to secure initiatives on housing matters which would benefit them and their clients.

Nevertheless, the rate of failure on initiative proposals, as we have seen, is such that no interest group can be sure of success in its efforts. More importantly, any interest group which seeks to get its proposals on the statute book through the initiative process must succeed in convincing the public through open debate when its proposals will be critically scrutinised by voters and by the media. It may be more difficult to convince the public through argument than to 'nobble' the legislature or the government. Nor is there any consistent relationship between the amount spent in an initiative campaign and the success of the side spending the money. There have been frequent cases where heavy campaign expenditure has not prevented a proposal being defeated. The initiative process is not necessarily dominated by the interests; it has been used in the western states to help in securing electoral control over them. On issues such as protection of the environment and consumer protection, voters have frequently been able to secure legislation through the initiative against the wishes of state legislatures dominated by powerful interest groups.

The initiative process, unlike the referendum, is not necessarily a conservative weapon. It has, it is true, exerted a conservative effect in Switzerland, but that is probably due as much to the conservatism of the Swiss electorate as to the nature of the machinery itself. In the American states, the initiative has on occasion yielded conservative results but it has also been used as a liberal weapon. In the state of Washington, for example, it has been used to secure primary elections, reapportionment and the expansion of welfare benefits. More recently, it has been enthusiastically adopted by the 'New Right' following the success of the Proposition 13 initiative in California. Broadly, the initiative has yielded liberal results on economic issues and conservative results on social issues, but that too, no doubt, reflects the attitudes of the American electorate.

In general, the initiative is likely to prove a transparent process. With a conservative electorate it will produce conservative results; with a liberal electorate, liberal results. Where the electorate is prone to extremism, it can be a dangerous weapon. For example, the two initiatives held in Weimar Germany in the 1920s each gave help to extremist forces at the expense of moderate opinion. In 1926, a popular initiative was held on the expropriation of the German Princes. This had been proposed by the Socialist and Communist Parties who had been weakened in the previous general election held in 1924. The Left-wing parties argued that the funds to be obtained from the expropriation of the Princes should be used for social welfare programmes. Clearly an issue of this kind lent itself to demagogic exploitation. The extreme Left attempted to whip up class hatred while the Nationalists insisted that anyone who supported expropriation would be regarded as a communist. In 1929, the Nationalists secured an initiative on the Young Plan, which had proposed a scaling down of reparations. The Nationalists called their proposal the Freedom Law, or the Law to Prevent the Enslavement of the German People, and the campaign enabled both the Nationalists and the Nazis to regain support which they had lost in the general election of 1928. Both of the initiatives in Weimar Germany, therefore, gave encouragement to extremists and weakened democratic forces loyal to the Republic; they may, therefore, have played some part in the destruction of democracy in Germany.

Nevertheless, there is no reason to believe that the initiative would be similarly exploited in Britain. Germany, it must be remembered, was new to the experience of democracy in the 1920s, and democratic forces there had to struggle against economic instability and resentment born of military defeat. Britain, on the other hand, is a mature and stable democracy, where support for anti-democratic parties has always been negligible. Indeed, even when there has been disillusionment with the two main parties, as in 1974, the British electorate has preferred to opt for strictly constitutional alternatives such as the Liberal Party or the Scottish National Party. It has shunned both the Communist Party and the National Front. If, therefore, an initiative does no more than reflect in a rather transparent way the opinions of the electorate, it would be unlikely to offer a stimulus to extremism in Britain.

Adoption of the initiative in Britain could yield considerable benefits. We have already seen that, in those areas where it is used, far from undermining democracy, it may serve to supplement the representative system by remedying some of its weaknesses. If it is merely an assumption that Parliament represents public opinion, the initiative offers an excellent method of testing that assumption. It provides a means over and above that offered by representative institutions through which the wishes of the electorate can be ascertained.

It could provide an even stronger check than the referendum on the power of party oligarchies, and thus encourage the growth of consensus. It could have similar results, in this respect, to the legislative referendum in Denmark, which has the effect, according to one authority on Danish politics, of making governments cautious about carrying through sweeping reforms in parliament: 'A Government in its evaluation of legislation must feel fairly certain that there is a sure majority in the population for important laws that are passed in the Folketing.'[27] It is possible that the initiative might have a similar effect on the pretensions of the political parties in Britain also.

The strongest argument, however, for the introduction of the initiative in Britain must be its educative effect upon public opinion. Almost all of the studies of political behaviour that have been made in Western democracies have noticed the low levels of knowledge and political awareness amongst the electorate as a whole, and the existence of such ignorance and apathy is frequently used to build up a case against 'populism'. But it is perfectly possible that public apathy is as much a product as it is a cause of the electorate's lack of impact upon the political process. It may well be that if citizens believed that their opinions were of importance and that politicians and civil servants would be required to take account of them, then their interest in and knowledge of political affairs would become greater.

Admittedly, this argument can be countered by pointing to the fact that referendums and initiatives generally attract lower levels of voter participation than elections. But it may be, nevertheless, that the referendum and the initiative, by encouraging concentration upon political *issues* rather than upon political parties or personalities, contribute more to the education of the electorate than a general election. For those in power the process may serve, as it has in the state of Washington,

> to call attention to the wishes of certain people who may not have as effective access to the Legislature as some others who have effective legislators to introduce and support their Bills. In short the process is an additional method for getting problems on the public Agenda.[28]

The initiative allows the electorate itself to define the issues, and it may well define them differently from the political parties or other political leaders. It might, therefore, encourage a sense of responsibility among the electors derived from the knowledge that they themselves are responsible for the legislation of the state. If bad legislation is passed they will be unable to blame the politicians, but will have to accept the responsibility themselves. In the words of James Bryce, 'the greatest, the most incontestable merit claimable for Direct Legislation' is that:

> It is unequalled as an instrument of practical instruction in politics. Every voting compels the citizen who has a sense of civic duty to try to understand the question submitted, and reach a conclusion thereon. Many, sometimes even a half, fail to come to the polls, yet even these may derive some benefit from the public discussion that goes on. . . . It is a good thing for the citizen to be relieved from the pressure of those personal or party predilections which draw him to one candidate or another and to be taken out of the realm of abstract ideology to face concrete proposals. Here is a plan which throws on him the responsibility of declaring a definite opinion on a specific proposition, forcing him to ask himself, 'Is it sound in principle?' 'Will it work?' 'Shall I vote for or against it?'[29]

Nevertheless, if the initiative were to be introduced into Britain, it would necessitate consequential reforms of a very radical kind. There would first have to be a statute delimiting those issues for which it was suitable. In Switzerland, the initiative cannot be used on matters connected with the budget or international treaties, and it would be generally agreed that issues broadly of foreign affairs and budgetary matters might be unsuitable for the initiative process. Moreover, although we have argued that the initiative would not in general lead to illiberal results, it would be wise to offer additional protection to minority rights so as to prevent such infringement in specific cases. In the United States and Switzerland, of course, minority rights are protected by the Constitution: and a number of successful initiatives in the American states have later been ruled unconstitutional by the Supreme Court. It would be better, however, if issues prejudicial to minority rights were prevented from being raised, rather than being ruled unconstitutional after having been passed, since clearly great hurt and humiliation could be suffered by minority groups simply by the discussion of certain extreme proposals. Great damage could be done to race relations, for example, by an initiative proposal to repatriate compulsorily coloured immigrants, even though such a proposal would almost certainly be rejected. Some kind of constitutional safeguard, therefore, would have to be developed if the initiative were ever to be applied in Britain.

Moreover, in order to ensure against the danger of legislative proposals being carried by a small minority of the electorate on a low turnout, it would be necessary to impose a requirement that a qualified majority, perhaps 40 or 50 per cent, should be required for success in an initiative. The need for this in the case of proposals which have not been considered by Parliament is more important than in the case of a referendum where the role of the electorate is restricted to approving or vetoing a legislative proposal which has already been accepted by Parliament.

In view of the constitutional difficulties of providing for the initiative in Britain, however, and because it would involve so radical a departure from her historic experience it might be best to delay its introduction until sufficient experience has been gained of the working of the referendum:

> Though Switzerland shows that referenda encourages responsibility and liberalism in electors, there are dangers during a transition period. It is one thing to have been drinking all one's life, another to start suddenly in middle age.[30]

CONCLUSION

To claim that the referendum can be a valuable and in certain circumstances a politically indispensable instrument is not to deny its limitations in the settling of contentious issues. Where it is of value is in resolving disputes in clearly circumscribed situations, but it cannot of itself yield the will to agreement where none exists. It can articulate a submerged consensus, but it cannot create one. The referendum will only succeed in settling a difficult dispute where there is some common ground between the contending parties. There are many examples of cases where this condition has been met and where, accordingly, the referendum succeeded in settling a dispute. Examples of such settlements are the plebiscite in Schleswig in 1920 which divided the province between Denmark and Germany after which 'the Schleswig Question, which caused three wars in the nineteenth century and rent the councils of Europe for some seventy years, . . . ceased to exist';[31] the referendums in Switzerland which consented to the creation of a separate canton of Jura, detached from Berne; and the referendums on the Sunday opening of public houses in Wales which were accepted on all sides as a fair method of resolving an emotive issue.

More frequently, however, the losing side is not fully committed to accepting the result. We have seen that after the EEC referendum, Tony Benn claimed that he had received from the British people 'a very big message . . . loud and clear', but the anti-Marketeers did not regard that as concluding the debate. Indeed, after a short pause, they again took up their policy, which they pursued with even more enthusiasm, of disentangling Britain from the EEC; and in Northern Ireland, the referendum is too blunt a weapon to resolve complex issues of nationality and allegiance.

It is not, however, an argument against the use of the referendum to say that it cannot provide a final settlement to constitutional problems by manufacturing the will to agreement where none exists. For it is not as if there is any alternative instrument which could succeed where the referendum fails. There is, as Disraeli noticed, no finality in politics, least of all over issues involving the volatile and sensitive emotions aroused by ethnic nationalism.

A further limitation of the referendum must be noted in that it cannot do much to solve the social and economic problems which are central to this country's future as an industrial nation. In September 1977, Mrs Thatcher, as Leader of the Opposition, indicated that, if involved in a crisis of industrial relations of the kind that had brought down Edward Heath in 1974, she would put the issue of 'Who governs – the government or the trade unions?' to the people in a referendum, rather than a general election. It is doubtful, however, whether the complex problems of industrial relations – problems essentially of bargaining rather than of constitutional principle – can be successfully put to referendum in this way. Indeed, there is no example of any other country in the world attempting to solve its industrial relations problems through this method – although in one or two American states, such issues have been put to referendum. Nor is it clear that a referendum is a genuine alternative to a general election in such a situation. For if the government lost a referendum on a 'Who governs?' issue, it would find it difficult to continue in office; and opponents of the government would use the opportunity of the referendum to seek to drive it from office.

It should not be thought, therefore, that wider use of the referendum could do very much for the progress of the British economy or for industrial recovery except perhaps indirectly by increasing the degree of rapport between government and people. The referendum is a weapon of very limited value in solving problems of economic management. The central contribution which constitutional reform can make to these wider problems is to provide a climate of political stability within which industry can operate effectively. Such an environment might result from a reform of the electoral system, but it will not come about solely through the introduction of the referendum. The very real value of the referendum would be undermined if it were misapplied to issues for which it was not suitable. It is for this reason that the referendum cannot provide a complete answer to the problems raised by the rigidity of the party system; it needs to be complemented by electoral reform.

We may conclude, nevertheless, that wider use of the referendum could offer real benefits in the operation of British politics. It would prove a powerful weapon against the condition described by Lord Hailsham as 'elective dictatorship', the attempt by governments to implement major changes without ensuring popular support for them. The referendum makes it impossible for such changes to occur unless there is a popular consensus behind them – a significant and important modification of the pattern of contemporary British politics. In doing this, the referendum could improve the quality of the relationship between government and people; and that constitutes the central argument in favour of its wider use. For, in the last resort, the arguments against the referendum are also arguments against democracy, while acceptance of the referendum is but a logical consequence of accepting a democratic form of government.

Part III

Proportional representation, 1831–1979

Our habit of treating the voice of a majority as equivalent to the voice of all is so deeply engrained that we hardly think it has a history.

MAITLAND

Chapter 1

1831–1931

INTRODUCTION

The most obvious way through which the people exercise their power in a democracy is by means of free elections. Indeed it is the ability afforded to the people to choose their representatives that constitutes the distinguishing mark of a democratic state. But this right can be exercised by means of a very large number of electoral systems, each having very different political effects.

In Britain, the electoral system has been a subject for debate since the time of the first Reform Bill. Indeed, motions advocating proportional or minority representation were proposed during the parliamentary stages of each of the great Reform Acts between 1832 and 1918. The debate has been an essentially practical one, and two interconnected aspirations have motivated most electoral reformers: first a desire to lessen the power of party; secondly, the urge to protect minorities. This second theme was particularly important in the nineteenth century as it became clear that extension of the franchise would lead inevitably to democracy. Indeed, the early and somewhat crude forms of proportional representation advocated in Britain are more properly understood as systems of minority representation – attempts to ensure that minorities were not excluded from Parliament.

The first occasion on which the electoral system was raised for discussion in Parliament was on 13 August 1831, when the poet, Winthrop Mackworth Praed, Tory MP for the rotten borough of St Germans in Cornwall, tabled an amendment to the Reform Bill calling for the 'introduction of a perfectly new principle into our representative system'.[1] He wanted to ensure that the new constituencies being created by the Reform Bill would secure 'the full representation of all classes of the community in Parliament'.

As a Tory, Praed was worried about the danger of placing 'a minority of number, but a majority of property and intelligence in opposition to a majority, perhaps a large majority, of number, but a minority, perhaps an insignificant minority, of property and intelligence'.[2] The new structure of representation being introduced by the Reform Bill would, if precautions were not taken, allow for a vicious form of class warfare, with the 'mob' overwhelming the civilised minority which had hitherto governed the country.

The cure for this condition was to appreciate that popular representation did not mean that only the majority should be represented. Representation was representation of all, and not merely representation of the majority:

If we desire that the Representatives of a numerous constituency should come hither merely as witnesses of the fact, that certain opinions are entertained by a majority of that constituency, our present system of election is certainly rational. . . . But if we intend, as surely we do intend, that not the majority only, but the aggregate mass of every numerous constituency, should, so far as it is possible, be seen in the persons, and heard in the voices of their Representatives – should be, in short, in the obvious and literal sense of the word 'represented' in this House; – then, Sir, our present role of election is in theory wrong and absurd.[3]

To ensure the representation of the community as a whole, Praed argued for a form of the limited vote such as was later applied in certain constituencies between 1867 and 1885. Until 1885, the basic unit of representation in England was not the single-member but the multi-member constituency: Praed proposed that in any of the seven county constituencies returning three members and in four-member seats, each elector should have not more than two votes. If the elector had as many votes as there were members returned, a bare majority would be sufficient to secure all three (or four) seats for the members of one party, and the minority would be totally unrepresented. With the limited vote, however, the minority, it was hoped, might be able to secure one seat.

Praed's motion was opposed by the Whig, Althorp, and it was not pressed to a division. In a later speech, however, in the Committee stage of the Reform Bill, Praed returned to the charge and alluded to another theme which was to become prominent in the writings of later advocates of proportional representation – the need for constitutional protection. He contrasted the situation in the United States, where democracy was circumscribed by checks and balances, with that in Britain:

But there is also another distinction between the U.S. and this country. The legislature of America had provided that no change should take place in the constitution of that country without the consent of at least two-thirds of the constituent body. We had no such security against great constitutional changes and were therefore bound to take care that a mere minority should be duly represented.[4]

Although his motion seemed conservative in spirit, Praed received no support from the leader of his party. 'Peel and our leaders thought it too speculative a notion, i.e. an idea by which the country might be benefited but the Party not,'[5] was Praed's own explanation for this lack of sympathy.

THE CUMULATIVE VOTE

By the 1850s, it was apparent that another Reform Act, further extending the franchise, could not be long delayed, and accordingly new schemes aiming to secure minority rights were presented. The most prominent of these schemes was the cumulative vote proposed by James Garth Marshall (1802–73) in his pamphlet *Minorities and Majorities: Their Relative Rights. (A letter to the Lord John Russell M.P. on Parliamentary Reform.)* Marshall was Liberal MP for Leeds from 1847 to 1852, and a member of the Leeds Parliamentary Reform Association. Unlike many electoral reformers of the period, he welcomed the extension of the suffrage to the working classes, but insisted that representative democracy was only tolerable if minorities were protected. There was, according to Marshall, 'an important defect in the mechanism of our Representative system as it now exists . . .'. This was the exclusion of minorities from proper representation. 'It is as if the majority in a simple democratic republic were to use their powers as a majority to disfranchise a minority and exclude them altogether from the National Legislative Assembly.'[6]

The instrument which Marshall proposed to secure minority representation was the cumulative vote. This gave to each elector in a multi-member constituency as many votes as there were candidates to be elected. The voter could distribute his votes as he wished and he could, if he so desired, cumulate votes on any one or more candidates. Thus, for example, if there were three candidates to be elected a voter could 'plump' by using all his three votes on one candidate. By doing this, any minority over the size of a quarter would be sure of gaining representation in a three-member constituency.

Moreover, through the mechanism of the cumulative vote, Marshall believed that it would be possible to secure the election of the best individual candidate, regardless of party. He hoped that the cumulative vote would ensure that the quality of support for a candidate would count as much as the quantity. It would be a means of giving:

> due weight to intelligence, education and character, without introducing any new class privileges, which might be more or less odious to those excluded.[7]

Marshall therefore sought, as Hare and Mill were later to do, through electoral engineering to combine democracy with enlightened government. In this way the advent of democracy might be made tolerable since it would not lead to the domination of the uneducated.

Marshall also hoped that the cumulative vote would moderate the extremes of the party system. Representative government suffered from a defect 'which may be admitted to increase in proportion as the popular element is strengthened . . . the want of fixed continuity of purpose in the conduct of public affairs. . . . Our present system of voting seems to be ingeniously contrived to encourage this tendency to extremes.' The tendency of the cumulative vote on the other hand, was 'to steady the utterance of the Will of the People, and to steady its influence upon the Government, which serves them'.[8] This was a theme which has retained its prominence in the thinking of many contemporary advocates of proportional representation.

In 1867, Robert Lowe, the vehement Liberal critic of democracy, tabled an amendment to the Second Reform Bill proposing the introduction of the cumulative vote for three-member constituencies. He saw this as a last desperate attempt to avoid the dominance of the 'mob' in politics, and to preserve something of the values of enlightened opinion which he saw as the hallmark of a Liberal society. He was supported by Gorst, a Conservative, later to be Disraeli's party manager, who believed that in its eagerness to indulge in a competitive auction for the extension of the franchise, the Conservative Party was in danger of forgetting Conservative principles:

> They were giving the country an extreme democratic measure and at the same time they shrank from all those checks and precautions that Honourable Members opposite had themselves suggested.[9]

Lowe's amendment was also supported by Lord Cranborne, later Lord Salisbury, as well as by the radicals Fawcett and Mill, who saw the cumulative vote as 'a makeshift',[10] a worthy but inadequate attempt to secure fair representation, an aim better secured by the single transferable vote. John Bright, however, saw the cumulative vote as:

> the most violent attack upon the principle of representation in this country that has ever been made in this House.[11]

and Disraeli believed that it was:

> Alien to the customs, manners and traditions of the people of this country,[12]

while Lowe, after the defeat of his amendment, claimed, no doubt rightly, that

> I don't think anyone in either House understood it.[13]

The cumulative vote was, however, adopted between 1870 and 1902 for the election of the school boards established under the Education Act, with the intention of ensuring that religious minorities were properly represented. It was hoped that in this way compromise between the different religious groups would be possible and asperities softened, so that parents of all religious denominations would gain confidence in the boards. The cumulative vote did, on the whole, succeed in securing the representation of the main religious groups on the boards. But it did so only at the cost of strengthening rather than limiting the influence of political organisation.

For if a particular group was to maximise its representation, it had to know where its supporters were located. Voters were then told by their party which candidates they should support. On a 15-member board, for example, a party would need eight members to obtain a majority. This meant that the vote had to be divided between two, three and three candidates in three divisions. So the voter lost the advantage which the cumulative vote had promised him, of being able to choose for himself which candidates were worthy of his vote. For this reason, the Royal Commission on the Elementary Education Acts recommended in 1888 the adoption of the single transferable vote in place of the cumulative vote, since the former would, in its view, do away with the need for rigid party organisation.[14] But in the event, the school boards were absorbed into the local authorities in 1902 for which the plurality method of election was in operation.

THE LIMITED VOTE

In the debates on the 1867 Reform Bill, Robert Lowe's amendment providing for adoption of the cumulative vote was, as we have seen, defeated. But the Reform Act of that year did provide for minority representation through another device known as the limited vote. This provided that, in all contested elections for the 13 three-membered constituencies created by the Act, no person should vote for more than two candidates and in the City of London, a four-member constituency, no elector would have more than three votes. This would ensure that two-fifths of the voters in a constituency would be able to elect a representative, and, it was hoped, allow the minority to be represented on as little as one-third of the vote.

The so-called minority clause formed no part of Disraeli's original reform proposals, and was indeed opposed by the Conservative Government, but it was put forward as an amendment to the Bill in the Lords by Lord Cairns, a Conservative peer later to be Lord Chancellor in Disraeli's 1874 administration. The motive was twofold; first there was the desire for 'fair representation', representation of individual opinion, of minorities as well as majorities; and secondly there was the conservative fear of the 'tyranny of the majority', and a desire to ensure that 'property and intelligence' were properly represented under the new dispensation. These two elements sat ill together, and easily lent themselves to satire:

> It was due to a combination of philosophers, who had persuaded themselves that it was in the interest of and furtherance of true democratic principles, with those on the other hand who feared the results of the Reform Act, and who regarded the principle as a means of checking Democracy, and as affording the opportunity for men with views unpopular to the general constituency to find their way into the House of Commons.[15]

In moving his amendment, Cairns asserted that the expansion of the franchise, by giving the vote to 'large masses in our large towns', would result in 'the great bulk of the property and intelligence' being 'found of necessity in the minority and not in the majority'. It would be in the minority in every constituency, and would therefore be in danger of securing no representation at all. Provision for the representation of minorities would improve the legislature; it would ensure 'diversity' of representation, so that the Commons was not dominated by one class, and the minority of 'property and intelligence' would provide a steadying element, thus providing a check on radical policies.

Cairns' amendment secured the support of Earl Russell who, as Lord John Russell, was a former Whig Prime Minister. Russell stressed the need for moderate men in Parliament whose influence 'is of much use in allaying the heat of party passion'. It was, however, opposed by both front benches, and Lord Malmesbury, speaking for the government, declared that his 'first objection' to the proposal 'is that it is entirely a new-fangled one'.

> The mind of an Englishman [he went on] is a very straightforward piece of machinery, and I may say he generally puts the question in black and white. Upon the subject of discussion he is accustomed, and has been accustomed, ever to obey majorities, to be ruled by majorities, and to be obedient to the decisions and verdicts of majorities.[16]

The peers, however, showed themselves less straightforward than Malmesbury had hoped, and passed Cairns' amendment by 142 votes to 51, the minority consisting largely of members of the government.

In the Commons, Bright urged, with considerable vehemence, the rejection of the Cairns amendment, regarding it as a usurpation of the functions of the Commons that the Lords should attempt to interfere with the electoral system. Sir Charles Russell, a Radical member, claimed:

> The arguments which had been used in support of the scheme were three phases of fear. The argument of the noble Lord the Member for Stamford [i.e. Cranborne] was that of alarm, the argument of Lord Cairns was one of anxiety, while that of the right hon. Gentleman the Member for Calne [i.e. Lowe] was one of woe. He did not share in the nightmare of any noble army of crochets. He felt no alarm. He had no anxiety. He conjured up no woe. What he had given, he had not given in distrust, but in confidence and faith.[17]

Gladstone, deeply conservative on electoral matters, urged the Commons to overturn the Cairns amendment – which was 'a great innovation', 'a causeless change in the institutions of the country'.[18] Disraeli, although also deploring the amendment, suggested, out of weariness rather than conviction, that it be accepted; and the Commons defeated Bright's motion of rejection by 253 votes to 204. So it was that the minority clause became part of the Act, although opposed by the three leading parliamentarians of the day – Bright, Gladstone and Disraeli.

EXPERIENCE OF THE LIMITED VOTE

The effects of the limited vote, however, were to be rather different from those anticipated. For in Glasgow and Birmingham, the Liberals were able to circumvent it; and in Birmingham, it stimulated the development of the Caucus, a political machine dominated by Joseph Chamberlain whose purpose it was to ascertain the location of Liberal strength so as to secure the election of all three Liberal candidates.

The Birmingham Liberal Association – the Caucus – appreciated that if, as appeared likely, it had the support of over 60 per cent of the electorate in the city, it could win all of the seats provided only that Liberal votes were distributed evenly amongst the candidates. They therefore instituted a canvass to discover where their support lay, and distributed to likely Liberal voters cards telling them to vote for candidates A and B; or A and C; or B and C. Thus each candidate would receive just the amount of support he needed to secure election without piling up wasted surplus votes which could have been used to assist other candidates.

The result of the 1880 election in Birmingham shows how this technique worked:

P. H. Muntz (Liberal)	22,969	Major F. Burnaby (Conservative)	15,735
John Bright (Liberal)	20,079	Hon. A. C. G. Calthorpe (Conservative)	14,208
Joseph Chamberlain (Liberal)	19,544		
	62,592		29,943

It can be seen that if care had not been taken with the preliminary canvass, 4,000 (say) of Joseph Chamberlain's votes might have been shared between Muntz and John Bright so that Major Burnaby, the Conservative, would have gained the third seat even though the total party vote was unchanged.

If, moreover, the Liberals had miscalculated the extent of their support, not only would they have failed to secure all three seats, but a wildly disproportionate result could have occurred, as at Leeds in 1874:

R. M. Carter (Liberal)	15,390	W. St J. Wheelhouse (Conservative)	14,864
E. Baines (Liberal)	11,850	R. Tennant (Conservative)	13,192
Dr F. Lees (Liberal)	5,945		
	33,185		28,056

The Conservatives, although securing 5,000 less votes than the Liberals gained two seats to the Liberals' one.[19]

Where, as in Birmingham, the Liberals were able to nullify the effects of the clause, this was done by telling Liberal voters which candidates they must support, and it gave great power to the party organisation.

The voter who had left the selection of the three candidates to the general committee was also to renounce the privilege of selecting from them the two which he preferred. 'Vote as you are told' was the password. . . .

'You must vote as you are told! We who have flattered and petted you when you had no vote – stating over and over again our entire confidence in your ability rightly to use it – now cannot trust you! I say it is an insult.' . . . Some Radicals of the old school, survivors of the 'glorious days' of 1831–1832, who had fought for the extension of the suffrage, were grieved to see that their fellow-citizens were about to exercise it not as free men but as puppets.[20]

But not only was the voter corralled by the party organisation. The candidate, too, found that, owing everything to the organisation, he could hardly afford to display the kind of independence in the Commons which supporters of minority representation such as Mill and Lowe had hoped to encourage. Far from turning the Commons into a deliberative assembly dominated by moderate men, therefore, the minority clause secured the return of members who owed election to the party machine.

It is ironic that the limited vote, designed to safeguard minorities, encouraged the development of a party machine whose purpose it was to ensure that only majorities were represented; and that the Liberal Party, which was to be a twentieth-century victim of the electoral system, should have been the first to apply the principles of modern party organisation so as to ensure the triumph of the majority.

The limited vote, like the cumulative vote, was but a crude precursor of Thomas Hare's system which became the single transferable vote. For this latter system, as we shall see, did not rely upon a party organisation to locate the vote. Under the single transferable vote, surplus votes were not wasted, as they would be under the limited or cumulative vote systems, but transferred to other candidates to assist in securing their election. Because the single transferable vote was so much more sophisticated than the crude devices of minority representation, it came to be the favoured instrument of electoral reformers from the 1880s, and support for the limited vote and the cumulative vote died away completely.

Unfortunately for the electoral reformers, however, the failure of the limited vote and the cumulative vote to achieve their aims cast doubt upon all schemes which sought to achieve proportional representation. Objections to a particular *method* of securing electoral fairness came to be identified with objections to the principle of proportionality itself. So it was that when in 1884 the advocates of the single transferable vote attempted to press their case in the Commons, they were met with arguments based upon the unsatisfactory working of the limited vote and the cumulative vote; and their case was treated with derision.

THOMAS HARE'S THEORY

The originator of the single transferable vote method of proportional representation seems to have been Thomas Wright Hill (1763–1851), a Midlands schoolmaster and father of Sir Rowland Hill, inventor of the modern postal system. It was developed independently in Denmark by Carl Andrae (1812–93), a mathematician, Minister of Finance, and 'A man of original and speculative intellect, a keen originator, a bold thinker, admitted by all his countrymen to be the first mathematician in Denmark.'[21] He applied his system in 1855 to elections to the federal chamber of Denmark in a vain attempt to conciliate the Germans of Schleswig–Holstein, the first occasion on which the single transferable vote system was applied to a national legislature.

But the elaboration of the single transferable vote was undertaken by Thomas Hare (1806–91), and this method of voting is often known as the Hare system in tribute to his memory. Hare was a Conservative free trader, and the keynote of both his advocacy of free trade and his attitude towards electoral reform was his desire to free the individual from all regulations which interfered with his choice. He became a Peelite in 1846, breaking with the Conservative Party, but he had no desire to be absorbed into the Liberal Party and sought to preserve his independent political identity. Indeed, part of his motivation in seeking electoral reform was to enable people like himself to remain independent and uncommitted.

Hare first published his views on electoral reform in a pamphlet entitled *The Machinery of Representation* (W. Maxwell, London) in 1857, but the principal source for understanding his ideas is his *Treatise on the Election of Representatives, Parliamentary and Municipal* (Longmans, 1859). Hare's theory was based upon a liberal conception of representation according to which the MP represented *opinions*, rather than social interests. The corollary of this view, he claimed, was that opinion could not be confined within the geographical boundaries of a parliamentary constituency. It was unfair that holders of a particular opinion should be unable to secure parliamentary representation because they happened to be scattered in different parts of the country, rather than concentrated within one parliamentary constituency. Under the plurality system, representation was *geographical*, and this was an unwarrantable limitation upon the free choice of the individual. Hare sought to transform a *geographical* system of representation into a system of *personal* representation. Indeed Hare preferred the name 'personal representation' to 'proportional representation' as a description of his system; for his central concern was that the individual should be properly represented, and this could occur only if he had an MP who shared his general outlook and would express it in Parliament. Later advocates of the system were to call it real representation.

In Hare's view, the individual should be able to choose his representative from any part of the country. His constituency ought to be a voluntary one composed of men of like-minded opinion, not a geographical one constrained by locality. In his original scheme, therefore, the elector would be able to vote for any candidate in any part of the country; indeed, there would be no list of candidates: the elector would write in the names of candidates himself. Of course the vast majority of electors would, no doubt, name candidates who lived within their local constituency and who were personally known to them. But there would be a significant and important minority, including, for Hare, the educated minority, who would name candidates from elsewhere.

Hare sought to avoid the defects of the limited vote and the cumulative vote by which votes cast for popular candidates would be wasted if they were in excess of those required for election. He proposed, therefore, that a quota be established consisting of the number of votes cast divided by the number of seats in the House of Commons. Thus suppose that every member of the electorate – 1¼ million in Hare's day – cast his vote: with 650 MPs to be elected, the quota would be 1¼ million/650, equal to 1,923. Voting would be preferential, the voter naming on his ballot paper an order of preference comprising as many candidates as he wished to support. If a popular candidate secured more than the quota, his surplus votes would be transferred to the next candidate preferred by his supporters. At the same time candidates at the bottom of the poll would be eliminated and their votes also transferred to other candidates. This process would continue until just 650 candidates had secured the quota. In this way no votes would be wasted and the elector would be enabled to choose from the whole country the candidate whom he most wished to see elected.

Hare's scheme formed the basis of what later became the single transferable vote. In its original form, it was of course hopelessly unrealistic and attracted much laughter and derision; and among Parliamentary wits, it became known as a Hare-brained scheme.

Nevertheless, it is worth investigating not the machinery of Hare's scheme but the aims which it sought to achieve, since these were also the aims sought by advocates of the single transferable vote. Hare was not altogether sympathetic to democracy, believing, with many Victorian intellectuals, that democracy could mean the rule of the ignorant and uneducated and the dominance of a single class, the manual labourer. This class would enjoy a majority in every constituency in the country so that, if the plurality system was retained, the minority would everywhere be totally swamped. The uneducated, lacking knowledge of the political process, would require organisations to tell them how to vote, and this would stimulate the growth of the party caucus, further constraining the enlightened voter and leading to social stagnation; for Hare believed, in common with most Victorian liberals, that progress depended upon diversity of opinion, which was an essential precondition of social improvement. Hare's aim, then, was to make universal suffrage tolerable by ensuring that minorities, and especially the educated minority, were properly represented in Parliament. The constraint which Hare's system would provide upon the tyranny of the majority was, moreover, a democratic constraint, and therefore, far superior to the 'fancy franchises' with which liberals had previously toyed. It would, in J. S. Mill's view, render unnecessary the introduction of educational qualifications or plural voting.

> I should not despair [said Mill] of the operation even of equal and universal suffrage, if made real by . . . Mr Hare's principle.[22]

It was for this reason that Mill believed Hare's scheme was making headway

> with the friends of democracy as a logical conclusion of their principles; with those who rather accept than prefer a democratic government, as an indispensable corrective of its inconveniences.[23]

Hare hoped that his scheme would greatly widen the choice available to the voter. It would free him not only from the natural constraints of geography, but also from the artificial constraints of party. Hare did not deny that parties were necessary for the effective working of representative governments, but like Mill and later Ostrogorski he believed that parties should be loosely organised structures representing broad categories of opinion rather than tightly organised machines requiring conformity and limiting the choice of the elector.

> The necessity of obtaining a majority involves the necessity of creating a party, adopting the party name, and putting forward some party tenet or dogma, to all of which the majority must lend itself. It is not usually the political tenet which has caused the party but the party which has created the tenet. . . .
>
> A system which forms the electoral body into adverse parties – arrayed under formal names which are themselves exaggerations calculated to excite hostility where none really exists – has thus the effect of preventing the expression of the true and individual opinions of the members who compose either party.[24]

Under Hare's scheme, parties would have to select their candidates more carefully since they could no longer be sure of getting them elected in safe seats. Under the plurality system, on the other hand, the elector is restricted to voting for the candidate presented to him by his party. The party nominee must be supported whatever his qualifications. The electors, in order not to split the vote of the majority party, are 'misrepresented, having been obliged to accept the man who had the greatest number of supporters in their political party, though his opinions may differ from theirs on every other point'. The parties, in order to avoid losing votes, would be likely to bring forward candidates without strong or distinctive qualities and 'Thus, the man who is chosen, even by the strongest party, represents perhaps the real wishes only of the narrow margin by which that party outnumbers the other.' Parliament would come to be composed of timid and weak personalities, men who would be only too willing to follow the lead of their party. Under Hare's system, on the other hand, the majority would have to seek members of higher calibre if they were to win seats. 'The slavery of the majority to the least estimable portion of their number would be at an end.'[25]

Therefore, the quality of MPs would be higher and the MP himself would become more independent of party ties since he would owe his election as much to his personal qualities as to his party allegiance. He might therefore hope to secure re-election even if the party which he supported was unpopular and suffered at the polls. Thus one important benefit of the Hare system was that it would improve the personnel of Parliament.

But Parliament ought not to be composed merely of representatives of the majority. For democracy entailed the right of the majority to rule; it did not mean that only the majority should be *heard*. Indeed, it was a basic premiss both of liberalism and democracy that all voices should be heard before decisions were made; for only in this way would it be possible for genuine debate and argument to take place. The legislature, therefore, should be a mirror of the nation as a whole. Under Hare's system, any minority whose views had significant support equal to that of the quota would be able to elect an MP. Hare and Mill had no doubt that it would be the educated minority which would be able to make itself felt in the Commons quite out of proportion to its numerical strength. Moreover, since there would be unlikely to be a solid party majority in Parliament, the executive would have to secure support in the Commons through reasoning rather than through the party Whip. Parliament would no longer be subordinate to the executive, but would become again a deliberating chamber peopled by the best minds. 'An assembly so chosen', Mill believed, 'would contain the elite of the nation.' 'Modern democracy would have its occasional Pericles, and its habitual group of superior and guiding minds.'[26]

The wider degree of choice which Hare's system gave to the voter would make him think more carefully about how he should exercise his vote. Hare saw the act of voting as a crucial exercise of personal responsibility:

> Personal representation encourages every man to do the best that is in him, and leaves him without excuse if he does not; and it therefore in the highest degree tends to promote individual effort.

and every detail of his scheme converged upon

one central point – that of making the exercise of the suffrage a step in the elevation of the individual character, whether it be found in a majority or a minority.[27]

This sense of responsibility was a vital constituent of a liberal society; together with the new-found independence of the MP and a Parliament composed of independent-minded members, it would play an important part in ensuring that liberal values were preserved even under a democratic regime.

Hare secured a distinguished convert to his scheme in John Stuart Mill who recommended it in his essay *Recent Writers on Reform* published in 1859, and in chapter 7 of his book *Considerations on Representative Government*, 1861. Mill had previously been sceptical of the value of democracy and had proposed that there be an educational qualification for the franchise. He then supported the cumulative vote which he hoped would assist in the election of educated candidates. But when he learned of Hare's scheme he wrote to him saying:

You appear to me to have exactly, and for the first time, solved the difficulty of popular representation; and by doing so, to have raised up the cloud of gloom and uncertainty which hung over the futurity of representative government and therefore, of civilization.[28]

In the debates on the 1867 Reform Act, Mill moved an amendment calling for the adoption of Hare's system. But he was regarded in the House as an impractical philosopher rather than a serious politician, and it looked as if his motion would not find a seconder, when the Commons was saved from disgrace by the intervention of Lord Cranborne, later to become, as Lord Salisbury, Prime Minister and leader of the Conservative Party. It was not that Cranborne welcomed the Hare scheme with great enthusiasm. Indeed, in his view, MPs

instinctively felt that it was a scheme that had no chance of success. It was not of our atmosphere – it was not in accordance with our habits; it did not belong to us. They all knew that it could not pass . . . every Member of the House, the moment he saw the scheme upon the Paper, saw that it belonged to the class of impracticable things.[29]

But nevertheless 'Any scheme which had been deeply thought over and earnestly advocated' by so prominent an intellect as Mill 'was worthy of respectful treatment by the House of Commons.'[30]

Mill, however, found no other supporters and his proposal was derided by one MP as

an emanation from Goosebery Hall. He asked the House to turn from the amusement they had had that night to more serious business.[31]

Mill did not press his amendment to a vote and shortly afterwards Hare's original system, which involved a nationwide constituency, was modified into the constituency scheme now known as the single transferable vote.

BAGEHOT'S CRITICISMS

The main contemporary attack on the arguments of Hare and Mill came from Walter Bagehot in his book *The English Constitution.* Of Hare's system, Bagehot wrote:

> One can hardly help having a feeling of romance about it. The world seems growing young when grave old lawyers and mature philosophers propose a scheme promising so much.[32]

Bagehot denied that Hare's system would stimulate the return of independent-minded candidates to Westminster since with voluntary constituencies organisation would become more and not less necessary if the names of the candidates were to be made known to the public. The educated minority would probably be less well organised than other interests, since:

> unfortunately the mere preference for intellectual and thoughtful men is faint in comparison with the special ties of sectarian and commercial interests. . . . Intellect is scarcely a uniting enough influence to be the basis of an association. We have heard of the Know-nothing ticket – but we should scarcely hear much of the Useful-knowledge ticket or the Social Science ticket.[33]

If, therefore, under Hare's scheme, organisation would be dominant, party men would be returned and they would owe their election to organisers and wire-pullers. This would encourage sectarianism. The interests of Nonconformists, for example, would have to be separately represented.

> Every chapel would be an office for vote-transferring before the plan had been known three months. . . . At present the Dissenters are a most energetic and valuable component of the Liberal Party; but under the voluntary plan they would not be a component – they would be a separate, independent element.[34]

If the MP owed his election to particular interests, he would inevitably become subservient to them. 'A voluntary constituency will nearly always be a despotic constituency.' Under the plurality system, on the other hand,

> The member is free because the constituency is not in earnest: no constituency has an acute, accurate doctrinal creed in politics. The law made the constituencies by geographical divisions; and they are not bound together by close unity of belief. They have vague preferences for particular doctrines; and that is all. But a voluntary constituency would be a church with tenets; it would make its representative the messenger of its mandates and the delegate of its determinations.[35]

Bagehot regarded Hare's plan as inconsistent with two of the fundamental features of parliamentary government – the independence of the

MP and the moderation of Parliament. The independence of the MP would be undermined by the organised interests to which he would have to pay allegiance to secure election, and the moderation of Parliament would be destroyed by the cacophony of sects which Hare's scheme would allow to be represented.

Bagehot was proved correct in his prediction that the adoption of Hare's scheme (in the modified form of the single transferable vote) would not do away with the need for organised parties. He appreciated, rather more than Hare or Mill, that parties perform important and indeed essential functions in a democracy, functions which would be less well performed if they disintegrated into noisy sects and interest groups. He may also have been correct in his view that a nationwide constituency scheme would strengthen party organisation and not weaken it. But the single transferable vote does not have this effect, for by offering the voter a choice of candidate, it can deprive the party organisation of much of its power.

Bagehot's criticisms, however, have proved extremely influential. His preference for strong government even when it conflicts with fair representation has in general corresponded to the priorities of the British electorate, and it was not until the 1970s that the plurality method of voting was questioned by more than a few enthusiasts. Bagehot reinforced the bluff, commonsense view that the plurality system was the most natural thing in the world, and proportional representation has never quite recovered from the aura of crankiness with which he associated it.

1884–5

Proportional representation was again to be considered during the years 1884–5 when the Third Reform Act and Redistribution of Seats Act were passed. Gladstone, faced with a demand from the Conservative Opposition that reform be accompanied by redistribution, had set up a Cabinet committee, led by the Radical Dilke, in 1884 to work out the details; and this committee had to decide whether or not to retain the limited vote or to make alternative provision for the representation of minorities.

Sadly for the advocates of proportional representation, Dilke's committee considered only the limited vote and the cumulative vote, but not the single transferable vote which, as he later said, 'was hardly known to politicians. It was known, of course, in literature.'[36] In practice, therefore, the issue of minority representation presented itself in the form of whether or not the limited vote should be retained. Dilke discussed this in July 1884 with Gladstone and concluded '. . . there was an almost universal consensus of opinion against that particular form of minority representation; and that no other form had powerful friends on either side of politics'.[37] He was supported in his opposition to minority representation by Lord Salisbury who, having in earlier days flirted with Hare's scheme, might have been thought to be more sympathetic to minority representation, as a means of preventing the tyranny of a Radical majority. But, as Roy Jenkins has noticed, 'there was an element of extremism in Salisbury's character – once he had accepted the need for change he was prepared for a drastic one'.[38] He had come to the conclusion, as his niece Lady Gwendolen Cecil relates in her biography of Salisbury, that single-member districts and the plurality system were by no means necessarily contrary to the interests of the Conservative Party.* Having come to accept that democracy was inevitable, he now had the self-confidence to believe that the Conservatives could compete successfully in the great centres of population.

> He repeatedly urged at the time, both in public and in private, his conviction that the traditional view had become obsolete, and that it was to the large centres of population that the Conservative party must henceforth look for its main urban support. For the next twenty years this forecast was justified by the election returns. He himself accounted for the fact by the demand upon the reasoning faculties which Conservatism makes. The intellectual activity engendered in great towns arms men both against the economic fallacies and the merely emotional appeals of Radical propagandists.[39]

Moreover, the abolition of multi-member constituencies would be likely to damage the interests of the Whigs who were accustomed to stand in harness with Radicals in two- or three-member constituencies. The Whigs were Salisbury's rivals for the leadership of a 'moderate' 'constitutionalist' alliance against the Left, and Salisbury suspected them of being in league with Northcote, his competitor for the Conservative leadership.

According to Dilke, Salisbury insisted that, as part of the Arlington Street compact between the parties, the principle must be accepted that 'Minorities not to be directly represented.'[40] He inserted on Gladstone's draft of the agreement, 'The above, i.e. that minorities be not directly represented, will be considered by the Government as vital – and the Government will resist as vital question the insertion in the Bill of any provision inconsistent with the above.'[41]

Gladstone was happy to comply with this proposal. 'Mr Gladstone', claimed Dilke, 'was a great conservative on redistribution – the strongest I ever met.'[42] He saw representation not as representation of opinion, but in terms of representation of communities as it had been in his youth. He ridiculed proportional representation as a '*pons asinorum*',[43] which few

*He was, however, prepared to accept the cumulative vote.

could understand, and claimed, when introducing the Redistribution Bill, that the scheme of single-member districts and plurality voting 'goes a very long way towards that which many gentlemen have much at heart – namely, what is roughly termed representation of minorities . . . there is no doubt that by means of one-Member districts you will obtain a very large diversity of representation'.[44] In other words, he believed that the plurality system would itself secure the aims which advocates of proportional representation sought through more radical reforms.

The only area for which minority representation was seriously considered was Ireland, where it was raised by Northcote with some tentative support from Salisbury. For Conservatives feared that the plurality system would compel a polarisation in Ireland between Unionists and Irish Nationalists, extinguishing moderate opinion, Liberal supporters of the Union together with 'the loyal minority' of Unionists in the South, and Liberal opinion in the North. Ireland was in any case over-represented in proportion to her population, and, without minority or proportional representation, the passage of the Reform and Redistribution Bills could well be, as Courtney was to predict in the debate on redistribution, 'the death knell of the Union'.[45] Indeed, Morley and Bryce were later to insist that the passage of these Bills had made Home Rule inevitable. Dilke, however, resisted the application of a minority system to Ireland on the grounds 'that no one could seriously propose to the House of Commons to have a minority system of representation in Ireland, and to have none, and even to extinguish the vestige of one, which existed in the rest of the United Kingdom',[46] and he succeeded in convincing Salisbury of this view.

Thus, the legislation of 1884–5 established the single-member constituency as the dominant unit of representation. It abolished the limited vote, and retained only 27 two-member constituencies in deference to the sentiments of Gladstone who favoured the system which he had known before 1832. The reform was shaped throughout by the needs and interests of the party leaders, and settled, symbolically, in a private inter-party conclave. Twenty-five years later, by which time he had become rather more sympathetic to proportional representation, Sir Charles Dilke reflected sadly:

> I am afraid that the party leader now, as in former times, takes the view that any resistance to that tendency, or that effect of single-member constituencies or of majority representation is a device to preserve in a glass case or under a glass shade a specimen on which he desires to trample with a boot. That, I think, is the party leader's usual view.[47]

Once the two party leaders had agreed upon a settlement, the chances of it being altered by others were remote. But in any case, there was no major political grouping which was sympathetic to, or willing to fight for, minority or proportional representation. The Radicals led by Joseph Chamberlain were particularly hostile to such schemes which would have weakened their hold in Birmingham and other urban centres. Radicals sought a majority in the Commons so as to form a strong government capable of resolving the social and economic issues of the future. With the extension of the suffrage, the old liberal fear of strong government was irrelevant. As Chamberlain put it to Arthur Balfour in 1886:

I think a democratic government should be the strongest government from a military and imperial point of view in the world, for it has the people behind it. Our misfortune is that we live under a system of government originally contrived to check the action of Kings and Ministers, and which meddles far too much with the Executive of the country. The problem is to give the democracy the whole power, but to induce them to do no more in the way of using it than to decide on the general principles which they wish to see carried out, and the men by whom they are to be carried out. My Radicalism at all events desires to see established a strong government and an Imperial government.[48]

The plurality method of voting clearly offered the best chance of securing such a strong government, a government backed by a loyal party majority in the House of Commons. Minority clauses and similar devices, on the other hand, would allow Whigs and moderate Liberals to run in harness with Radicals. The resulting government would be a coalition of Whigs and Radicals, such as Chamberlain had been compelled to endure between 1880 and 1885, incapable of effective action and obscuring the true battle between progressive and reactionary.

At the first conference of the National Liberal Federation in 1877, Chamberlain spoke of

Liberals ignorant of what are the first elements of Liberalism, and whose lingering distrust of the good sense and the patriotism of the people has found expression in machinery – cumulative vote, minority representation, and I know not what of the same kind, which tends to divide the party of action in face of the ever united party of obstruction.[49]

In 1883, the NLF passed a resolution declaring that 'the attempt to secure the representation of minorities by special legislative enactments is a violation of the principles of popular representative government';[50] and, speaking at Hanley on 7 October 1884, Chamberlain warned his audience that the Whigs and the Tories would combine in an attempt to retain minority representation:

What is the object of a representative system? Surely it is to secure that the majority shall rule. . . . Minority voting in every form . . . secures an over-representation of crotchets, which misrepresents great principles, which tempts the exhibition of personal ambition and personal vanity, which confuses the great issues we are called upon to decide, which divides the point of progress, and by all these means plays into the hands of the party of privilege. . . . The majority has the right to enjoy the fruits of victory.[51]

Chamberlain's fellow Radicals, Bright and Morley, had little doubt that the 'diversity of representation' desired by the advocates of minority and proportional representation was merely an excuse for the preservation of class privilege.

All these schemes [said Morley] were but new disguises for the old Tory distrust of the people.[52]

The Radical Programme, published in 1885 with an introduction by Chamberlain, welcomed the end of the minority vote 'which was an insidious device to cripple popular strength, to throw the balance of power into the hands of the Whigs, and to create dissensions amongst the majority'. 'An equitable system of parliamentary representation' was 'entirely inconsistent with the minority vote, and no sound Radical can acquiesce in such a device for minimising, and it may be for nullifying altogether, the power of the majority.' The Radicals believed that the single-member seats would help them since they would

remove the possibility which has hitherto existed of arranging – even where the majority of the voters may have been of a decidedly Radical complexion – for the return of one Moderate in conjunction with one Radical. There will be no room for these convenient understandings, these amicable parliamentary bargains . . . the buffers on which timid Liberalism has hitherto relied against advanced Liberalism will henceforth disappear.[53]

In the general election of 1885, Birmingham was divided into seven single-member constituencies. All seven were won by Radicals, although two Conservatives – Lord Randolph Churchill and Henry Matthews – came within a few hundred votes of securing election, and the Liberals secured in total only 33,423 votes, as compared with the 23,694 for their Conservative opponents. It was the plurality system which allowed Chamberlain to retain his hold on the West Midlands, and this regional base enabled him to preserve his political position even after he had broken with Gladstone on the issue of Irish Home Rule.

The conception of democracy held by the Chamberlainites contrasted in an important way with the outlook of an earlier generation of radicals. The radicalism of Mill had been individualistic, and had sought to strengthen the deliberative role of Parliament. For Chamberlain, however, collective action was necessary if radical aims were to be achieved, and this necessitated disciplined organisation. The function of Parliament was not primarily to discuss, but to sustain an executive capable of rapid and effective action. MPs could not afford the luxuries of deliberation and debate; their central responsibilities were to Radical voters outside Parliament by whose mandates they were elected. Indeed, in 1877, Chamberlain went so far as to call for 'A truly Liberal Parliament outside the Imperial legislature'[54] which would formulate policy and hold MPs accountable for carrying it out.

Chamberlain was carrying to its extreme a conception of the role of the political party still held by many on the Left. According to this conception, the central elements in radical politics are the development of a programme by political activists, and the construction of an organisation to ensure that MPs carry it through. From this viewpoint, not only is any restriction upon the rule of the majority anti-democratic, but a special role in the formulation of policy is given to political activists who begin to assume the role of a Calvinist elect. The analogy with the contemporary Left is indeed a close one, for the germ of its conception of democracy is to be found in Joseph Chamberlain's philosophy of political organisation. As Ostrogorski put it, 'The majority has a monopoly of the representation, and the Caucus has a monopoly of the majority'; but with proportional representation, 'the Caucus, now the arch-monopolist, would have to submit to the law of competition'.[55] For the single transferable vote would allow the elector rather than the Caucus to select the candidate, thus depriving the organisation of much of its power.

The only major group in whose interests it might have been to support proportional representation was the Whigs. For it was only if some provision was made for multi-member constituencies and minority representation that they could hope to survive as an independent force within the Liberal Party. But Hartington and Goschen seem to have given little attention to the issue or to have realised that it could provide security for the 'moderates' in the Liberal Party.

This meant that the only MPs to champion proportional representation were a disparate group of individuals without a mass following either in the House or in the country. Their only unifying link was their concern with Ireland. According to Andrew Jones, 17 of the 73 Liberal supporters of proportional representation sat for Irish constituencies, 15 of the 23 Liberal members of the Proportional Representation Society who remained in the House in 1886 voted against Gladstone on Home Rule in 1886, while another 15 members of the Society were to emerge after 1886, as Liberal Unionists.[56] In 1884, the Proportional Representation Society issued a circular claiming that under the plurality system in Ireland, the extension of the franchise would mean that 'those who hold moderate and loyal opinions, although numbering more than one third of the whole electorate, may be everywhere outvoted and reduced to silence'. In November 1884, Courtney wrote to Gladstone:

If the threatened Parliamentary representation did truly correspond with the division of opinion in Ireland the conscience of the nation would not endure to maintain the Union. Home Rule would be inevitable ... yet ... it cannot be doubted that there must still remain within its confines a large number of temperate opinion ... both liberal and conservative, which is failing to secure Parliamentary expression and is in imminent danger of being soon entirely deprived of it.... There is a strong case in Great Britain for large efforts to secure proportional representation, but in Ireland it is clamourous.[57]

The advocates of proportional representation, as Jones notices, 'used the language of high morality to confess their faith, but it was perfectly clear to Gladstone that the premium so innocently placed on independence of mind in fact foreshadowed a destructive independence'.[58]

The Proportional Representation Society had been in existence for only a few months, since January 1884, when the Redistribution Bill was introduced, and it did not make many converts. *The Pall Mall Gazette* claimed that 'the principle of minority representation has been badly compromised by the three cornered constituencies which, without in any way affecting the balance of parties have made the very name of proportional representation stink in the nostrils of keen politicians on both sides of the House'.[59] Leading advocates of proportional representation were regarded as eccentrics; the hobbies of one of them, Sir John Lubbock (later the first Lord Avebury), included teaching dogs to read. It was no wonder that Arthur Balfour, although nominally a member of the Proportional Representation Society, declared that he could not vote for it, since he believed that it was 'a perfectly hopeless crusade. It was not so much the case that the question was dead, as that it had never been alive.'[60]

Beatrice Webb, attending a meeting of the Proportional Representation Society in 1885, came to the same conclusion:

The subject, I fear, is at present a dead one; the educated classes are far too cynical as to the possibility of foretelling the result of any scheme to take much interest in this one; the uneducated classes, struggling for their bare existence, do not see in it any help towards solving that great problem – How to get more from those who have, – that will be the practical question of the future.[61]

It is hardly surprising that Courtney's amendment to the Redistribution Bill providing for proportional representation received no more than 31 votes.

The settlement of 1884–5 determined the shape of party politics until the First World War. Its prime beneficiaries were Gladstone and Salisbury, the leaders of the two parties who had negotiated the settlement. It enabled Gladstone to retain tight control over a naturally fissiparous Liberal Party, and to insist in 1886 that Liberals either supported him on Irish Home Rule, or left the party. Leonard Courtney believed that under a system of proportional representation Gladstone 'would not have been able to carry with him that great array of waverers, who, knowing all was lost unless they followed him, consented to adopt his policy though detesting it'.[62] It was the electoral system which prevented the Liberal Unionists from remaining as an independent element within the Liberal Party.

For Salisbury, the single-member system enabled him to head off demands to merge with a Whig/Liberal Unionist/Conservative 'constitutionalist' alliance. He was prepared in 1886 to allow Liberal Unionists a free run against Gladstonian Liberal candidates; but the central precondition of the Unionist alliance was that it accepted the leadership of Salisbury and the Conservative Party. The Liberal Unionists, apart from the Chamberlainites, were unable to resist precisely because their electoral survival depended upon Conservative goodwill.

Similarly, the Unionist Free Traders after 1903 found themselves forced to decide which was their priority – the Union or Free Trade. They could not remain as an independent grouping within the Conservative Party since Chamberlain, extending the methods of the Birmingham Caucus to the country at large, encouraged constituency organisations to treat support for the Tariff as an essential test of party loyalty, and not to adopt Unionist Free Traders as candidates. Thus, by the time of the 1906 election, only 3 per cent of Unionist candidates were prepared to declare that they supported Free Trade.[63]

Moreover, the settlement of 1884–5 effectively militated against the formation of a Centre Party in British politics. Such a party was mooted many times between 1885 and 1914, and there were a number of different variants – a party of Radicals led by Chamberlain and Lord Randolph Churchill, a 'moderate constitutional' party led by Hartington and supported by moderate Conservatives, an alliance of Unionist Free Traders and Liberal Imperialists led perhaps by Rosebery or by the Duke of Devonshire (as Hartington had now become), or finally a union of laissez-faire Liberals hostile to Lloyd George's 'People's Budget' of 1909, with Unionist Free Traders. But on each occasion, the creation of such a party was to remain nothing more than the gossip of the dinner-table. Any attempt at the practical realisation of such a plan would have immediately come up against the difficulty of securing a foothold in the constituencies when faced with two powerful and solidly entrenched party organisations. Sir John Lubbock, himself a Liberal Unionist Free Trader, admitted:

> Without Proportional Representation, a central party is, I believe, impossible. A system of election such as ours favours two extremes, and crushes out moderate men and independent thinkers.[64]

The only group which was able to make an incursion into this territory was the Labour Party, and this was because it was able to secure solid majorities in certain working-class areas; but, even in the case of the Labour Party electoral survival until 1914 was, as we shall see, very much dependent upon the grace and favour of the Liberals.

Thus in Britain, the settlement of 1884–5 reinforced the two-party system and prevented party fragmentation. In Ireland, on the other hand, it led to one-party dominance, giving the Nationalists a clean sweep of all seats except two in the South, and the Unionists a monopoly of seats in the Protestant areas of north-east Ulster. Moderate opinion – Liberals in the South and North, and the Unionist minority in the South – remained unrepresented, and politics in Ireland came to be dominated until 1918 by the seemingly unbridgeable conflict between Home Rulers and Unionists. After the 1885 election in which no Liberals were returned in Ireland, the O'Conor Don, a leading Irish Liberal, wrote to Courtney:

> This is the result of the single-seat constituencies without provision for minority representation. No one that knows anything about Ireland can maintain that this is a true representation of the feelings of the country. One necessary consequence of the present representation is that every Catholic who wishes to have any voice or influence in the Legislature or government of the country must join the Nationalists, and it seems to me that it will be next to impossible to govern Ireland constitutionally against the will of 86 per cent of the representatives.[65]

This proved to be an all too accurate prophecy, as from 1886 to 1922, British politicians sought desperately for a way of resolving what turned out to be irreconciliable differences between Irish Nationalists and Unionists.

1905–1914[66]

After its failure in 1885, proportional representation disappeared from public view for some years. There was a brief flurry of activity in 1888, with an unsuccessful attempt to convince the government to adopt proportional representation for the election of the new local authorities established by the Local Government Act. But otherwise the issue remained dormant until 1905, when the Proportional Representation Society was re-formed.

The period between 1905 and the First World War was one in which constitutional issues such as Home Rule, reform of the Lords and the referendum were again in the forefront of political discussion. Proportional representation was bound to take its place amongst these issues. This renewed interest in the constitution had its roots in a certain disenchantment with the working of liberal democracy. To many of those whose task it was to reflect on government, the representative system seemed far from ideal; far from liberating the citizen, it seemed only to have subordinated him to even more complex forms of political authority. Social scientists such as Michels and Max Weber showed that representative government could not work without political organisation; yet these very organisations served to undermine the autonomy of the individual voter. Graham Wallas argued that liberals had failed to take sufficient account of the strength of non-rational motives at work amongst the electorate. Ostrogorski showed how the workings of party prevented the free expression of the opinion of the electorate; and Lowell spoke of 'discontent with some of the results of democracy, a feeling which finds vent in widespread criticism of representative institutions'.[67]

It was against the background of a further extension of the franchise that Edwardian politicians came to consider electoral questions. In 1905, the government promised in the King's Speech to introduce a new reform bill; and, although the Fourth Reform Bill was not in fact passed until 1918, politicians realised that they would have to resolve not only issues such as plural voting and women's suffrage, but also the vexed question of the electoral system.

The Liberal Government, however, was by no means enthusiastic about electoral reform. The general election of 1906 had given the Liberals a vastly disproportionate number of seats in the Commons – 397 – instead of the 285 to which their percentage of the vote would have entitled them under a proportional system. It was hardly surprising, then, that the Liberal Party was at this time particularly hostile to proportional representation, and there were only a small number of Liberal MPs, mainly uninfluential backbenchers, who favoured it.[68]

The Liberal tradition, as we have seen, was hostile to proportional representation. Its leaders in the 1880s – Gladstone, Chamberlain and Bright – regarded it as an instrument for securing the election of 'faddists' and cranks to the Commons. The plurality system, on the other hand, would impose unity and coherence upon a naturally fissiparous Left-wing Party, always in danger of disintegrating into congeries of competing pressure groups.

Moreover after 1906, the Liberals, if they were to limit the power of the Lords to destroy their legislation, desperately needed the large overall majority which only the plurality system could provide. Proportional representation would have made it more likely that they would be dependent upon the Irish Nationalists for their parliamentary majority. The Liberals had endured that experience between 1892 and 1895, and they had no wish to repeat it, for it deprived them of the moral authority needed to combat the Lords and prevented them from carrying out their legislative programme. According to J. Renwick Seager, the Secretary of the Registration Department of the Liberal Central Association, in evidence to the Royal Commission set up by the Asquith Government,

> Proportional representation is a matter scarcely ever talked about. . . . The Liberal agents as a whole, so far as I know, are none of them in favour of it; and as to the organisations, I do not know of one Liberal organisation that has ever passed a resolution in favour of it.

Seager was himself opposed to proportional representation, since 'the effect to my mind would be that the number of bores and cranks in the House would be largely increased, apart from the personal interests of trade or religion'. It was, he said, in language reminiscent of Chamberlain, 'the duty of the minority to turn itself into a majority by reason and in course of time'.[69]

Nevertheless, the Liberals could not remain entirely indifferent to the weaknesses of the plurality system, for the structure of politics had been complicated by the birth of the Labour Party which in 1906 succeeded in returning 29 members to the Commons. In 1903, the Liberals had come to an agreement with the Labour Party – the Gladstone–MacDonald pact – through which the two parties agreed not to encroach upon each other's electoral territory. This agreement succeeded in preventing a split in the Left-wing vote in 1906 and in the two general elections of 1910, but it was accepted more readily by the parliamentary leadership of the two parties than at constituency level, where Labour activists resented being forced to stand down in favour of Liberal candidates. There was, throughout this period, the possibility that Labour would attempt to break out of the constraints imposed by the Liberals. If such a strategy were to look like being successful, then the Liberals would have to consider the alternative vote – preferential voting in single-member constituencies – if they were not to hand a number of seats to the Unionists on a split vote.

It was for this reason that Liberals such as Asquith and Churchill made sympathetic noises towards the alternative vote or two-ballot systems after 1905; and for this reason perhaps that Asquith agreed, in response to a request from Courtney, to establish a Royal Commission on Electoral Systems in 1908. This Commission, which reported in 1910, recommended, with one dissentient, adoption of the alternative vote. Its Report is, however, a curious document, since the evidence which it elicited and the chain of reasoning in the Report itself, point rather to proportional representation than to the alternative vote. There is some substance in Earl Grey's complaint that the Royal Commission 'refused to give a report in conformity with the evidence'.[70] For it came to the following conclusion on the working of the plurality system in single-member constituencies established in 1885:

> Whether the authors of the Bill of that year did or did not believe that the single-member constituency would secure a general correspondence between the support in votes and the representation of the two great parties, such a belief was no doubt widely held at the time. It has proved to be unfounded. Majorities in the House have since shown a very great, and at the same time variable disproportion to majorities in votes, and there is nothing in the system to warrant the belief that such exaggerations will not recur.[71]

The plurality system, moreover, 'misleads the nation as to the actual state of feeling in the country. In the House of Commons it encourages ambitious legislation for which there is no genuine demand.'[72] In the light of such conclusions, it is surprising that only Lord Lochee, the one dissenting member of the Royal Commission, recommended proportional representation, especially as the Commission conceded that its advocates were in a stronger position in 1910 than in 1885, since they now agreed on the best scheme – the single transferable vote – and had entirely abandoned the limited vote and the cumulative vote.

The Royal Commission's Report was published in August 1910; and, coming as it did at a time when the energies of politicians were engaged in the struggle over the Lords, it made little impact. Indeed, it was not even debated in either House of Parliament.

The Liberal Government was not, however, wholly unsympathetic to the alternative vote, and the first draft of the abortive franchise bill of 1912 provided for its adoption. But, before the First World War, the challenge from Labour cannot have appeared strong enough to compel the Liberals to regard such a reform as pressing. For, although the alternative vote would benefit the Liberals by preventing Unionist victories on a split vote, it would allow the Labour Party to extend its organisation into Liberal territory, and therefore undermine the Liberal strategy of containing Labour. The Liberals, therefore, had to make a difficult calculation as to whether the danger from Labour was great enough to make electoral reform a matter for urgent consideration. There is little evidence to suggest that leading Liberals had reached such a conclusion by 1914.

The infant Labour Party found itself frustrated by the success of the Liberals' strategy of restricting their candidatures. By 1914, only nine out of the 39 seats which it held had been won against Liberal competition. If it sought to broaden its electoral base this would mean retaliation from the Liberals, 'and that retaliation would probably mean the loss of 50 per cent of the seats now held'.[73] It seemed that Labour would never be a genuinely independent party, able to stand on its own feet, but would always remain an appendage to the Liberals. So those in the Labour Party who placed a high priority upon independence were the most likely to be sympathetic to proportional representation; and it was for this reason that the Independent Labour Party at its conference in 1911 voted in favour of it.

The leading advocate of proportional representation in the Labour Party before the First World War was Philip Snowden. Snowden was a member of the ILP and, significantly, MP for Blackburn, relying heavily on the votes of the 'Conservative working-man' as did other Labour MPs in Lancashire, where there was a genuine tradition of 'Tory Democracy'. Snowden, therefore, could not be expected to look with favour upon increasing co-operation between the Liberals and the Labour Party, for this might cost him the support of Conservative-inclined voters. He argued that the plurality system made Labour permanently dependent upon the Liberals.

There was not a Labour Member today but knew that he was dependent for his seat in the House of Commons upon the goodwill of those who belonged to other political parties. As long as they had Members returned by Liberal votes they could not expect independent action from their Members.[74]

Unlike MacDonald and Lloyd George, Snowden did not assume that the Liberals and Labour were part of one Progressive alliance. The Liberal Party was a capitalist party, and its co-operation with Labour was merely a tactic to weaken the working-class movement. Labour therefore had to *attack* Liberal representation, but it was not yet strong enough to win three-cornered fights, or even necessarily to come second in such contests, so neither the plurality system nor the alternative vote would be of much assistance to it.

There might be, as in certain municipal elections, a combination of capitalist forces against Labour. Even a combination of one capitalist party with a section of another might be sufficient to deprive Labour of victory.[75]

Labour representation would thus be at the mercy of others. There was a salutary lesson to be learnt from Germany where, in the election of 1907 under the two-ballot system, the Social Democratic Party had been head of the poll in the first ballot in 44 out of 90 constituencies where it was involved in a second-ballot contest, but it succeeded in winning only 14 of them.

Introduction of the alternative vote was therefore 'full of grave dangers for Labour. It is not too much to say that if this is introduced for the next general election the Parliamentary representation of the Party may be wiped out.'[76] With proportional representation, on the other hand, Labour organisations in different parts of the country would be encouraged to put up candidates in the knowledge that even if they secured only a seventeen per cent vote in a five-membered constituency, they would be sure of representation. Moreover, the Labour candidates elected under proportional representation would owe their election to Labour voters, not to Liberal support. This would enable Labour MPs to display greater independence in the Commons. 'Each quota of Labour voters polled will return a Labour member, and the member so returned will have a position of security and of independence which the Alternative Vote cannot possibly give him.'[77] Nor, of course, could the plurality system provide that security. Proportional representation, therefore, offered the only route for Labour to win seats and for Labour MPs to retain their independence from the two major 'capitalist' parties. This would enable Labour to campaign on a genuinely socialist programme, rather than a compromise put together to induce Liberal support.

Arguments of this kind had convinced every other socialist party in Europe to support proportional representation before 1914. But at its conference in 1914, the Labour Party decisively rejected proportional representation at the behest of the Party's Chairman, Ramsay MacDonald, and in large part as a tribute to his personal authority over the movement. MacDonald's hostility to proportional representation derived from his conception of the future development of socialism which differed in important respects from that held by Snowden. For MacDonald, society developed not through class conflict but through organic evolution, and socialism marked 'the growth of society, not the uprising of a class'. It was 'the stage which follows Liberalism, retaining everything of value in Liberalism by virtue of its being the hereditary heir of Liberalism'.[78] For this reason, MacDonald, although he favoured an independent Labour Party, saw it before 1914 as a unit in a wider Progressive Alliance. He sought a

> fusion . . . of all members of Parliament whose policy made for Socialism. It would not matter if this united party disowned the name of Socialism. All he was concerned about was that the policy should be based upon the present principles of the Labour Party.[79]

For MacDonald, therefore, proportional representation would be harmful because it would encourage Labour to differentiate itself from the Liberals. Political opinion in the constituencies would 'be divided into watertight compartments . . . Socialists should vote for Socialists, Labour Party electors for Labour Party candidates, Liberals for Liberals and so on'. But 'nothing has hampered our Movement in the country more than this false idea of independence, that only Labour or Socialist votes should be given to Labour or Socialist candidates. It is humbug.'[80] For in Parliament Labour could secure its ends only by combining with Liberals. What was the point, therefore, of encouraging Labour to commit itself over a wide range of constituencies, and to compete electorally with the Liberals? There would be a contradiction between the attitudes of the Left in the constituencies, where it would be competing, and its attitudes in Parliament where it would have to co-operate.

Moreover, MacDonald held a strongly collectivist conception of the nature of political action. He deprecated the liberal view that the Commons existed to represent individual opinion. Instead the legislature was 'not merely a mirror of public opinion, but an expression of the public will'. It was therefore 'none the worse for having active political elements slightly over-represented in it',[81] for only in this way could a strong government be formed able to implement radical social measures.

It seemed that MacDonald's policy would confine Labour to the role of junior partner in the Progressive Alliance. It would forever remain within the limits assigned to it by the Liberals. But MacDonald, although extremely cautious about Labour's prospects in the short run, was optimistic about the long run when the inevitability of gradualness would make Labour the dominant power in the state. When that stage had been reached, of course, the plurality system would work to Labour's advantage, and enable it to squeeze out its competitors for the Left-wing vote. In accepting MacDonald's case in 1914, the Labour Party was showing an uncanny prescience as to what would be in the Party's future self-interest.

After their crushing defeat in 1906, it might have been expected that the Unionists would have become more sympathetic to proportional representation. But it was mainly the Unionist Free Trade faction within the Party, now in rapid decline, which called for change; and when, in February 1908, the Proportional Representation Society began publication of a journal, *Representation*, it made an explicit appeal for free trade support. 'The Conservative Free Trader of today is like the Liberal Unionist of twenty years since. The one had to give up Liberalism if he would be a Unionist in active life: the other may have to give up Free Trade if he is to be an active Conservative.'[82] The Free Traders were being driven out of the Unionist Party by the Tariff Reform Caucus, and Central Office would not exert itself to defend them: 'I cannot use our Central Office to return to Parliament a group of men who, when we get a majority, will either refuse to support or will oppose the chief measures on which a majority has been returned,' declared Acland-Hood, the Conservative Chief Whip.[83] But, if the free trade faction within the Unionist Party disappeared and all free trade voters were forced to support the Liberals, then the electoral swing of the pendulum could jeopardise free trade, even though that cause might command overwhelming support in a referendum. In the general elections of 1910, three issues were at stake – the future of the House of Lords, the Union with Ireland and free trade. How was a 'moderate constitutionalist', wishing to preserve the position of the Lords but hostile to Home Rule and Tariff Reform, to cast his vote? However he made his decision, his vote would be appropriated by one of the parties and used to claim a mandate for a radical policy of which he disapproved.

With proportional representation, however, the moderate voter would come into his own. 'In such circumstances', wrote Lord Hugh Cecil to Strachey, 'people like you and I will begin to be appreciated at our proper value.' The Unionist Free Traders stood on its head the traditional criticism made of proportional representation that it would lead to governments with small majorities. For 'nothing would suit us better', replied Strachey 'than a small majority for the tariff reformers. It would entirely sterilise them and their schemes.'[84] With small majorities, tariff reform, Home Rule and radical reform of the Lords would be equally impossible unless the voters positively desired such changes; and Parliament would reflect the view of the electorate more accurately.

Since, however, it was so explicitly aimed at the dominant Tariff Reform faction in the Unionist Party, it was not to be expected that the Unionists would embrace proportional representation. They had no interest in encouraging the growth of a 'Unionist Free Trade' constituency which might include 'moderate' elements in the Liberal Party and defeat the Tariff. The Chamberlainites who had been firm against proportional representation in 1885 as tending to the frustration of social radicalism, were equally staunch in 1910 in rejecting a reform whose effect would have been to entrench Free Trade. By 1910, they were near to destroying the Unionist Free Trade faction in the Commons which, by 1914, had ceased to exist as an independent political constituency.

THE FIRST SPEAKER'S CONFERENCE

It needed the impetus of war to induce agreement on the shape of a new Reform Bill. The World War made the old party squabbles seem irrelevant, and in May 1915 Asquith formed a Coalition Government which included Conservatives and Labour. Faced with the prospect of a long war, it was clear that there would be a massive task of social and economic reconstruction when it was over. This task could only be carried out by a government resting upon the authority of a wider franchise.

In July 1916, Asquith confessed to the House of Commons that the Cabinet had been considering the problems of franchise and registration for some time, but it had been unable to find a solution to them. Since these matters affected Parliament as much as the government, Asquith hoped that a Select Committee could be established to secure agreement. This suggestion was, however, laughed out of court by the House. In August Walter Long, the President of the Local Government Board, proposed the setting up of

> a representative conference, not only of parties, but of groups, a Conference which would really represent opinion on these three subjects: electoral reform, revision of your electoral power when you have got it – and registration.[85]

The Speaker agreed to chair this representative conference, and it was as a result of Long's improvisation that the curious institution of the Speaker's Conference was born.

The first Speaker's Conference was a product of the wartime Coalition spirit; in the words of one of its members, 'an experiment – an experiment that many people were sure would fail, and that few anticipated would be as successful as it proved to be'.[86] It met from October 1916 to January 1917 during one of the most testing periods of the war, after the first battle of the Somme when daily reports were bringing evidence of the carnage in

France and Flanders. The members of the Conference felt that if they could reach agreement upon a measure of electoral reform, they too would be making a contribution to the national struggle. In his letter to the Prime Minister reporting the resolutions agreed by the Conference, the Speaker paid tribute 'to the admirable temper and conciliatory disposition' of its members, who

> were desirous of rendering at a time when the national energies were almost wholly centred upon the successful prosecution of the war, a service which might prove of the highest value to the State, and result in equipping the nation with a truly representative House of Commons, capable of dealing, and dealing effectively, with the many and gigantic problems which it will have to face and solve as soon as the restoration of peace permits of their calm and dispassionate consideration.[87]

The Conference grappled courageously with the difficult problems of electoral reform; party conflict was suspended and it reached its conclusions through a process of consensus. It made a large number of recommendations, the most important of which were that there should be, in effect, manhood suffrage; extension of the Parliamentary franchise to women who had attained a specified age, such as 35 or 30 years; proportional representation in borough constituencies, and the alternative vote in all other constituencies. Of the 37 resolutions passed by the Conference, all but three were carried unanimously; the three passed by majority included the recommendations for women's suffrage and the alternative vote (but not proportional representation which was carried unanimously).

Since the deliberations of the Conference have never been published, it is not possible to discover with any degree of certainty how the recommendation of proportional representation came about. During the parliamentary debates which followed, a number of members of the Conference claimed that the proposal to adopt proportional representation was part of a bargain which could not be broken. But such evidence must be treated with caution since this claim would be a natural one for advocates of proportional representation to make when they saw that support for it was seeping away, or for opponents seeking an excuse for having given way.

There is also evidence, however, from one of the members of the Conference, who agreed to proportional representation against his better judgment, that it was part of a bargain. It was, said Willoughby Dickinson, 'recommended as part of the compromise because certain members held that so large an extension of the franchise could not be accepted unless accompanied by a method whereby the minority could be sure to secure some representation'.[88] When proportional representation was defeated in the Commons, Dickinson confided to his diary with relief,

I had to vote for it in loyalty to the compromise as it was an essential part of the bargain. We could not have got a unanimous vote to extend the franchise if we had not consented to support Proportional Representation. But I consider it entirely a mistake and fought it unmercifully in the Conference. So, tonight I have salved my conscience and yet had my way.[89]

It would seem from these remarks that it was Conservatives, and perhaps those Liberals still sceptical of the value of democracy, who pressed for proportional representation as their price for agreeing to an extension of the franchise. But a majority of Conservatives voted against proportional representation on every occasion on which it was debated in the Commons. So Dickinson's comments do not solve the problem of how proportional representation came to be unanimously recommended.

It is not necessarily naive to speculate that at the Speaker's Conference party considerations were genuinely forgotten. Politicians thought that the postwar period would herald a new style of politics, but no one could discern how the new electorate would use its power. In the eyes of the prudent, proportional representation would provide an insurance policy against a Left-wing Labour Party; but it also offered the hope of building a new moral and social order upon the co-operation of different classes. In Parliament, some of its supporters referred to proportional representation as an analogue to the Whitley Councils designed to encourage capital and labour to resolve disputes in a spirit of compromise.

'We have formed a Coalition', said Sir Alfred Mond,

of all parties to work together to guide the country in its most perilous hour. We have surely learnt that co-operation of different parties produces more rapid progress than the idea that we can only go on with extreme party men and party majorities. I hope I have learnt . . . that there is another way of governing a country besides the old way of parties in and out of office opposing each other, not on principles but on party lines.[90]

However, the recommendation to adopt proportional representation was weakened by the fact that it was only to apply to about one-third of parliamentary constituencies. It could be argued that, if proportional representation was a sound principle, it should be applied universally; if it was a dubious one, it should not be recommended even as an experiment. The agricultural interest was particularly disappointed that proportional representation was not to be applied to the rural constituencies, believing that unless there was representation of agriculture in all parties, it would be ignored in a reformed parliament. Moreover, proportional representation in the boroughs might be expected to benefit the Conservatives who could secure minority representation in radical strongholds. Many Liberals found it difficult to see how they would gain from it. They might hope to benefit from the alternative vote in the remaining single-member constituencies, but the alternative vote was entirely unacceptable to the Conservatives who saw it as an attempt by the two Left-wing parties to gang up on them, and deprive them of their fair share of representation.

It soon appeared that most of the advocates of proportional representation represented constituencies which would not be affected by the recommendations of the Speaker's Conference; while those who would be affected were almost unanimously opposed to them. The alternative vote was seen as a merely partisan ploy, and had no chance of all-party acceptance. The government, therefore, was faced with a difficult dilemma. There can be no doubt that proportional representation would have been carried if the government had supported it. But the leaders of both elements of the Coalition – Conservative and Liberal – were suspicious of it as likely to weaken party discipline. Lloyd George himself gave little thought to electoral problems, but reacted instinctively at this time against proportional representation which, he told C. P. Scott, was a 'device for defeating democracy, the principle of which was that the majority should rule, and for bringing faddists of all kinds into Parliament, and establishing groups and disintegrating parties'.[91]

The government decided to accept all the recommendations of the Conference except those relating to women's suffrage, the alternative vote and proportional representation, the only unanimous recommendation of the Conference which it refused to accept. It proposed instead a free vote on the choice of electoral system.

The result was that the issue shuttlecocked back and forth between the Commons and the Lords. The Commons rejected proportional representation on no less than five occasions, substituting for it the alternative vote, twice by a majority of only one. The Lords, on the other hand, twice reinserted proportional representation into the bill and rejected the alternative vote. In the end the plurality system was retained, in part by default, but also because many of the supporters of electoral reform feared that, if they continued to make an issue of it, the whole bill would lapse. The bill therefore passed into law without provision for either the alternative vote or proportional representation, except that, as a rather picturesque anomaly, proportional representation was retained for elections to four of the seven university constituencies. In withdrawing their protection from proportional representation, the government thus 'threw it to the wolves', and ensured its defeat.

A breakdown of the Commons vote on proportional representation shows that no party was united on this issue except for the Irish Nationalists, who supported it despite the fact that it was not to be applied to Irish constituencies. The pattern of voting was as follows:

1. 12 June 1917

	For PR (143)	Against PR (151)
Con.	38	85
Lib.	77	53
Lab.	13	11
Irish Nat.	14	–
Others	1	1
	143	150
		(only 150 names printed)

2. 4 July 1917

	For PR (171)	Against PR (203)
Con.	40	137
Lib.	90	58
Lab.	13	7
Irish Nat.	27	–
Others	–	1
	170	203
	(only 170 names printed)	

3. 22 November 1917

	For PR (128)	Against PR (204)
Con.	29	125
Lib.	57	70
Lab.	15	8
Irish Nat.	25	–
Others	2	1
	128	204

4. 30 January 1918

	For PR (115)	Against PR (225)
Con.	59	96
Lib.	43	110
Lab.	5	18
Irish Nat.	6	1
Others	2	1
	115	226
		(226 names printed)

5. 13 May 1918

	For PR (112)	Against PR (168)
Con.	43	104
Lib.	61	55
Lab.	7	9
Irish Nat.	–	–
Others	1	1
	112	169
		(169 names printed)

Source: Elizabeth Lyon: *PR and Parliament: Round One 1886–1931* (Parliamentary Democracy Trust, n.d.)

It will be seen that, if the final vote on 13 May 1918 is excluded, proportional representation was rejected by increasing majorities on each occasion. In the first vote on 12 June 1917, it was rejected by only eight votes, and the advocates of proportional representation were unable to recover from this narrow defeat: for when it was seen that one recommendation of the Speaker's Conference could be rejected without endangering the others, MPs such as Willoughby Dickinson, who had supported proportional representation with misgivings only because it had the authority of the Conference behind it, felt free to vote against it.

Although the Conservative peers strongly supported proportional representation, there was never a Conservative majority for it in the Commons. Austen Chamberlain spoke for the Conservative leadership in arguing against it. He reminded the House that he 'was brought up as a Radical' and 'sat at the feet of John Bright', when 'the whole of the Liberal party with the exception of a few theoretical philosophers regarded this proposal . . . as a Tory doctrine to defeat the democracy'.[92]

The Liberal and Labour parties were deeply divided on proportional representation. The Labour Party Conference had in 1918 for the first time voted in favour of it, but there were nevertheless majorities against it on two of the five divisions, and a minority remained opposed in the other divisions. One may contrast this with the three divisions on the alternative vote when no Labour MPs could be found to go into the division lobby against it. For the alternative vote would be more advantageous than proportional representation to Labour in its attempts to break out of the confines of the Gladstone–MacDonald agreement by extending its candidatures into Liberal territory: and Arthur Henderson, when asked by C. P. Scott how a Labour Party intending to run candidates over the whole country could secure co-operation with progressive Liberals, said that 'he would depend on the alternative vote and on a friendly understanding between Liberalism and Labour to give each other their second choice'.[93]

The Liberal Party was as divided as Labour. Had it been united in favour of proportional representation, the first two votes would have been carried, and proportional representation would almost certainly have been enacted. But there was never more than a three-fifths Liberal vote in favour, and on two occasions there was actually a Liberal majority against. No doubt many Coalition Liberals, noticing the government's lukewarm attitude, were hesitant to support the change; while Asquith refused to give a lead to the Independent Liberals, declaring that 'The matter is not one which excites my passions, and I am not sure that it even arouses any very ardent enthusiasm.'[94] Although he indicated that he was now in favour of proportional representation, he did not vote in any of the divisions and objected to his constituency of East Fife being merged with the surrounding constituencies – although, ironically, this might have saved him from defeat in the 'Coupon Election' of 1918. One may again contrast Liberal uncertainty on proportional representation with the divisions on the alternative vote which secured Liberal majorities of between 78 and 150, while not more than 13 Liberals could be found to go into the lobbies against it.

THE DEFEAT OF ELECTORAL REFORM

The recommendations of the Speaker's Conference undoubtedly offered advocates of proportional representation the best opportunity they have ever had of securing reform of the electoral system. It was, in the words of Lord Burnham,

> the first Reform Bill in which proportional representation has had a chance. In the past it has been greatly prejudiced by the assumed pedantry of its antecedents. Its sesquipedalian title is against it, and may I say it has suffered from association with the figure of John Stuart Mill, who was always called a philosopher in politics, and anything he advocated was supposed to be incapable of understanding by the multitude.[95]

Public opinion was more likely to prove sympathetic to proportional representation at a time when a large extension of the franchise was being made under conditions of considerable uncertainty. Moreover, on political as on other questions, the war brought men face to face with first principles, compelling a re-examination of hitherto hallowed practices. Proportional representation was, as we have seen, in tune with the spirit of co-operation to which the war had given rise, and which many hoped would survive the conclusion of hostilities. It might have made coalition government the norm in postwar politics, and encouraged a more fluid and flexible grouping of parties.

The Lloyd George Coalition was not, of course, insensible to this atmosphere. Its political approach owed a good deal to Joseph Chamberlain's 'social imperialism' as it attempted to cut across the sterile dispute between advocates of laissez-faire and state socialism. There followed intermittent attempts to 'fuse' the Coalition Liberal and Conservative Parties and to create a Centre Party as a more satisfactory instrument of class conciliation than a diehard Conservative Party.

Many of the constitutional measures proposed by the Coalition provided for the introduction of proportional representation. In 1918, the Education (Scotland) Act introduced the single transferable vote for education authorities in Scotland; in 1919 the Local Government (Ireland) Act provided for this method of election for all local authorities in Ireland; while in the Government of Ireland Act 1920, proportional representation was accepted without demur by Westminster for the Home Rule Parliaments in Ireland. In 1919, it was proposed on an experimental basis for India in the Government of India Act, while in 1921 the new constitution of Malta framed by Milner and Amery provided for parliamentary elections in the colony to be conducted by the single transferable vote; and in 1922, the Irish Free State (Agreement) Act provided for this method in elections to the Irish Dáil.

It seemed indeed at this time as if there was a tendency for all democracies to move towards proportional representation. Belgium, Finland and Sweden had already adopted it in 1899, 1906 and 1907 respectively; Denmark followed in 1915, to be succeeded by Switzerland and Austria in 1918, and Italy and Germany in 1919; while the new states created by the Versailles Treaty such as Poland and Czechoslovakia also adopted proportional representation for elections to their legislatures.

But a number of different reasons can be cited to explain why Britain did not follow in the footsteps of these countries. One of the factors making for the adoption of proportional representation on the Continent was a fear by Liberal parties that, under universal suffrage, they would be squeezed by clerical and socialist parties. Conservative parties also feared that universal suffrage would be inimical to their interests. These had been crucial factors in Belgium and Sweden where the farmers and urban Conservatives had pressed for proportional representation as the price for agreeing to manhood suffrage.

In Britain, on the other hand, the Conservative Party had the self-confidence – justifiably as it turned out – that it could compete successfully against the Left, even under a regime of universal suffrage. The Conservatives would be difficult to dislodge in rural constituencies, and their powerful party machine ensured that they would continue to dominate cities where the Caucus was strong, such as Birmingham and Liverpool. Moreover, in 1917, the Party was anticipating that the patriotic enthusiasm aroused by the war would bring it a large election victory. 'The

Tadpoles and Tapers of the Party are opposed to (PR) because they believe the next Khaki Election will return them by a large majority.'[96] But even if they had looked further ahead, the Conservatives need have seen no cause for alarm. It would, in the view of many (including most Labour politicians), be a long time before Labour could hope to compete with the Conservatives on equal terms: and meanwhile, the Conservatives could hope to profit from the split between the Liberals and Labour on the Left. Perhaps, also, the more far-sighted Conservatives discerned what Baldwin understood, that Labour in office would be far too timid and subservient to offer any serious threat to the established order. As Sir Reginald Hall told his constituents at Newport, the country had nothing to fear from Labour except incompetence.[97] The best hope for the survival of the established order lay not in estranging Labour by forming parliamentary combinations preventing it coming to power, but in bringing Labour within the pale of the constitution, and adopting a conciliatory attitude towards it.

The Liberal failure to vote solidly for proportional representation must be accounted the Party's most disastrous decision this century. Of course the decline in the Liberal vote in the 1920s, which was to reduce the Liberals to the status of a minor party within seven years, could not be foreseen by the leaders or the Party. By 1922 the Asquithian Liberals were advocating proportional representation in their election manifesto, the first party in Britain officially to do so; but by then it was too late. In the general election of 1924, with one-sixth of the vote, the Liberals secured 40 seats. They had become irretrievably the third party in the system, 'a dying party set between the upper and nether millstones', in Asquith's words.[98]

The opportunity lost in 1918 was not to recur. As the Labour Party came to benefit from the relative majority system, so its MPs hardened against proportional representation, and it became a purely party issue. In May 1924, a private member's bill providing for proportional representation was introduced into the Commons. The vote on Second Reading was as follows:

	For PR (146)	Against PR (240)
Con.	8	147
Lib.	107	1
Lab.	28	90
Others	3	2
	146	240

The pattern was set for a two-party system in which the Conservatives and Labour opposed any change in an arrangement from which both benefited; while the Liberals, now outsiders, saw proportional representation as the only means of recovering the position which they had lost.

The public atmosphere also became less sympathetic as the contrast between Britain's political stability and the instability of many of the Continental democracies became apparent. In 1927, Lord Burnham, who had been so enthusiastic a supporter of proportional representation in 1918, was telling Humphreys, the secretary of the Proportional Representation Society,

> I have not ceased to believe in the merits of Proportional Representation, but I am bound to say that public opinion in this country is, so far as I can see, becoming increasingly hostile to its adoption. It is not that anybody questions its justice and perfection, but it is said that everywhere it has been tried it is being turned down for some reason or another, and undoubtedly it will not be adopted here for a long time if at all.[99]

1918–31

The prime beneficiary of the decision to retain the plurality system was the Conservative Party, and its judgment that proportional representation would not have been to its advantage was soon vindicated. The election of 1918 produced a wildly unbalanced Parliament. The Coalition gained roughly five-ninths of the vote in contested seats. This gave it an overall majority of 239 in the Commons (311 if the Sinn Féiners, who did not take their seats in the Commons, are excluded) instead of the 82 (or 154 if the Sinn Féiners are excluded) to which it would have been entitled in terms of its proportion of the vote in contested seats, together with unopposed returns. Its large majority meant that the Coalition could be impervious to parliamentary criticism, and the bitterness of industrial relations in the immediate postwar period might well have been exacerbated by a feeling that the forces opposed to the Coalition were under-represented in the Commons.

The election appeared to give Sinn Féin which gained 72 of the 101 Irish seats a mandate for breaking the British connection. But if the results in contested seats are examined, the electorate's verdict does not appear quite so clear-cut:

Party	Votes	Seats	Seats in proportion to votes
Sinn Féin	495,345	47 (+25 unopposed)	37 (in contested seats)
Unionist	289,213	23	22
Nationalist	228,902	6	17

Nationalist support was fairly evenly distributed across Ireland, and so more votes were needed to elect a Nationalist MP than a Sinn Féin MP or a Unionist, whose strength was concentrated in North-East Ulster.

The consequence was that (excluding unopposed returns), the Unionists secured 23 seats on 28.4 per cent of the vote, while the Nationalists secured only six seats out of the 56 they contested, with 22 per cent of the vote. The results of the 1918 election in Ireland constitute, therefore, an object lesson on how the plurality system can encourage the forces of separatism in a divided society.

The triumph of the Coalition in 1918 was a victory not merely for the Conservative Party, but also for those politicians drawn together by Lloyd George and seeking to reorientate postwar politics away from traditional party doctrines. But in 1922 the Conservatives decided to break up the Coalition, and fight the general election as an independent party. The election destroyed the hopes of Lloyd George and his supporters. For the Lloyd George Liberals were able to field only 154 candidates, and would thus be in no position to form a government. They had to rely upon constituency pacts either with sympathetic Conservatives or Asquithian Liberals. The Conservatives succeeded in gaining an overall majority of 73 although in the contested seats (excluding university seats), they won under 5½ million votes, while the total vote of the non-Conservative candidates exceeded 8½ million. The Conservatives secured 38 per cent of the vote – over five per cent less than it had won in 1922 – and it was the electoral system which enabled them to form a single-party government on such a small share of the vote.

After the election result had been announced, Lloyd George who, together with other Coalitionists, had not believed that the Conservatives would secure an overall majority, remarked that

> the most notable feature of the elections is the return of a decisive majority of members by a very definite minority of the electors. . . . A minority of three millions in a national referendum could hardly be claimed as a vote of confidence. . . . It would be idle to pretend that in a democratic country like ours, thoroughly imbued with the spirit of representative government, this does not weaken the moral authority of the government of the day.[100]

The Conservative *Morning Post* then commented that having lost the game Lloyd George was now trying to change the rules.[101]

The Conservative victory of 1922 began the process of restoring the two-party system. Lloyd George now realised how mistaken he had been in 1917, and in November 1925 C. P. Scott spoke to him on proportional representation,

> as to which George evidently felt that he had made a great mistake. 'Some one ought to have come to me', he said, 'in 1918 and gone into the whole matter. I was not converted then. I could have carried it then when I was prime minister. I am afraid it is too late now.' When I told Lady Courtney of this at lunch afterwards [Scott continued], she mocked at him. Why, she said, he was in constant com-

munication with my husband. But of course it was not the general principle which needed explaining to him, but its special application to the interests of the Liberal Party, as to which Lord Courtney would have been an imperfect expositor.[102]

The Labour Party, of course, seemed a joint beneficiary with the Conservatives of the decision to reject proportional representation. In the short run, however, the split in the ranks of the Left between Labour and the Liberals meant that the Conservatives were in power for most of the interwar period.

It would be wrong to regard the electoral system as the only or even the prime cause of this state of affairs. For there was considerable social as well as ideological hostility between Labour and the Liberals. In 1918, the Labour Party had committed itself to a socialist constitution, and the prewar conception of a 'Progressive Alliance' against the Conservatives was replaced by a socialist/capitalist division in which the Liberals were no longer on the side of progress. Indeed, for most socialists in the 1920s, one of Labour's aims was to drive out the Liberals, so that the battle between the forces of light and the forces of darkness could be properly joined.

This ideological conflict was powerfully reinforced by the deep social and psychological resentments felt by many Labour leaders, reacting against the patronising treatment which they had endured from the Liberals for so many years. In conversation with C. P. Scott in July 1924, Ramsay MacDonald

reverted again and again to this dislike and distrust of the Liberals. He could get on with the Tories. They differed at times openly then forgot all about it and shook hands. They were gentlemen, but the Liberals were cads. . . . The feeling against the Liberals was general in the party. Social intercourse had almost ceased. J. H. Thomas was perhaps now the only man who ever asked a Liberal to tea.[103]

This feeling was powerfully reinforced by the experience of Labour participation in the Asquith and Lloyd George Coalitions; and Henderson, who believed that he had been humiliated by Lloyd George, declared at the Labour Party Conference of 1918 that 'as long as he ever lived he should never be a member of any other Government, whatever its colour, unless Labour was in control'.[104]

Yet, even when due allowance has been made for this hostility, it remains true that the electoral system can play a significant role in inducing different types of political behaviour. The differences between Labour and the Liberals were barriers to co-operation; but another electoral system could have made it easier to surmount these barriers. With Labour determined to extend its candidatures, and compete with the Liberal Party, clearly no electoral pact was possible. This meant that under the plurality system, the only possible form of electoral co-operation was the reciprocal withdrawal of candidatures, something which would not appeal to constituency activists, and was bound to cause friction at constituency level. But the alternative vote would have allowed Liberals and Labour to compete without splitting the progressive vote; while the single transferable vote might have encouraged co-operation because Labour's aim of destroying the Liberals would have been incapable of fulfilment.

Labour's eagerness to destroy the Liberals made it impossible for the Party to enjoy any constructive tenure of government during the interwar period. In 1923, Labour's National Executive Committee had called upon the parliamentary leadership 'to accept full responsibility for the government of the country without compromising itself with any form of coalition'.[105] Yet how could such full responsibility be exercised by a party which had won only 30.5 per cent of the popular vote? Labour's attempt to govern on its own meant that the first Labour Government could be nothing more than a propaganda exercise whose purpose was confined to proving to the electorate that the Party was 'fit to govern', unable to pass constructive measures, but able respectably to occupy Cabinet seats. The government could be no more than, in Beatrice Webb's words, 'a scouting expedition in the world of administration – a testing of men and measures before they are actually called to exercise majority power'.[106] The first Labour Government, therefore, lasted only nine months, although in the view of the *New Statesman*, if MacDonald 'had treated his Liberal allies with even common courtesy he might have remained in power not merely until 1925, but for some years to come, possibly even for a decade'.[107]

By the time of the second Labour Government in 1929, MacDonald was beginning to appreciate that if Labour was to govern constructively, it had to do so in co-operation with other parties. This was not merely a matter of the survival of a minority government, but essential if the government was not to be overwhelmed by the world slump. In the King's Speech of 1929, before his government was in any danger of defeat, MacDonald wondered

> how far it is possible, without in any way abandoning any of our party positions, without in any way surrendering any item of our party principles, to consider ourselves more as a Council of State and less as arrayed regiments facing each other in battle . . . so that by putting our ideas into a common pool we can bring out . . . legislation and administration which will be of substantial benefit for the nation as a whole.[108]

A committee was set up to consider electoral reform, but it could make no progress in the light of Labour's opposition to proportional representation and Conservative hostility to the alternative vote. Eventually, in September 1930, an understanding seems to have been reached between Labour and the Liberals: in return for the alternative vote, the Liberals would keep Labour in power for the two years which would be needed to pass an Electoral Reform Bill over the opposition of the Lords by means of the

Parliament Act procedure. Writing to Lansbury in February 1931, Lloyd George could still hope that 'through the agency of the Alternative Vote there will be such co-operation at the polls as will ensure a fresh opportunity for a progressive Government to complete the great programme upon which we are agreed'.[109] But it was not to be. The Lords rejected the Electoral Reform Bill; and before it could be introduced into the Commons again, the financial crisis of 1931 swept away both the Labour government, and all possibility of co-operation on a 'progressive' policy.

The electoral system was thus one amongst a number of factors which both inhibited co-operation between the Liberal and Labour Parties, and prevented the Liberals, as a minor party, from exercising influence in the 1920s. This had important political consequences for a political system which was becoming increasingly polarised by conflicting ideologies. Indeed, it could be argued that the existence of a centre party, neither Protectionist or Socialist, was a vital prerequisite of a representative Parliament. 'To divide either the nation or the politicians into those who advocate the taxation of imports and those who advocate the public ownership of the means of production is obviously not an exhaustive classification.'[110] Without the Liberals, there was no way in which a voter could express his disapproval of both Protection and Socialism. Since a majority of the electorate in the 1920s was probably opposed to either policy, a Parliament in which the parties were more balanced would have been more representative of the will of the electors than one dominated by either of the major parties.

The case for the two-party system in this period was that the political strength of the Liberal Party would not be lost if the Party broke up, but would be used to imbue the other parties with the spirit of liberalism. The events of the 1930s, however, were to show that the Liberals could amalgamate with the Conservatives only at the price of accepting Protection; while in the 1920s, Liberals feared that joining Labour would mean abandoning the mixed economy and the sophisticated intellectual justification of it which the 'Yellow Book' provided.

Under the influence of Keynes, the Liberals in the 1920s were pioneering the development of the new economics – a form of interventionism which sought to conquer unemployment while yet preserving the essentials of the private enterprise system and avoiding the state planning associated with socialism. The Labour Party failed at this period to comprehend the Keynesian revolution, and believed the mixed economy to be an unhappy compromise between laissez-faire capitalism and socialism. The mixed economy, in the eyes of MacDonald, was an unworkable 'medley',[111] and socialists did not believe that the capitalist system could be patched up in the manner suggested by Keynes.

Yet experience of the two Labour Governments of the interwar period showed that Labour lacked any practical cure for unemployment. There was no majority for socialist policies, and in any case 'socialism' was as much an incantation as a practical programme of action. It has been persuasively argued[112] that the dispute between capitalism and socialism was of importance in the interwar period only at a rhetorical level; the real issue lay between laissez-faire capitalism and interventionist capitalism, between economic conservatives, represented on the front benches of both major parties, and economic radicals led by Lloyd George and Keynes. The failure of co-operation between the Liberal and Labour parties, therefore, prevented the implementation of a new economic policy capable of challenging the orthodoxies of the day; and Labour, in driving out the Liberals, found that it lacked any alternative domestic programme capable of solving economic problems. 'It seems', declared W. J. Brown in 1931, 'that we have spent twenty years destroying the Liberal Party in order to get a Government whose policy is less radical in relation to the needs of to-day than that of the Liberals was in relation to the needs of 1906–14.'[113]

The financial crisis of August 1931 destroyed all hope of co-operation between the Liberal and Labour parties and it led to the collapse of the Labour Government. In the ensuing general election, the Liberals, far from co-operating with Labour, allied themselves with the Conservatives and with the small number of National Labour candidates (followers of MacDonald), against Labour. As a result of constituency pacts, there were three-cornered fights in only 58 seats. It was as if the alternative vote system was in operation enabling the 'capitalist' parties, having chosen one preferred candidate, to gang up against Labour. The result in terms of seats exaggerated the size of the National Government's popular support. With 67 per cent of the vote, it secured a majority of over 500 seats. Labour, which in 1929 with 37 per cent of the vote had won 285 seats, now found that with 30.7 per cent of the vote, it could secure only 52 seats, as compared with the National Government's 554. Nor have even the most determined of revisionist historians been able to do much to refurbish the reputation of the 1931–5 Parliament which is generally regarded as one of the worst this century.

CONCLUSION

The period between 1885 and 1931 was one in which proportional representation was a live issue and a genuine topic of political debate. With the exception of the years 1917–18, however, the advocates of proportional representation never really looked like being successful. For, as the inter-party agreement of 1885 showed, the leaders of the two main parties had a powerful interest in preserving an electoral system which worked, on the whole, in their favour and against third party breakaways.

The plurality system was a powerful inducement to party orthodoxy, and a disincentive to rebellion; and this, too, served the interest of party leaders.

The Liberal Party which, from 1922, advocated proportional representation as part of its official programme, was not especially sympathetic to this reform when it had the opportunity to change the system, and the leaders of the Party – Gladstone, Asquith and Lloyd George – were particularly hostile to it when in government. In their opposition to change, the Liberals were supported by the Radical wing of the party, which followed the lead given by Chamberlain in deploring 'minority devices' as tending to muddy the pure waters of democracy. Democracy was majority rule, and the main right enjoyed by minorities was the right to be outvoted. The Labour Party, which as a third party might have been expected to be more sympathetic to proportional representation, was lukewarm since its concentrated geographical strength allowed it to secure a firm foothold in Parliament; while its confidence in the trends of social evolution led it to think that in the future it too would benefit from the plurality system. Until threatened by Sinn Féin, the Irish Nationalists also favoured a system which made it appear that they had uanimous support in Ireland outside north-east Ulster. They too benefited from the advantage which the plurality system gave to a regionally concentrated party.

The main advocates of proportional representation were the 'moderates' such as the Liberal Unionists and Unionist Free Traders, groups which seemed to be shut out of the parliamentary system by the operation of the party machine. The tightening of parliamentary procedure during this period and the development of new methods of political organisation made the position of 'moderates' increasingly uncomfortable. For minorities, complained *The Times* on 16 May 1910, 'there is the guillotine inside the House if they speak their minds. There is outside the House another guillotine in our electoral system to prevent them entering.' There was, Courtney wrote to Gladstone shortly before resigning from his government in 1884, an

> injury done to our national life by the deleterious training more or less undergone by every one who is drawn into the political world, and by the loss of men who are shut out of it as refusing to submit to this training. There are men who cannot serve the state just as there are men who cannot serve the Church because they cannot subscribe, except in a non-natural sense, to all the articles imposed on those admitted to service.[114]

Proportional representation by the single transferable vote system – the only method seriously considered during this period – would have alleviated the position of such men, since it would have allowed the electorate to support Liberal Unionist or Unionist Free Trade candidates against an official party candidate without the fear that they would be handing the seat over to the opposite party through a split vote. So an MP who disagreed with his party would have the security of knowing that he could not be removed, because his supporters could not be faced with the dilemma of voting for the official candidate or handing the seat to the Opposition. 'Its fundamental principle', claimed Hare, 'is, in fact, a corollary of that of individuality. It puts forward in a practical shape the necessity of freedom for individual action.'[115] It was pressed by politicians such as Courtney whom Graham Wallas described as 'the last survivor in public life of the personal disciples of Mill'.[116] It is not surprising that such a cause failed to make very much headway at a time when individualistic assumptions in politics, as in other spheres of social life, were being rapidly undermined: and it did not prove difficult for the men of government to defeat them. It was only in a situation of party fluidity, such as characterised the years 1917–18, that proportional representation had any chance of success.

What is perhaps more surprising is that the advocates of proportional representation were able to make so little impact upon public opinion. Support for reform was confined to a small number of enthusiasts who had studied the question carefully; but they proved unable to convince the public of the strength of their case. There was, throughout this period, hardly any public pressure for change, and the issue never appeared likely to excite public passions in the way that extension of the franchise or female suffrage were to do. Such lack of public pressure proved a handicap to the reformers, and it may well be that the existence of an organised public opinion favourable to change could have persuaded enough waverers in 1917 to swing the vote in the Commons in favour of proportional representation. In 1930, Sir Samuel Hoare, a member of the Committee on Electoral Reform, conscientiously seeking information about the working of proportional representation, was struck by

> the almost complete lack of interest in PR. I had imagined from circulars of the PR Society and the entire propaganda in the press on the subject that there was a strong movement in the country behind PR. When I made tentative enquiries as to the possibility of a compromise upon a PR basis, I found that the Society was little more than an office and that its Chairman, Lord Grey, was not in the least anxious to make any move in the Lords on the subject.[117]

The public were not very much moved by the theoretical deficiencies in the electoral system pointed out by reformers. They saw that the system operated with a rough and ready justice – if it had given the Liberals an overwhelming majority in 1906, it did the same for the Conservatives in 1924 and favoured Labour in 1929. They accepted Bagehot's view that

> The judgment of the Parliament ought always to be coincident with the opinion of

> the nation; but there is no objection to its being more decided. . . . It is therefore no disadvantage, but the contrary, that a diffused minority in the country is in general rather inadequately represented. A strong conviction in the ruling power will give it strength of volition. The House of Commons should think as the nation thinks; but it should think so rather more strongly, and with somewhat less of wavering.[118]

Between 1885 and 1931, the House of Commons on the whole lived up to this precept. Fundamentally the electoral system survived because the theoretical defects, to which reformers drew attention, did not appear sufficiently blatant to justify reform. It was not until the general elections of 1974 that the electorate saw the grotesque anomalies of which the system was capable; and proportional representation was not to become a major issue in British politics until the operation of the electoral system came to be linked to a critique claiming that it produced not only unfair results but also unstable government.

Chapter 2

1974–1979

THE POLITICS OF CLASS

With the overwhelming victory of the National Government in 1931 constitutional issues disappeared from the mainstream of British politics until the 1970s. In 1944 and 1965–8, two further Speaker's Conferences debated proportional representation, but the subject aroused no interest, and the Conservative and Labour Parties were nearly unanimous in rejecting it.

A central reason for the eclipse of proportional representation was the rapid reassertion of the two-party system after 1931. Until 1974, every general election produced an overall majority for one of the two major parties (although in 1950 and 1964, this was scarcely large enough to be dignified by the term 'working majority'). Minor parties continued to compete in parliamentary elections, but only the Liberals succeeded in gaining representation regularly, and, until 1974, they never secured more than 11.2 per cent of the vote. The electoral system, therefore, did not seem to involve any blatant injustices and its legitimacy was unquestioned by the vast majority of electors.

However, the two-party system had re-established itself in a very different form. For the rise of Labour introduced not just a new party into the political system, but also a new conception of representation which had the effect of making the conflict between the parties far more rigid and inflexible than it had been before the First World War.

The substitution of Labour for the Liberals as the dominant party of the Left was primarily a result of the extension of the franchise to include the bulk of the working class, and the allegiance of this class to a party whose *raison d'être* was representation of its collective interests. Long-term social and economic changes 'were simultaneously uniting Britain geographically and dividing her inhabitants in terms of class'.[1] As class feeling came to be the central determinant of political allegiance, so the Liberal Party which saw itself as representing a 'Progressivism' transcending class found itself eclipsed. Liberalism was an individualistic philosophy seeking to establish a community based upon diversity and mutual respect. Liberals conceived of party, therefore, as a group of like-minded individuals, bound together by specific programmes to which they had given voluntary assent. The touchstone of a man's Liberalism lay in whether he accepted the programme. If he ceased to accept a particular item of policy, be it Home Rule or Free Trade, he was no longer a Liberal.

For Labour, on the other hand, political allegiance was defined in socio-economic and in class terms. As Aneurin Bevan put it in his book *In Place of Fear*,

> The texture of our lives shaped the question into a class and not into an individual form. . . . For us power meant the use of collective action designed to transform society and so lift all of us together. . . . We were the products of an industrial civilisation and our psychology corresponded to that fact. Individual initiative was overlaid by the social imperative. The streams of individual initiative therefore flowed along collective channels already formed for us by our environment. Society presented itself to us as an arena of conflicting social forces and not as a plexus of individual striving.[2]

This meant that the tie binding an individual to his party was inevitably tighter than had been allowed for in the Liberal conception:

> not that of mere voluntary association which stresses common ideas and moral judgments. On the contrary, its integration is seen as arising especially from objective conditions that give its members a function, and are the ground for deeply rooted, continuing – even 'fixed' – interests.[3]

Whereas, for the Liberal Party, identification had been the result of an act of the rational intellect, identification with Labour was a natural and primary response of the working class to its social environment. It was, therefore, far more difficult to break with Labour than it had been to defect from Liberalism; for to break with Labour was not merely to alter one's political views, but to break with one's class, to betray the experience which had shaped the very texture of one's life. Thus, for a member of the Labour Party 'The basis of his party allegiance is not so much that he *agrees* as that he *belongs*.'[4] It is partly for this reason that Labour has been so suspicious not only of coalition, but also of co-operation with other parties in peacetime, and has so excoriated the renegade. MacDonald's crime in 1931 was not that he disagreed on policy with others in the Labour Movement – for the policy differences which led to the breach were in reality far narrower than they were later made to appear; moreover, those ministers in the second Labour Government who agreed with MacDonald's views on the economy cuts but remained in the Party were quickly forgiven. MacDonald's crime lay rather in deserting the Labour Party, and therefore betraying the class which he had been called upon to serve.

Labour's conception of party differed from that of the 'capitalist' parties, therefore, in that it was derived from a model of trade union and factory discipline. The working class, it was held, could only improve its lot through collective action, and that required solidarity. Party lines had to be very strictly drawn, and the MP was to regard himself first and foremost as a delegate of the Party who had been sent to Parliament to uphold the decisions of the Party.

The Liberals, then, had claimed to represent individual opinion. Labour claimed to represent a class, and the rise of Labour became 'the principal means by which a new theory of representation has been propagated'.[5] According to this theory the purpose of a general election was not so much to elect a deliberative Parliament, a Parliament representative of opinion, but to choose a government which represented certain social interests. The focus of political action moved away from Parliament, towards government and its relationship to the social forces outside Parliament. Society was divided essentially into two camps, and the parties faced each other in the Commons like two disciplined armies between which communication was difficult and uncertain, and desertion to the enemy unthinkable. The political system reflected a model of democratic class conflict, and the parties in Parliament represented the great social interests which both sustained and financed them.

There can be no doubt that for much of the period between 1931 and 1974 this conception of politics corresponded with the behaviour of the electorate. For during these years, identification with the two main parties was largely a function of class and of attitudes towards class. Public attitudes were reflected in the broad geographical homogeneity of the national vote and in the stability of electoral patterns between 1945 and 1966. When in 1963 he investigated voting patterns in four English-speaking democracies, Robert Alford found Britain to be the most class-based in its political behaviour.[6] Within this context proposals for proportional representation, or indeed for constitutional reform in general, were bound to appear as irrelevant diversions from the battle which had to be joined. During the period of Labour/Conservative dominance, therefore, the electoral system remained unchallenged, and politics came to be dominated by class feeling. It was not until the sense of class identification had become seriously eroded, that the two-party system came under threat, and a political space was created within which there was room for issues of constitutional reform to return to the agenda.

'RED LETTER YEAR'

It was the result of the two general elections of 1974 which transformed proportional representation from a fringe issue in British politics to a central place on the political agenda. But the ground had already been prepared for serious discussion of the question by the opening up of other constitutional issues in 1973. Indeed it was the year 1973 which the Electoral Reform Society called in its newsletter a 'Red Letter Year'.[7]

Britain's entry into the EEC in January 1973 was particularly likely to assist electoral reformers in the long run since it would expose Britain to the political systems of the other members of the Community, characterised by coalition governments, and (with the exception of France) by the use of one or other of the list systems of proportional representation in electing their legislature. Moreover, entry into the Community carried with it commitment to a uniform system of direct elections to the European Assembly, and of course a proportional system would be the most likely candidate for such a uniform system. Indeed, in the long debates over direct elections to the European Assembly, it was noticeable that the most fervent supporters of the Community were also, in general, those most strongly committed to using proportional representation in direct elections to the Assembly, while the anti-Europeans tended also to be hostile to changing the electoral system.

Encouragement for electoral reformers also came from Northern Ireland where sectarian conflict had led to the breakdown of both the provincial government (Stormont) and local government. In reconstructing these institutions, the Heath administration embraced the concept of 'power-sharing' since it was hoped that if the Catholic community was given a guaranteed role in the government of the province, then extremists would be isolated. As part of this policy it was decided that the new district councils in Northern Ireland, and the assembly which was to replace Stormont, should both be elected by the single transferable vote; and since 1973 all elections in Northern Ireland, other than elections for the House of Commons, have been conducted by this method. So for the first time since the abolition of the university seats in 1948, a system of proportional representation was actually in use in a part of the United Kingdom, for parliamentary and local elections.

Although the elections to the short-lived Northern Ireland Assembly yielded a majority in favour of power-sharing, the new electoral system has not been able to produce a permanent structure of stable and moderate government in the province. Nevertheless use of the single transferable vote has benefited the cause of electoral reform since it has disarmed many of the 'practical' objections made against it. The system of election rapidly gained the confidence of the electorate and the elections themselves were administered extremely smoothly. Turnout in the 1973 local government elections was high even after allowance is made for personation which seems to have been a feature of elections in Northern Ireland since time immemorial. It varied from 43 to 90 per cent despite intimidation by the Provisional IRA. In the Assembly elections, turnout varied from 62 per cent in Belfast West, a Catholic constituency where intimidation probably kept many away from the polls, to 84 per cent in Fermanagh and South Tyrone. Nor did the system prove complicated for voters. The government carried out an effective campaign of instruction in the new method of voting with the aid of a cartoon character called 'PR Pete' who told the electorate that 'PR is as easy as 1, 2, 3...'. In the district council elections, only 1.5 per cent of the ballot papers were invalid, while in the Assembly elections, the figure varied from 1.2 per cent in North Down to 6.4 per cent in West Belfast, where the Provisional IRA had urged voters to spoil their papers. Figures for invalid ballots have been lower in later Northern Ireland elections. Thus the elections in Northern Ireland showed that the single transferable vote method was both technically and administratively feasible, and that any objections to it would have to be couched in terms of substantive political principle.

Devolution also brought electoral reform to the forefront of the political debate. In October 1973, the report of the Royal Commission on the Constitution was published, and amongst its few unanimous recommendations was a proposal that any assemblies established in Scotland, Wales or the English regions should be elected by the single transferable vote, this being particularly important 'in any region in which there were likely to be long periods without alternation of parties in power'.[8] The electoral gains of the SNP in 1974 and the Labour Government's commitment to devolution soon brought the Royal Commission's conclusions into the centre of political debate, and the Electoral Reform Society was well justified in claiming that there was

> a radically changed climate of opinion. The reform this Society seeks is no longer an academic matter, capable of being dismissed as the concern of a few enthusiasts; it is now something actually operating within the UK and recommended for extended use by a distinguished official body.... The whole subject is topical as it has not been for half a century.[9]

THE ELECTIONS OF 1974

The general election of February 1974 might almost have been designed by the Electoral Reform Society to display the anomalies of the plurality system. The election had been called by Edward Heath following a miners' strike which led to the introduction of a three-day week. The Conservatives invited the electorate to decide 'Who governs' while Labour mounted a vigorous attack against the Government's 'confrontation' with the trade unions. The electorate, however, refused to polarise on class lines and the result is shown in the table.

The most obvious anomaly in these results was the gross disproportion between the Liberal vote and the number of Liberal seats. With over one-half of the votes of the Labour and Conservative parties, the Liberals secured only 14 seats rather than the 122 to which they were proportionately entitled. The small number of Liberal MPs elected meant that

1974–1979

	Votes	%	Seats	%
Labour	11,645,616	37.2	301	47.4
Conservatives	11,872,180	37.9	297	46.8
Liberals	6,059,519	19.3	14	2.2
SNP	633,180	2.0	7	1.1
Plaid Cymru	171,374	0.6	2	0.3
United Ulster Unionist Coalition	366,703	1.3	11	1.7
SDLP	160,437	0.5	1	0.1

a Liberal/Conservative or Liberal/Labour coalition could not command a parliamentary majority, even though either combination could lay claim to the support of a large majority of votes in the country. Given the unlikelihood of a Labour/Conservative coalition, this meant that the new government would have to rely upon the support of the Liberals as well as the SNP or UUUC. The SNP had secured half as many seats as the Liberals with under one-ninth of the Liberal vote; while the UUUC, with 51 per cent of the vote in Northern Ireland and one-fifteenth of the Liberal vote, secured 11 out of the 12 Northern Ireland seats, a result dealing a serious blow to the chances of success of the power-sharing assembly in Northern Ireland which had begun its work in January 1974.

When the election result was announced, Heath proposed to Jeremy Thorpe, the Liberal leader, a formal Coalition involving 'full Liberal participation in government. . .'. Mindful of the Liberal commitment to electoral reform, and the moral strength of the Liberal case in the light of the election result, he proposed that a Speaker's Conference be set up to consider the issue. He admitted that he could not bind either his Party or Parliament, but promised that the recommendations of the Conference would be put to Parliament for a free vote.

There was never any likelihood that such a proposal would prove acceptable to the Liberals. They had, after all, campaigned strongly against what they claimed were 'confrontationist' tactics on the part of Heath, and many of their votes must have been gained from disillusioned Conservatives. It was hardly realistic to ask them to sustain the very government which they had just fought to defeat, and participation in a coalition on such an unequal basis might well have led to the Liberals being swallowed by the Conservatives. Even if Heath had been more forthcoming on proportional representation, he would not have been able to deliver the votes of his backbenchers, and Liberals knew full well that a Speaker's Conference would be unlikely to make any recommendations against the interests of the major parties who would nominate the majority of its members. In addition there was no sign that Heath would be able to secure the extra support (either the Scottish Nationalists or the United

Ulster Unionists) necessary if the coalition was to be able to command a majority in the Commons.

Nevertheless the Liberals were put in an uncomfortable position by refusing Heath's offer. It seemed odd for a party which supported proportional representation to baulk at the chance of participating in a coalition, since proportional representation would make coalition more likely. The Liberals' counter-proposal of a government of national unity combining all three United Kingdom parties hardly looked a plausible alternative, especially as Harold Wilson, immediately the election results were known, declared that Labour was prepared to govern on its own and would not enter a coalition. Wilson then proceeded to form a minority government, and the minor parties were unable to exert any real influence upon it.

Thus the seemingly strong bargaining position held by the Liberals rapidly evaporated. It is difficult to judge whether more could have been achieved. Jeremy Thorpe's action in meeting immediately with Heath after the election has been criticised as a failure to make the most of the Liberals' electoral success.[10] Instead, it is argued, Thorpe should first have approached Labour before treating with the Conservatives, since Labour, by winning more seats than the Conservatives, had denied Heath his mandate. Only if such an approach had failed would the Liberals have been in a strong position to seek a Liberal/Conservative agreement. It may well be that such a stratagem would have induced one of the major parties to make a stronger commitment to electoral reform: but still more promising, perhaps, would have been an attempt by a respected elder statesman such as Jo Grimond, the former Liberal leader, to negotiate for *all* the minority parties, parties which had won 25 per cent of the total vote. This might have capitalised upon the strong moral position which the Liberals held, for many who had not voted Liberal were compelled to admit the force of the case for electoral reform.

The Labour Party, which proceeded to form a minority government, had won the election only in the sense that it was the largest party in the Commons. It had fewer votes than the Conservatives; and its vote had fallen since the election of 1970 by 5.9 per cent, the largest fall in votes for any major Opposition party since the war. Indeed the central feature of the general election of February 1974 was the low percentage of the vote polled by both major parties, and Labour won not because it was particularly popular but because it lost less of its 1970 vote than the Conservatives.

In forming his minority government, Harold Wilson's intention was to dissolve Parliament as rapidly as possible so as to secure a working majority. The general election of October 1974 barely gave him that, however, since Labour was confined to an overall majority of 4, and the election gave rise to distortions almost as great as those which had been so apparent in February.

	Votes	%	Seats	%
Labour	11,457,079	39.2	319	50.2
Conservatives	10,462,565	35.8	277	43.6
Liberals	5,346,704	18.3	13	2.0
SNP	839,617	2.9	11	1.7
Plaid Cymru	166,321	0.6	3	0.5
UUUC	407,778	1.4	10	1.5
SDLP	154,193	0.5	1	0.1

The Liberals again found themselves grossly under-represented, securing only 13 seats for 18.3 per cent of the vote, while the UUUC gained 10 seats for 1.4 per cent of the vote. Paradoxically, the UUUC had increased its vote from 51 per cent of the Northern Ireland total to 58 per cent, but nevertheless found that it had lost one seat.

In Scotland, the performance of the three main parties was as follows:

	% of Scottish vote	No. of Scottish seats
Labour	36.3	41
Conservatives	24.7	16
SNP	30.4	11

The Conservatives found themselves with more seats than the SNP, although they had secured fewer votes. Labour secured 41 out of the 71 Scottish seats, although polling just a little over one-third of the Scottish vote. The SNP, discriminated against by the voting system, needed an extra uniform swing of just 6.8 per cent to secure a majority of seats in Scotland, upon which it would have claimed a mandate for independence, despite having only a minority of the Scottish vote.

The Labour Party, although winning an overall majority of seats, secured its lowest percentage of votes since the war, except for the general election of February 1974. It gained less of the vote in October 1974 than in 1959 or 1970 which were, until 1979, its worst postwar defeats. Nevertheless, although it had lost one-tenth of its 1970 support, Labour was able, until it lost its majority in 1976, to govern untroubled by having the support of only 39 per cent of the voters, and 29 per cent of the electorate.

It is not surprising that support for proportional representation spread rapidly amongst the general public. On 25 March 1974, *The Times* published the results of an opinion poll in which the public had been asked whether it would be a good or a bad idea to introduce a new system of voting so that the number of seats won by a party reflected the votes it received. One must interpret the result of such a poll with great caution, since other polls have shown that only a minority of the electorate understands what proportional representation actually is, and an even smaller minority possesses sufficient knowledge about the different systems to be able to evaluate them properly. Nevertheless, the results of the ORC poll are significant as indicating a public mood.

	All	Con.	Lab.	Lib.
Good idea	70	74	59	87
Bad idea	15	16	19	6
Don't know	15	10	22	7

Opinion polls published since 1974 have continually indicated majorities in favour of proportional representation, although, as these various polls have also shown, many who support change do not necessarily favour the probable consequence of more frequent coalition government; it does not follow that electoral reform would secure a majority in a referendum if the issue were actually presented for decision.

Reinforcement for the cause of electoral reform came in 1976 with the report of the Hansard Society's Commission on Electoral Reform, chaired by Lord Blake, the historian and Conservative peer. This questioned many of the assumptions held by supporters of the plurality system, and in particular the view that the alternation of majority governments made for a combination of stability and democratic choice. On the contrary, the Commission argued, it was 'a recipe for instability of the most damaging nature'.[11] The report unanimously advocated a change in the electoral system, although preferring a variant of the West German system to the single transferable vote hitherto advocated by most electoral reformers.

The Commission was a self-appointed body, and although it began as an all-party Commission, two of the three Labour members soon dropped out, and the Labour Party refused to supply it with evidence. Of the remaining members, two were Conservatives, one (Lord O'Neill of the Maine) a former Ulster Unionist Prime Minister of Northern Ireland who had been disowned by his party for attempting to bridge the gulf between the two communities in the province, and two were industrialists. The members of the Commission, because of their sympathy with the complaints of the business community and their concern at the damage done to industry as a result of continual shifts of policy, were predisposed in favour of electoral reform. Nevertheless, the public reputation of the Commission's members ensured that the Report would make a considerable impact. Previously, criticism of the plurality system had been confined to Liberals and members of the Electoral Reform Society 'regarded until recently as political flat-earthers. . . . Supporters of the status quo are now on the defensive; they have lost the best arguments and have largely retreated to positions of raw self-interest.'[12]

To coincide with the publication of the Commission's Report, an all-party National Committee for Electoral Reform was set up, chaired by Lord Harlech, a former Ambassador to Washington, and containing amongst its members two former Speakers, Lord Selwyn-Lloyd and Lord Maybray-King and such non-political figures as Lord Ramsey, the former Archbishop of Canterbury, and Diana Rigg, the actress, as well as many other academics and celebrities. This was clear evidence that electoral reform was now advocated by many of the leading figures of British public life, and had become not only respectable but also distinctly fashionable. But of course a change in the electoral system depended not primarily upon the state of 'Establishment' opinion, but upon the attitudes of the party leaders whose prospects of office it would affect.

THE LABOUR PARTY

The Labour Party has, not surprisingly, in recent years been the least sympathetic of the three United Kingdom parties to electoral reform. By 1979, it had been in power for eleven out of the past fifteen years, a period during which the Conservatives had succeeded in winning only one election; and at the 1975 Labour Party Conference, Harold Wilson claimed that Labour was now 'the natural party of government'. Electoral reform would have prevented Labour from governing on its own unless it secured the votes of 50 per cent of the electorate, something it did not look like being able to achieve.

It might have been expected that Labour's Right wing, under increasing pressure from the Left in the constituencies and the Party Conference, would have looked sympathetically at proportional representation. For the single transferable vote system would have taken away from constituency activists the power to foist Left-wing candidates upon a 'moderate' Labour electorate; while coalition with the Liberals could have been acceptable if it meant that the influence of those Liberals orientated towards social democracy replaced that of the Left.

But the Right hardly concerned itself with electoral reform. It was as much affected as the Left by the trauma of 1931, and therefore unsympathetic to coalition. Moreover, the Right continued to believe that it could control the Labour Party through the methods so well described by Robert McKenzie in his book *British Political Parties* (1955). According to McKenzie, the Right-wing leadership of the Parliamentary Labour Party would be able to dominate the extra-parliamentary wing of the Party by virtue of the union block vote at Conference, so ensuring that the Party's National Executive contained a loyalist majority. In this way, the Party Constitution which assigned primacy in policy-making to Conference and the National Executive could be by-passed. The Party would be led by a moderate parliamentary leadership allied to loyalist unions.

After 1974, Labour's hopes in government rested upon a 'social contract' agreed with the unions, and the Labour Right hoped that the unions would play their traditional role in maintaining the stability of the Party. The Right, however, placed an exaggerated confidence in the manipulative abilities of Harold Wilson and James Callaghan so to 'manage' the party as to defuse any threat from the Left. Callaghan's methods were graphically described by one backbench Labour MP as being 'to let an unrepresentative minority within the party make the running in public debate while he slipped round quietly to the back room and tried to fix the votes against them; and if the fixing failed he either compromised or accepted defeat'.[13] By the time that these methods had been shown to be inadequate, the position of the Right in the Party had been seriously weakened.

There was, however, in the 1974 Labour Cabinet a group of what Barbara Castle in her diaries calls 'the hard core of Jenkinsite coalitionists',[14] by which she means Roy Jenkins himself, together with Harold Lever, Shirley Williams and Reg Prentice, who were becoming increasingly sympathetic to electoral reform. A Speaker's Conference which Heath had called into being in 1973 to discuss various technical aspects of electoral procedure lapsed with the general election, and, in the confused parliamentary situation which followed the February election, Roy Jenkins sought to reconstitute the Conference, including in its terms of reference 'the matter of the single transferable vote'. Otherwise, in his view, 'we should look as though we were the only party not interested in electoral reform. As the Liberals were very likely to propose its examination, it would be better for us to take the initiative.' However Willie Ross, the Secretary of State for Scotland, pointed out in Cabinet that 'If we were not careful we could see the end of any possibility of a Labour Government,' and, according to Barbara Castle, the Cabinet concluded that 'It was obviously best to let this sleeping dog lie as long as possible. So we sent Roy away with a flea in his coalition ear.' Jenkins tried again at a Cabinet meeting in November 1975, but was attacked by Denis Healey who 'with good pragmatic vigour, denounced the idea as "absolute madness"', while Barbara Castle reflected that 'these rightists will go on beavering away . . . until they have finally destroyed the Labour Party's independence and power to govern single-handedly'.[15] In the light of its setbacks since 1979, however, it would not be surprising if the Right wing of the Labour Party began to display more open interest in proportional representation; and indeed, it is a main policy plank in the platform of the new Social Democratic Party which would perhaps be the party most likely to benefit from electoral reform; for if the British electorate is in reality, as has been frequently suggested, mildly left of centre, then proportional representation might ensure long periods of social democratic government, as it has done in the Scandinavian countries and in West Germany.

Ron Hayward, the General Secretary of the Labour Party, has epitomised its traditional attitude to electoral reform when he declared that 'Proportional representation means coalition government at Westminster, on the lines of our European partners, and it is goodbye then to any dreams or aspirations for a democratic socialist Britain.'[16] He did not, however, ask himself how it was that the democratic socialist parties among 'our European partners' such as West Germany, Norway, Sweden and Denmark had succeeded, under various systems of proportional representation, in enjoying longer periods of government, and rather more success in achieving their objectives, than the Labour Party had done. It is ironic that under either the single transferable party vote system as used in Ireland or the West German additional member system of proportional representation, the voting figures of May 1979 – Conservatives, 43.9 per cent; Labour, 36.9 per cent; Liberals, 13.8 per cent – would have been insufficient to yield Mrs Thatcher an absolute parliamentary majority, and Labour, had it been able to renew its pact with the Liberals, would have been able to continue in government.

THE CONSERVATIVES

The Conservative Party has in general been far less confident in its support of the plurality system than Labour. Indeed, after 1974 there was a vigorous and lively debate within the Party on the electoral system, a debate that was by no means concluded with the Conservative election victory in 1979.

Most Conservatives were deeply disturbed by their election defeat in February 1974. Believing that they had been driven from power by the trades unions, they began to ask themselves how government could acquire the authority to deal with such a threat in the future. They observed the Labour Government, although supported by less than one-third of the electorate, proceeding to implement controversial and, in the Conservative view, damaging legislation for which it had received no mandate. One result of this was that little remained of the achievements of the Heath Government. The Industrial Relations Act was repealed and replaced with legislation restoring and extending the privileges of the trades unions. Britain's entry into the EEC came under question as the Labour Government proceeded to renegotiate the terms accepted by Heath; the Housing Finance Act was repealed; and the Pay Board was abolished together with the rest of the machinery of the Heath Government's incomes policy. It was natural, therefore, for Conservatives to ask whether a broader-based government such as they hoped might be produced by proportional representation, would not command wider authority in the country and therefore be more successful in resolving national problems.

Many supporters of the Conservative Party in industry and finance shared these fears. They sought a stable political climate within which investment plans could be framed in the knowledge that they would not be undermined by continual reversals of policy as government swung from Right to Left. Some looked longingly at West Germany where, so they claimed, changes of government did not involve the wholesale repeal of previous policies and there was a basis of agreement on economic fundamentals which allowed for steady industrial progress. In Britain, no programme of industrial reconstruction could be completed within the lifetime of one Parliament, and therefore continuity of policy was an essential precondition of economic revival.

Heath's response to this feeling was to fight the October 1974 election on an explicit appeal for a Government of National Unity to meet the economic crisis. Such a government

> would seek to put aside party bickering and concentrate on mobilising the full resources of a nation united to beat the crisis. The crisis of authority in our democratic system represents a problem for any government. To tackle it, we need a broadly based government to call on the support of the whole community and protect the public interest. The strength of such a government lies in the national unity that backs it.[17]

But Heath was unwilling to advocate proportional representation, and he was unable to erase past memories of confrontation in government or of the 'Who Governs' election in February. Indeed, many electors feared that the return of a Conservative government, far from securing national unity, would lead only to renewed industrial strife.

The second Conservative defeat stimulated further discussion of proportional representation, which seemed to many to be implicit in Heath's call for a coalition. Indeed, some Conservatives believed that if only Heath had been able to make some explicit commitment to electoral reform, then he rather than Harold Wilson would have been occupying Downing Street. The mood in the Conservative Party following the second election defeat is well captured in a letter written by Jeremy Thorpe in November 1974.

> The hopeful thing is that we have (except for Ted, who is going anyway) convinced some Tories (e.g. Du Cann and Whitelaw) that we are here for good, and may accept (a) that the Labour Party will never and has never polled 50% or more of the votes but (b) under the present electoral system 39% of the vote can and has given one party a majority. . . . In October we proved that there was a 3 party system linked to a 2 party electoral system. All of this has to be achieved *before* the Tories recover and start to think they can win without us! I think we can do it.[18]

Heath was indeed replaced as Conservative leader, but, unfortunately for Thorpe, his successor was not William Whitelaw but Mrs Thatcher who soon revealed herself as an implacable and determined opponent of proportional representation. Mrs Thatcher turned out to be a devotee of the free market school of economics: she believed fervently that inflation could be controlled by monetary methods and that the forces of economic liberalism would then work to stimulate industrial recovery; she saw no reason to share power with those who did not accept this philosophy. During the general election campaign of 1979, speaking at Cardiff on 16 April, she was to affirm that she was 'a conviction politician', adding 'The Old Testament prophets did not say "Brothers, I want a consensus." They said: "This is my faith. This is what I passionately believe. If you believe it too, then come with me."'

But Mrs Thatcher's election as leader of the Conservative Party did not end the debate on electoral reform. Indeed, the stridency with which she advocated policies contrary to those pursued by the Heath Government alarmed many Conservative MPs who supported proportional representation as an instrument to secure less dogmatic policies. They were encouraged by the EEC referendum campaign which showed that there was a much greater degree of consensus amongst politicians of different parties than was reflected in the country's political arrangements.

Moreover, the course pursued by the Labour Government deeply disturbed most Conservatives who believed that, with the support of only 39 per cent of the voters and 29 per cent of the electorate, Labour lacked a mandate to implement its policies. Yet the Government proceeded to implement its programme as if it had a comfortable overall majority, phasing pay beds out of the National Health Service, imposing comprehensive education upon local authorities and nationalising the aerospace and shipbuilding industries and the docks. Conservatives began to ask themselves whether it was right that a radical government enjoying office through the support of a minority of the voters, should be able to impose irreversible social changes upon the country. Indeed, it was to describe this situation that Lord Hailsham in his Dimbleby Lecture of 1976 coined the phrase 'elective dictatorship'. Proportional representation was obviously one way by which the risk of such dictatorship could be avoided, and it therefore had a powerful appeal for some Conservative leaders.

Nevertheless, the new Conservative leadership was determined to have nothing to do with electoral reform. In 1975, the annual Conservative Conference debated the subject for the first time since the war. The debate was carefully 'managed' by the platform to ensure that electoral reform was rejected 'by a very substantial majority'. The Conference had received 23 motions from Conservative Associations on electoral reform, of which 18 were in favour, and five hostile; it was, however, a hostile motion that was called for debate. The mover was given 8 minutes to make his speech, and then four other speakers were called for 8 minutes each: the debate was concluded by Angus Maude who spoke for 25 minutes. Maude delivered a blistering attack on proportional representation, ending with a rhetorical flourish accusing the electoral reformers of defeatism.

Or do perhaps these people just lack confidence in the ability of our own Party to win? Is it that they think the Conservative Party cannot win an election and could not govern effectively if it did? Now, if you do not believe that the Tory Party, under new leadership, coming to the next election with practical policies to save the country and with the courage and resolution to carry them through; if you do not believe that the Tory Party can win and can govern, then in God's name what are we all doing here now in this hall at this Conference? Why are you all sweating away in your constituencies raising money, holding meetings, selecting candidates, if you do not think we can win and we can govern?[19]

The force of Maude's rhetoric obscured the fact that he had not resolved the dilemma facing those Conservatives who did not believe that a single election victory would be sufficient to restore Britain's fortunes, especially when a new Conservative government would be confronted by a hostile trade union movement and a Labour Party dominated by the Left and committed to repealing most of the measures enacted by a Conservative government. Maude's prescription would work only if the Conservatives succeeded in winning not only the next election, but the election after that as well, and many Conservatives were sceptical of the Party's ability to do so.

Moreover, Maude proved more explicit than any politician had yet been in public on the criterion by which to judge the merits of electoral reform: it was simply whether reform would assist the Conservative Party in winning power; and his speech drew a caustic comment from a leader in the *Guardian* which declared that Maude's message was 'likely to achieve a somewhat less universal acclaim from audiences where the essential test of an electoral system is something more than its probable effects on the fortunes of the Conservative Party or indeed the Labour Party', while *The Times* commented that the Conservative Party 'wants to keep our unfair electoral system in order to have an unfair share of power'.[20]

The Conservatives won the general election of 1979, securing an overall majority of 43 seats. Yet their election victory did not end the debate within the party on electoral reform, for the new government proceeded to implement its own controversial economic programme based upon monetary deflation and the cutting of public expenditure. These policies aroused disquiet not only amongst the government's political opponents, but also amongst Conservatives belonging to the Party's moderate wing, both inside the Cabinet and on the backbenches. It was natural for Conservative critics of the government to believe that electoral reform would be able to provide a government with a broader basis of support so giving it more authority to carry out the policies needed to effect economic recovery.

In its hostility to electoral reform, the Conservative Party faced the difficulty that its stance was in direct contradiction to the instincts of many of its supporters in the country. For the Conservative Party in Parliament generally relies for its success upon the conservative interest in the country, a sentiment favouring continuity and stability rather than radical change and upheaval. It was this interest which had been so deeply offended by the policies of the Heath Government because they had seemed to lead to 'confrontation' with the unions and endless industrial strife. Indeed the appeals of both Harold Wilson and Jeremy Thorpe in 1974 had, in their different ways, been directed to the electorate's yearning for peace and stability. In 1979, the Conservatives explicitly appealed to the electorate as a radical party determined to introduce new policies in an attempt to reverse a seemingly inexorable economic decline. These policies could be justified only by success; for, like those of the Heath Government they were bound to offend the natural instincts of Conservative supporters in the country. As the Labour Party swung to the Left, following its election defeat, and in 1980 chose as its new leader Michael Foot, who had been hitherto identified with the Left wing of the party, some Conservatives began to ask whether the plurality system was really in the best interests either of conservatism or of industrial progress. This gap between the official attitudes of the Party leadership and the natural interests of its supporters is potentially a dangerous one for the future of the Party.

THE LIBERALS

The Liberals, of course, were not in doubt as to the merits of proportional representation, a precondition of their re-emergence as a major party. Their problem was to obtain a strong enough bargaining position to be able to press for change. The election successes of the Liberals in 1974 – by far their best results since 1929 – had put them tantalisingly close to power, and in March 1974, they had been offered places in a Coalition Cabinet if only they would agree to sustain Heath in office. Yet both power and influence had seemed to slip away, and after the October election they seemed as far from their objective as ever.

In the early 1960s, Jo Grimond had attempted as Liberal leader to redefine the role of a Party which could not hope to be elected to government in the near future. Instead of aping the functions of the other parties Liberals should act as a catalyst for change. They should seek party realignment as the divisions between Left and Right in the Labour party worsened. Moreover, the Liberals 'could not by some miracle of parthenogenesis spring from six MPs to a majority in the House of Commons.

They would have to go through a period of coalition.' Yet 'The prospect of coalition . . . scared Liberals out of their wits' since, remembering the Lloyd George Coalition and the National Government, they feared that they would be swallowed up by their senior partner. Nevertheless, it was odd that those who cried most loudly for electoral reform were 'also the most adamant against any Coalition with other Parties', although 'If electoral reform led to the results for which Liberals hoped and which statistics foretold, that is the fifty to seventy MPs to which our vote entitled us, then if government was to be carried on, coalitions of some sort would often be essential.'[21]

In 1976, when David Steel became Liberal leader, he sought definitely to reorientate the Party's tactics towards coalition. He had already achieved considerable parliamentary success through cross-party co-operation in the Abortion Act of 1967 and in his campaign against the Labour Government's bill of 1968 restricting the entry of Kenyan Asians into Britain. He was, unlike many Liberals, eager to exert a practical influence upon public affairs, and was attracted, rather than repelled, by the prospect of power. He was especially determined to make the maximum use of his tiny forces in a Parliament in which, by the end of 1976, the Labour Government had lost its overall majority.

His opportunity came when the first devolution bill – the Scotland and Wales Bill – foundered in Committee. The Liberals had refused to continue with their support for this bill unless concessions were made to their point of view, but the government remained rigid and inflexible in its approach. By voting against a guillotine motion, the Liberals ensured its defeat, and effectively killed the bill. The SNP's 11 members immediately decided that they would do all they could to bring the government down, believing that they could capitalise electorally upon Labour's inability to secure devolution. Thus Labour, in order to survive, needed to secure co-operation from either the Liberals or the Ulster Unionists, and in March 1977, the Liberals agreed to support the government until the end of the parliamentary session. So began the Lib–Lab pact which lasted until the summer of 1978.

The pact was not a formal coalition. For it was hardly possible for a small party of 13 MPs to join in government with a party of over 300 MPs. It was instead, in David Steel's words, 'a parliamentary but not governmental coalition – a unique experiment'.[22] For Steel the central aim of the pact was to show that the Liberals could act as a responsible party of government rather than remain a mere sectarian fringe party; in this way it would encourage the notion that coalition government could solve the country's problems more successfully than single-party government, and would therefore increase support for proportional representation so as to produce such a government.

In addition the Liberals could hope for electoral gains. They would undoubtedly lose votes from disillusioned Conservatives but such voters would in any case have returned to their traditional home as soon as they appreciated that a Liberal protest vote was a luxury leading to a Labour government. It was, therefore, inevitable that the Liberals would achieve fewer votes in the next election; on the other hand they might well secure more *seats* as a result of tactical voting by Labour supporters in constituencies where the Liberals were a reasonably close second to Conservatives elected on a minority vote. There were in fact over 30 seats in the general election of October 1974 where the Labour vote was significantly larger than the Conservative majority over the Liberal; and if this Labour vote could be squeezed, then the Liberals could hope to win seats such as Bodmin, Skipton, Leominster, Hereford, Chippenham and Bath. Unfortunately for the Liberals, however, this strategy needed more time to work than the 15 months of the Pact allowed. For most of the period of the Lib–Lab Pact, the Labour Government was still so unpopular that many Labour voters were themselves switching to the Conservatives, and were unwilling to thank the Liberals for keeping what they saw as an incompetent government in power.

Moreover Steel's strategy was by no means accepted by the Liberal Party as a whole. Jo Grimond took the view that realignment was no longer an option since it was no longer possible to believe that the social democrats would gain the upper hand in the Labour Party, and the Labour Right had been irretrievably weakened by continual accommodation to the demands of the Left. The Liberals 'must therefore obtain something from the pact which would, in the medium term at least, strengthen the hand of the non-socialist but progressive element in our politics. The only immediate way to achieve this was by electoral reform. That was therefore the prize, the only prize, which could have justified the pact.'[23] The Labour Government would hardly have agreed to introduce electoral reform, but Grimond was prepared to carry his argument to its logical conclusion and face the electorate since he believed that the Liberals could put up a creditable performance in the ensuing general election. However, an election would almost certainly have resulted in a Conservative overall majority, and the Liberals would have lost their bargaining power in the new Parliament. So the majority of the Parliamentary Liberal Party were not prepared to accept Grimond's argument.

But they hoped, nevertheless, for some specific gains from the Pact, and in particular they hoped to secure proportional representation for the elections to the European Assembly which was of vital importance to Liberals since they believed – correctly as it turned out – that otherwise they would win no seats, even if they secured one-eighth of the vote. For Steel, however, the aim of the Pact was not to secure such specific gains, but to show that a parliamentary coalition could work successfully to provide economic improvement and stability. But this meant that in the negotiations which took place during the period of the Pact, the Liberals had no sticking point, no point at which they were prepared to bring down the government; and this undoubtedly weakened their bargaining position. Partly for this reason, the legislative gains which they achieved were very meagre.

There is some evidence that Steel and Callaghan came to think in terms of the German model of government whereby an alliance between the Social Democrats and the Free Democrats gave the country continuous government of the moderate Left, and kept the Right-wing party out of power even if, as in 1976, it proved to be the largest single party in terms of votes and seats. In February 1978, Callaghan told Steel that 'he needs a good size Liberal vote, and that the next parliament may well be hung'; in April he 'says there could be a minority Labour government after the next election, which is why he agrees the present pact should not end in a row. . .'; and in July he 'raises FDP comparison . . . (The FDP in Germany campaign for coalition stating their partnership intentions).' There was even a hint that Callaghan would have liked to see Lib–Lab co-operation at electoral level when he told Steel, regretfully, 'He doesn't see Labour candidates standing down in third places – they tend to be extreme there.'[24] Such a degree of electoral co-operation would have ensured that the Conservatives could not have won an overall majority in an election fought in the autumn of 1978.

There was thus, parallel to the formal Lib–Lab pact, a burgeoning personal sympathy between Steel and Callaghan which could have led to the transformation of British politics. But Callaghan's view of the possibilities of co-operation was hardly accepted in the Labour Party as a whole, since most Labour supporters saw the pact as a device to enable the Party to struggle through a period of unpopularity, and they hoped to win an overall majority in the next general election. Michael Foot, the Deputy Leader, gave voice to the real feelings of the Party when he said:

> What we want to do is to prepare for the time when we can get a full majority again in the House of Commons. There is nobody who wants that more than I do. But if we had not had an arrangement with the Liberals we would have thrown away that chance of getting a real majority not merely for months but maybe for years.[25]

In the event Callaghan threw away the prospect of continued Lib–Lab co-operation when he decided not to call an election in September 1978 on the grounds that a hung parliament would not be in the country's best interests; and the Conservative victory in May 1979 put paid to Liberal hopes of continued co-operation. Like Edward Heath, Callaghan found himself a victim of the search for total power for his own party because of his unwillingness to continue sharing power with another like-minded party. In gambling *va banque*, he lost all.

The election of 1979 consisted in reality of two separate contests. There was first the battle between the Conservative and Labour parties, but also the struggle by the minor parties to obtain enough seats for another hung parliament, an outcome which did not, of course, depend upon their efforts alone. Speaking at Peebles in August 1978, Mrs Thatcher insisted that there were only two ways to run the country, the Tory way and the socialist way. 'You cannot', she declared, 'run for a hung parliament. How do people vote for a hung parliament?' David Steel, on the other hand, insisted that a hung parliament was 'a people's parliament', since

> To the electorate the difference between these two [i.e. Lib/Lab or Lib/Con] would be much less than the difference between a Lib–Con government and a Thatcher–Joseph government, or the difference between a Lib–Lab government and a Foot–Benn one. The next election, therefore, will provide a solid choice which is both proven and credible. No democrat can complain about that.[26]

The result of the election showed that the third force did not command sufficient support to ensure a hung parliament, and that its strength had receded since October 1974, although the Liberal vote held up rather better than at previous elections when there had been a swing to the Conservatives. The period 1976–9 had, moreover, brought the Liberals no nearer solving the problem of how to bring electoral reform on to the practical agenda of politics and ensure that they themselves could exert a continuing influence upon government policy. The Lib–Lab Pact was, inevitably, a highly temporary arrangement; and even if it had been buttressed by an electoral pact, this could not be a substitute for electoral reform. For it would be as objectionable on grounds of democratic principle to deprive Labour voters of their choice in Roxburgh, Selkirk and Peebles as to deprive Liberal voters of their choice in Hertford and Stevenage, Shirley Williams's seat. 'No: the real answer is electoral reform, not the rigging of an already unsatisfactory system.'[27] The increasing polarisation of politics after the 1979 election made it more urgent than ever for the Liberals, representing one-seventh of the electorate, to bring their influence to bear upon a political system becoming increasingly discredited by the failures of successive governments.

DIRECT ELECTIONS TO THE EUROPEAN ASSEMBLY

For many Liberals though not for David Steel, the adoption of proportional representation for elections to the European Assembly was the cornerstone of the Lib–Lab Pact. Article 138 (iii) of the Treaty of Rome committed the British Government to 'election by direct universal suffrage in accordance with a uniform procedure in all member states'. If there were to be a uniform system of election, it would almost certainly have to be a proportional one, since seven of the nine EEC countries use a proportional system for their domestic legislatures. There were, moreover, strong grounds for Britain abandoning the plurality system for the European elections. The traditional arguments in defence of this system as providing stable government and constituency links between the voter and his MP were irrelevant since the 'government' of the European Community – the Council of Ministers – was not responsible to the Assembly; and the 81 seats which Britain was allotted in the Assembly meant that constituencies under the plurality system would contain half a million electors, so there could hardly be close contact between the member and the voter.

The plurality system's most characteristic feature is an exaggeration of the number of seats gained by the winning party in an election. The larger the constituency the more difficult it becomes for minority parties to secure representation, and the greater the degree of exaggeration. If support for the two main parties was fairly evenly divided, the outcome might not be too disproportionate as between them. But it would be likely, especially if direct elections fell between general elections, that the government would be unpopular and that voting patterns would be influenced by the desire to protest against government policy. If that were the case, there could be a very considerable disproportion between votes and seats. In July 1977, David Butler calculated the likely result of direct elections held under the plurality system, assuming that the average by-election swing from Labour to the Conservatives of 15 per cent between October 1974 and June 1977 was reflected in the election to the European Assembly. The result would be that the Conservatives would win 71 seats and Labour only 7.[28] Moreover Labour's seats would be concentrated north of the Trent, so that Labour voters in the Midlands and the South of England would be totally unrepresented. With an unpopular Conservative government, the opposite result could of course occur, and in that case, the Conservatives might well not succeed in returning any Euro MPs in the North of England, Scotland or Wales.

Moreover, Britain by 1977 was no longer a two-party system. The SNP was maintaining a powerful challenge following the failure of the first devolution bill, and polls in Spring 1977 indicated that it could be the leading party in Scotland. If one in twenty of those who had voted Labour in October 1974 swung to the SNP, then the SNP would scoop all eight of the proposed Euro-constituencies under the plurality system. If, on the other hand, SNP support fell from the 30 per cent which it secured in October 1974 to just 27 per cent, it might well win no seat at all.[29] The Conservatives who won a quarter of the vote in October 1974 would also be unlikely to secure any seats in the election. Thus the campaign in

Scotland would be dominated by the prospects of the SNP, rather than the future of the EEC, and 'Those who hope that the electoral campaign will promote informed and intelligent discussion of the future of the Common Market and the role of the European Assembly will be brushed aside.'[30]

In Northern Ireland, use of the plurality system would prevent the election of a Catholic, since, even if the Unionist vote was split, 'there is simply no contiguous group of four constituencies where the Catholic-based parties could beat a Unionist'.[31] It was for this reason that the Government decided that 'Whatever electoral system is used in the rest of the United Kingdom it would be appropriate for these elections to be conducted by a system of proportional representation,' and 'If the rest of the United Kingdom uses the simple majority system, STV would be used in Northern Ireland.'[32] An attempt by the Ulster Unionists to delete the provision for the single transferable vote in the European Assemblies Bill on the grounds that the whole United Kingdom ought to use the same system was resisted by the Government and comfortably defeated. So it was that, for the first time since 1918, the whole of Ireland elected members simultaneously by the same electoral method to the same Parliament. Before the Lib–Lab Pact, however, the Government took a less sympathetic line to the Liberal minority in Britain which would also be grossly under-represented. Indeed, the Liberals would need to secure 28 per cent of the vote to win a single seat in the Euro-election – nearly 2½ million votes more on a similar turnout than their February 1974 vote.[33]

The Government took the view, nonetheless, that the plurality system should be preserved. In August 1976, the Second Report from the Select Committee on Direct Elections argued for the status quo, and its Labour and Conservative members combined against the lone dissentient, Jeremy Thorpe. The Committee presented a number of rather inadequate administrative arguments for its final decision, and its work has been described, not unfairly, as 'characterised by a narrow vision, a failure to search out and investigate real alternatives'.[34] It conducted no research into the effects of different electoral systems, and it seems to have been mainly motivated by the fear that proportional representation for elections to the European Assembly would prove 'the thin end of the wedge' for proportional representation to the House of Commons.

The Lib–Lab Pact, however, transformed the situation, for its terms committed the Government not only to introduce legislation for direct elections, but also to 'consult' on the choice of electoral systems, to make no 'recommendation' before considering the Liberal Party's views, and to allow a free vote in the Commons.[35] One month after the Pact, a 'White Paper with Green edges' appeared, *Direct Elections to the European Assembly* (Cmnd. 6768, 1977) in which the government offered a choice of three electoral systems – the plurality system, the regional list system and the single transferable vote.

Advocates of proportional representation now had to consider which system would be likely to offer the best chance of winning the vote in the Commons. For this purpose, the ideal system would have to be one which, since 'there is no Parliamentary majority for domestic electoral reform at this stage' would not 'be seen as a stepping-stone to a more general move towards electoral reform in Britain'.[36] Moreover, if proportional representation was to have any chance of securing all-party support, its advocates would have to avoid any system which was already the preferred favourite of reformers in one particular party. These criteria excluded both the single transferable vote, which was closely identified with the Liberals and advocated by them for use in Westminster elections; and also the German system or the additional member variant proposed by the Blake Commission for elections to the House of Commons, both of which were identified with the Conservative Party and would be difficult for Labour MPs to support.

It was Michael Steed, a lecturer in Government at Manchester University and a prominent expert on electoral systems, who proposed in a pamphlet *Fair Elections or Fiasco?* that the electoral system used in Finland and known as the regional list system be adopted: and it was this system which the Government agreed to recommend in the European Assemblies Bill published in November 1977. But the Government took account of the fact that the Commons might well not be persuaded to support this system, and the first schedule to the bill provided, as an alternative, what it called 'the simple majority system' (i.e. plurality system) for Great Britain, with STV for Northern Ireland.

In accordance with its pact with the Liberals, the Government allowed a free vote on the issue and made strenuous efforts to persuade Labour MPs to support proportional representation. The Conservatives, out of loyalty to Mrs Thatcher, who was known to be hostile to proportional representation, and in order to destroy the pact, opposed the change. George Gardiner declared that the bill should be called the 'Lib–Lab Pact (Preservation) Bill'. He argued that the regional list system would deprive the voter of any direct relationship to his Euro MP since the smallest Euro-constituency would have a population of one and a half million, while the largest, South-East England, would comprise over seven million voters. He also claimed that it would give too much power to the central party machines, that it would be seen by the electorate as an alien system imported from the EEC like the juggernaut lorry, and would therefore increase the unpopularity of the Common Market.[37] Douglas Hurd, although a member of the National Committee for Electoral Reform, declared that he could not support a system 'discovered by a Liberal professor in the forests of Finland'.[38] But Conservative 'moderates' such as Edward Heath, Francis Pym, James Prior, Sir Ian Gilmour and Peter Walker all voted for proportional representation and they succeeded in attracting the support of a respectable minority of Conservatives. Callaghan succeeded in persuading 147 out of 308 Labour MPs to support proportional representation, but nevertheless it was heavily defeated. The voting is indicated in the table.

	For PR	Against PR	Did not vote
Labour	147	115	46
Conservative	61	198	22
Liberal	13	0	0
SNP	0	0	11
Plaid Cymru	2	0	1
Ulster Unionists	0	8	2
Others	1	0	3
	224	321	85
Labour ministers	64	14	
Labour backbenchers	83	101	

It is perhaps not surprising that the turnout for the first election for the European Assembly in Great Britain was 32.4 per cent, by far the lowest for any European country. In Northern Ireland, on the other hand, where the single transferable vote was used, the turnout was 57.1 per cent, although Northern Ireland, as had been shown by the 1975 referendum result, was one of the areas of Britain least sympathetic to the Community.

The result of the election for the European Assembly held in Great Britain in June 1979 was as follows:

	% Votes	Seats
Conservatives	50.6	60
Labour	33.0	17
Liberals	13.1	0
SNP	1.9	1
Others	1.4	0

The Conservatives, with just over one-half of the vote, secured over three-quarters of the seats; Labour, with one-third of the vote, secured just over one-fifth of the seats; the Liberals, with over one-eighth of the vote, secured no seats at all; while the SNP, with less than one-sixth of the Liberal vote, did succeed in securing a seat. Plaid Cymru which secured 11.7 per cent of the Welsh vote, slightly higher than their best ever performance in any Westminster election, failed to win a seat.

As important as the misrepresentation of parties, however, was the misrepresentation of opinion on the future development of the EEC. For the supporters of each party were divided between those who favoured Britain remaining in the EEC and those who wanted her to leave; between those who favoured rapid movement towards European federalism and those who believed that the Community should remain a 'Europe des patries'. Yet the balance between these opinions in Britain's representatives in the Parliament was determined not by the voters, but by the decisions of selection committees. However, because the Labour Party was under-represented, so also was the attitude of hostility to the Community which is widespread in Britain. The absence of Liberals from the Assembly means that federalist attitudes are probably totally unrepresented. On the other hand, the dominance of the Conservatives probably meant 'that one particular British attitude (limited pragmatic acceptance of the idea of European unity) is far more dominant among British MEPs than it is in British political opinion'. 'Paradoxically', Michael Steed has written, 'the 36 nominated British MEPs were more representative than the 78 elected members are.'[39]

It is little wonder that the result of the election produced scathing comments from the European press. Henri Pierre of *Le Monde* declared that the British electoral system had given an 'extremely distorted and incorrect representation of the electorate', while the *Gazet van Antwerpen* claimed that the plurality system was an 'idiotic electoral system', and the *Neue Zürcher Zeitung* spoke of 'absurd distortion . . . a colourless British delegation'.[40] The elections to the European Assembly, far from extending its legitimacy, probably contributed both to the apathetic way in which the campaign was fought, the low turnout and the grossly distorted result which ensured that Britain's delegation would find it hard to represent Britain's interests in the Community.

DEVOLUTION

The other major constitutional reform of the 1974–9 Parliament was devolution, a topic which occupied a considerable amount of parliamentary time for no tangible result, since Welsh devolution was decisively rejected by the electorate in the referendum, while Scottish devolution received an insufficient 'Yes' majority and the Government was unable to implement it. The Government's refusal to accept proportional representation for the Scottish assembly was probably one cause of the failure of devolution in Scotland.

One of the few unanimous recommendations of the Royal Commission on the Constitution was that if devolved assemblies were to be established, they should be elected by the single transferable vote method of proportional representation. Indeed, the majority Report declared that

An *overriding* requirement for the regional assemblies would be to ensure the proper representation of minorities. . . . This would be particularly desirable in any region in which there were likely to be long periods without alternation of parties in power. We therefore favour the single transferable vote.[41]

This argument was also accepted by Lord Crowther-Hunt and Professor Peacock in their Memorandum of Dissent.[42]

The Labour Government, however, at an early stage in its deliberations, proposed in its White Paper, *Democracy and Devolution: Proposals for Scotland and Wales* (Cmnd. 5732, 1974) that 'Membership [i.e. of the assemblies] will be on the same system as membership of the United Kingdom Parliament,' that is it decided to use the Westminster system for elections to the Scottish and Welsh Assemblies. Because of the difficulties of drawing new constituency boundaries in time for the first Assembly elections, the Government proposed to use the existing parliamentary constituencies in Scotland and Wales, each of which would return two members to the Assemblies, except for constituencies with electorates more than a quarter over the average, which would return three members; and Orkney and Shetland which would be divided into two single-member constituencies. For subsequent elections the Boundary Commissioners would have worked out individual Assembly constituencies.

But the consequences for the first election would have multiplied the distortions of the plurality system. First, the great disparity in constituency sizes would mean that both Glasgow Central, with an electorate in 1976 of 22,338, and Clackmannan and E. Stirling, with an electorate of 65,405 – almost three times as large – would each return two members to the Assembly. In addition, it would be possible for each constituency to return two or three members to the Assembly on a minority vote; and in the four-party system which characterised Scottish politics, it is not surprising that in the general election of October 1974, 56 out of the 71 Scottish seats were held on a minority vote. In Inverness, for example, the result in October 1974 was:

Party	% Share of vote
Liberal	32.4
SNP	29.6
Conservative	22.0
Labour	15.6
Independent	0.4

Assuming that few voters split their vote, the Liberals could secure two seats in the Assembly on only 32.4 per cent of the vote.

Paradoxically the most marginal seat in Scotland, E. Dunbartonshire, where the result in October 1974 was:

Party	Votes	% Share of vote
SNP	15,551	31.2
Conservative	15,529	31.2
Labour	15,122	30.3
Liberal	3,636	7.3

might well return three SNP members to the Assembly, enjoying the support of one-third of the voters in the constituency.

Of the other five Scottish constituencies which would return three members, four – East Kilbride, West Renfrew, West Lothian and Midlothian – were held by Labour in October 1974, but were vulnerable to small swings to the SNP, a swing which could yield them 12 seats in an Assembly of 148 members on a vote of under 40 per cent in each constituency.

The proposed Scottish Assembly would be established for a fixed term, and could be dissolved only on a vote of two-thirds of its members – an unlikely occurrence. This meant that a party which succeeded in getting its nose in front during the election could, under the plurality system, retain an overall majority in the Assembly for four years, even though it rapidly lost popular support amongst the electorate. In October 1974, the share of the vote of the four main parties in Scotland was:

Labour	36.3%
SNP	30.4%
Conservative	24.7%
Liberals	8.3%

If voting habits remained the same, and voters did not split their votes, this would have probably yielded the following result:

Labour	86 seats
Conservatives	33 seats
SNP	23 seats
Liberals	6 seats

The system was, however, extremely vulnerable to a swing to the SNP. With a ten per cent swing to the SNP, for example, the result would probably have been an Assembly composed in the following way:

SNP	93 seats
Labour	28 seats
Conservatives	23 seats
Liberals	4 seats

Advocates of a Scottish Assembly who saw devolution as a middle way between the status quo and Scottish independence had a particular incentive therefore to support proportional representation. They could remind themselves of the situation in Quebec where the separatist *Parti Québec-*

qois had succeeded in gaining an overall majority in the provincial parliament on a minority of the vote.

1973	30%	6 seats out of 110
1976	41%	65 seats out of 110

The result of the 1976 election in Quebec plunged Canada into a constitutional crisis which was alleviated only when, in 1980, the Quebec electorate rejected separatism in a referendum.

In Wales, Plaid Cymru was far weaker than the SNP, and the danger of separatism remote. The result of an election to the Welsh Assembly under the plurality system would be to ensure an overall majority for Labour, even on a minority vote. On October 1974 figures, the probable composition of a Welsh Assembly would have been

Labour	50 seats
Conservatives	19 seats
Liberals	4 seats
Plaid Cymru	6 seats

There were strong arguments for the introduction of proportional representation for elections to the new Assemblies; for in Scotland it could prevent the SNP from winning a majority of the seats on a minority of the popular vote; whilst in Wales, it would have compelled Labour to co-operate with other parties if Labour support fell below the October 1974 level.

One of the conditions of the Lib–Lab Pact was that the Government would allow a free vote on the issue. However John Smith, the minister in charge of the bill, spoke against proportional representation, and ministers were whipped to vote against it. According to David Steel, John Smith had told him that 'There was no point discussing the intellectual or political merits of the case: The Scottish Executive of the Labour Party would not have it, and that was that.'[43] The Government was to pay a heavy price for its obstinacy.

During the long passage of the two devolution bills, various amendments attempting to secure proportional representation were presented but regularly rejected in the Commons by large majorities, although the Lords twice reinserted provision for PR. When John Mackintosh proposed the system of election recommended by the Hansard Society Commission, his speech was punctuated, as John Stuart Mill's had been over a hundred years ago, with laughter which reached a crescendo when he declared that 'Other countries have worked this system . . .'[44] Few MPs appreciated the connection between proportional representation and the success of the devolution experiment.

In Wales the rejection of devolution was so massive and overwhelming that it cannot seriously be argued that the question of the voting system affected the issue. In Scotland, however, where the 'Yes' vote was marginally higher than the 'No' vote, but some way short of the 40 per cent laid down by Parliament as the minimum requirement for establishing the Assembly, the absence of proportional representation might well have affected the result. There were 'No' majorities in all the rural areas of Scotland except for the Highlands and the Western Isles, and it is reasonable to suppose that Conservative and Liberal voters were unwilling to endorse an Assembly in which they would be in permanent opposition to a Labour majority dominated by Strathclyde. Moreover, many voters were driven into the 'No' camp because they believed that the Assembly would be used by the SNP to break up the United Kingdom. This belief might have appeared less plausible under a different electoral system.

Lord Home had articulated these fears when, in the debate in the House of Lords on proportional representation for the Scottish Assembly, he had declared, 'I am . . . a devolutionist although I do not much like this Bill. . . . I am bound to say that my attitude to the whole of this Bill will depend very much on whether the Government agree to adopting some form of proportional representation for elections to the Assembly.'[45] During the referendum campaign, he made a highly publicised speech advocating a 'No' vote, and gave as one of his reasons the absence of proportional representation in the Scotland Act. Lord Home exerted a strong influence upon Scottish Conservatives, and, given the narrow margin by which Scottish devolution failed, it may well be that his intervention was decisive. If so, the Labour Government's rejection of proportional representation was an important cause of the defeat of devolution.

CONCLUSION

The Parliament of 1974–9 was dominated to an unusual extent by constitutional issues, in particular the EEC referendum, direct elections to the European Assembly and devolution. Yet, in retrospect, what is perhaps surprising is the extent to which the Constitution so easily withstood the challenge of those who favoured change, whether electoral reform, reform of the Lords or a Bill of Rights.

The shift, both of popular and elite opinion, in favour of electoral reform had led to no tangible legislative result; and the election of a Conservative government with an overall majority in 1979 removed the issue from the immediate political agenda. For this election restored the two-party system in the Commons if not in the country. In the Commons, the Conservative and Labour Parties between them gained 608 seats out of 635 – 95.7 per cent – but the two-party share of the vote was 80.8 per cent – lower than at any election since 1945 except for the two general elections of 1974. There were, moreover, signs that the setback for the minor parties might be only temporary. Despite the fact that the Party's former leader Jeremy Thorpe was to face a conspiracy to murder charge shortly after the polls closed (he was in fact acquitted), the Liberals lost only two seats net, and their share of the vote was 13.8 per cent, a better result than in any general election since 1929, again excluding the two elections of 1974. The Liberals had succeeded in holding their position in the face of a swing to the Conservatives which, when it had occurred in the past – in 1950, 1951 and 1970 – had led to a Liberal collapse. In Scotland, the SNP's share of the vote – 17.3 per cent – was not reflected in its parliamentary representation, which fell from 11 seats to two – but it could hope to benefit from the unpopularity of a Conservative government which had managed to secure only a minority of the seats in Scotland.

Moreover, the Conservative election victory in 1979 could not allay a deep public anxiety over the effectiveness of Britain's political institutions. The election itself had taken on much of the character of an unpopularity contest, and the Conservative victory owed as much perhaps to fear of the Labour Left and the trade unions as to positive enthusiasm for Conservative policies. After the election, however, Lord Thorneycroft, the Party Chairman, claimed that the electorate had given the Conservatives 'a great mandate', oblivious of the fact that the Conservative share of the poll – 43.9 per cent – was the lowest enjoyed by any party with a secure absolute majority in the Commons since 1922. The Conservatives had accused the Labour Government elected in 1974 of abusing the mandate argument by implementing socialist policies which enjoyed the support of, at most, 39 per cent of the electorate. It was difficult to believe that an extra 5 per cent of the vote gave the Conservatives the privilege of the mandate which, they had argued, the preceding government lacked.

The process of political polarisation was increased by developments in the Labour Party. After its election defeat, the Callaghan Administration was assailed by the Left which claimed that it would have been more successful had it taken more notice of the policies laid down by the activists at Party Conference. In 1980, Callaghan resigned as leader of the Party and was replaced, not by Denis Healey, the firm favourite both of Labour voters and of the electorate as a whole, but by Michael Foot, one of the candidates of the Left.

This meant that both parties seemed to be led, not from the centre, but from a position much nearer their extreme wings. But it was not clear that this centrifugal tendency corresponded to the wishes of the electorate, nor even of the dwindling number of those who continued to identify with the two major parties. In such a political atmosphere, electoral reform would not lose its relevance for those who believed that Britain's economic difficulties had their roots in a political structure increasingly unsuited to the complex world of the last quarter of the twentieth century. For it was beginning to seem as though the plurality system of election which had once appeared a guarantor of stability and progress, was now a prime factor in the survival of a discredited political system. It is to an examination of the actual working of the plurality system, therefore, that we now turn.

Part IV

The case for electoral reform

Indeed, it could be argued that the electoral system has lagged behind the perceptions, however imprecise, of the people.

HANSARD SOCIETY COMMISSION ON ELECTORAL REFORM

Chapter 1

The British electoral system

THE WORKING OF THE SYSTEM

The plurality system of election, often known colloquially as the 'first past the post system', is regarded by the vast majority of people in Britain as something natural, as the very basis of stable democracy. Yet Britain is the only democracy in Europe to employ it; only four other democracies in the developed world – the United States, Canada, New Zealand and South Africa – use it for electing their legislatures; three of these were once British colonies of settlement. The plurality system is confined to Britain and to countries influenced by British conceptions of government.

In Britain it has always been strongly associated with the idea of the representation of communities. The House of Commons was originally a house of communities, and from the time of Simon de Montfort's Parliament, constituencies representing local communities returned two members to the House of Commons. In 1430 an act was passed formalising the principle of election by relative majority in country constituencies, and analogous legislation was soon passed for borough elections. The majority principle, however, was applied in a very different way from that customary in modern democracies. For from 1430 until the Reform Act of 1832, 'the *preponderant tradition* in English electoral practice was probably *the tradition of uncontested elections*';[1] and between 1868 and 1922 a level of 110 uncontested constituencies in each general election tended to be regarded as the norm.[2] Adoption of the majority principle, therefore, long preceded the nationalisation of politics or the growth of modern political parties, both of which profoundly altered its working. For a central presupposition of the majority principle had been that the proper units of representation were geographical constituencies which were integers with particular interests of their own. But with the growth of party feeling MPs came to represent, not primarily geographical constituencies, but party opinions and collective interests.

The plurality system came to be defended not on the grounds that it made possible the representation of geographical units – the sort of defence offered by Gladstone as late as 1885 – but that it offered an accurate picture of the state of party feeling in the country as a whole. Thus, an MP from Oxford is seen as a representative not primarily of Oxford, but of certain political ideas which he attempts to implement through supporting a government or opposition in the Commons; or he may be conceived of as the representative of a class – of the working class or of business interests. Increasingly, general elections came to be seen as plebiscites to determine which of two opposing teams, each representing a large social block and a large section of public opinion, should have the right to rule.

The plurality system cannot, therefore, be defended as it was in the mid-nineteenth century as a system which makes for the representation of locality. Instead, it requires a new and more realistic defence to take account of twentieth-century conditions. Yet, curiously enough, the plurality system operating within a framework of disciplined parties, has never received such a defence. As A. H. Birch noticed in 1964, 'while British political practice is now dominated by the assumption that the Parliamentary parties will behave as disciplined blocks, British political thought still lacks any justification of party discipline that is generally accepted'.[3] In place of a justification in theoretical terms, the defence has been a pragmatic one. For, whatever its defects in terms of an abstract conception of fairness, the system provides, so it is argued, 'strong' and responsive government; while the single-member constituency makes for close contact between the elector and his MP, thus linking the interests of the state with those of the citizen.

The system has thus been justified with the type of argument that Bagehot would have understood; and it is in these terms that we must evaluate it. We begin, therefore, by considering how the plurality system actually operates in Britain today, and whether the claims made for it are still justified.

One of the most obvious features of the plurality system is that the number of seats which a party receives in the Commons is dependent not only upon how many votes it gains, but also where these votes are located. A 15,000 majority for Labour, for example, in a safe seat in Durham is of less value to the Party than seven majorities of 2,000 each scattered amongst the marginals. In the one case 15,000 votes yield one seat; in the second case, 14,000 votes yield seven.

It might seem at first sight as if there is no consistent relationship at all between the number of votes won and seats gained under the plurality system, and that the result, therefore, can be nothing but a gamble. Consider, for example, the results in the general elections of 1966 and 1970 in the Wrekin constituency.

	1966		1970	
Conservative	22,846	49.1%	26,282	50.5%
Labour	23,692	50.9%	25,764	49.5%

If results like this were multiplied across the country, Labour in 1966 and the Conservatives in 1970 would seem to be able to win every seat in the country on less than 51 per cent of the popular vote.

Studies of the operation of the plurality system in many different countries, however, have shown that it is very rare for a party to win an election with fewer votes than its main competitor. For, whatever the bias in a few seats – anomalous results occur far more frequently in local and provincial than in national elections – it is likely to cancel out over 635 constituencies. Socio-economic factors, which are the crucial determinants of voting behaviour in most democracies, ensure that the electorate will not be distributed at random across the country, but will be clustered in groups.

Nevertheless, anomalies can occur. If the votes of one party are excessively concentrated as compared with its main rival, it can win a majority of the votes but not a majority of the seats. In South Africa, for example, the general elections of 1948 and 1953 resulted in Nationalist victories although the Nationalists secured fewer votes than the United Party. These anomalous results were not due to candidates winning on a minority vote, since nearly all the seats were fought by only two candidates. Disparities in constituency size helped the Nationalists, but more decisive was the geographical concentration of votes for the United Party which resulted in it piling up safe majorities in urban areas. These election victories in 1948 and 1953 allowed the Nationalists, supported by a minority of the voters, to introduce the system of *apartheid*.[4]

In Britain, at two general elections in the postwar period the party with the most votes has failed to secure the largest number of seats in the Commons – in 1951 and February 1974. In the former, however, the Conservatives were unopposed in four Northern Irish seats which if contested would have given them large majorities and thus narrowed the difference. In February 1974, tactical voting by Labour supporters in Conservative-held constituencies was the primary factor responsible for the Labour vote being lower than the Conservative. Moreover, in both cases, the party ill-used by the electoral system was the outgoing government, and a fully proportional result might merely have kept an unpopular government in power for a few more months until a further general election confirmed the swing against it.

Gross anomalies are rare, and there is in general a predictable relationship between votes and seats in plurality systems. For Britain, the relationship was formalised by Kendall and Stuart in 1950 as the cube law, but it had been first stated by J. Parker Smith to the Royal Commission on Systems of Election in 1909, and rediscovered by David Butler in 1949.

According to the cube law, if two parties in a general election held under the plurality system receive votes in the proportion A:B, then the seats will be distributed in the ratio $A^3:B^3$. But the cube law is usually stated with qualifications. For Parker Smith, it applied only when the two parties are nearly equally divided. If there is any great disparity, the exaggeration of the majority increases at a much more rapid rate. Implicit in this statement is the further precondition that there are only two parties competing for votes, and Parker Smith excluded Ireland from the operation of the law. For Kendall and Stuart, the law rested upon the empirical fact that the distribution of population is nearly normal; while for Butler it depended upon a two-party system, constituency boundaries which were fairly drawn and broad political homogeneity so that there would be 'universal and equal swings from one party to another in all constituencies'.[5]

Parker Smith preferred to call the cube law a 'formula' rather than a law, since he could offer no causal theory to explain why the relationship is as it is. Moreover, it is not invariant in time and place – as indeed the different preconditions laid down imply. Tufte has shown that the relationship which he calls the *swing ratio* is higher in Britain than in the United States or New Zealand and, having studied 132 elections in six two-party systems,* he came to the conclusion that only in Britain did the relationship expressed by the cube law actually hold.[6] This analysis, however, was published in 1973, and since then, as will be seen, the cube law has ceased to hold in Britain also.

Nevertheless, the so-called cube law does bring out a central feature of the plurality system, namely that it produces exaggerated majorities, translating a small plurality of the popular vote into a safe, working majority for the winning party. It secures disproportional representation, which is held by the defenders of the system to be an advantage since it increases the likelihood of a single-party government with a majority in the Commons, an alleged precondition of stability in government.

The manufacture of majorities allows a government to be elected on a plurality rather than a majority of the vote, and no government since the war has won 50 per cent of the popular vote – but this does not matter provided the government seeks to broaden the basis of its support; and the system itself provides an incentive for parties to do this since they must bid for moderate support if they wish to form a government. The voter in the centre of the political spectrum becomes pivotal under the plurality system, which therefore makes for strong and effective government.

The plurality system discourages extremism in another way by discriminating against small parties – parties which win less than 30 per cent of the vote in a general election. Votes cast for the Liberals, for example, may be wasted, but as they are a centre party their policies will be adopted by one of the other two parties in their search for a majority. Votes for the National Front and, in the 1930s, for the British Union of Fascists, are also

*Britain, New Zealand, the United States, Michigan, New Jersey and New York.

wasted, and extremists are therefore isolated by the electoral system. It is argued, therefore, that the plurality system strengthens national unity by discouraging splinter groups and party splits. It compels voters to decide between two parties; so that a party which seeks to win control of government must appeal to all sections of the community. It will therefore have to seek unifying themes in its policies, and not rely upon purely sectional or regional appeals. Discrimination against minor parties therefore has a positive function, allowing a government to be formed which represents the nation as a whole.

Of course, the system has never worked as smoothly as this in Britain, which has rarely enjoyed a pure two-party system. At the beginning of the century, the Liberal Unionists were still separate from the Conservatives, and the Labour Party was gradually making its presence felt in Parliament. After the First World War the Liberals retained a parliamentary presence, and secured 10 per cent of the vote until the election of 1935. In Ireland first the Nationalists and then Sinn Fein were able, with the assistance of the plurality system, to wipe out any opponents and secure a one-party dominance in the whole of Ireland outside north-east Ulster. In tacit recognition of the preconditions for the success of the plurality system, politicians were far more willing to recommend proportional representation for Ireland than for Great Britain.

Nevertheless, the existence of third parties has not, in general, made elections a gamble. If it had regularly done so, it would have become unacceptable. The plurality system has survived in Britain because the preconditions – two main parties, absence of sectional parties (except in Ireland) and electoral homogeneity – have on the whole been satisfied. But in addition, it has seemed peculiarly appropriate to the British structure of government, one in which the government of the day can control Parliament. Proportional representation would, so it is argued, make such control impossible since the Commons would become a coalition of groups each of which would have to be conciliated on every issue, and since such coalitions would have to be constructed in secret, this would weaken the influence of the electorate. The plurality system is therefore held to be peculiarly suited to the age of popular control of government since it allows the electorate rather than Parliament to choose the government. The Commons is, in fact, less a legislature than an electoral college; and the central aim of a general election is not to choose a representative Parliament but to choose a government; a general election is a plebiscite between two opposing governmental teams. Thus the institutional structure of British democracy and the country's political homogeneity seemed to provide the essential preconditions for the effective working of the plurality system which used to be regarded as a model for democratic governments everywhere.

CHANGES IN THE WORKING OF THE PLURALITY SYSTEM

The defence of the plurality system rests upon two contingent assumptions: that the electoral system effectively translates a plurality of the vote into a majority of seats, and that two single-party majority governments alternating in office can provide stable and effective government. If these assumptions no longer hold, the plurality system would have to be reappraised.

In fact, social and political changes have combined to invalidate both of these assumptions. The electoral system no longer works so predictably as it did, and cannot be relied upon to produce a one-party government with a safe working majority in the Commons; while changes in political attitudes and the movement of the two main parties away from the centre of politics mean that the regular alternation of one-party governments does not necessarily provide stable or effective government, but might instead produce instability of a most damaging kind.

We have seen that the predictability of the relationship between seats and votes rests in part upon the postulate of uniform swing. Yet in recent years there has been a differential variation in swing between urban and rural seats, a variation which has been cumulative since 1970, as the table demonstrates.

Type of constituency	Mean percentage swing to Conservatives, 1970–9
Largely rural	8.45
Somewhat rural	6.27
Conurbations	0.86
Cities with over 200,000 population (in 1974)	−2.19

Source: John Curtice and Michael Steed, 'Electoral choice and the production of governments: the changing pattern of the UK electoral system, 1955–79' (unpublished paper, delivered to PSA Conference, 1981).
Note: 'Somewhat rural' is defined as between 6 and 15 per cent employed in agriculture; 'largely rural' is with over 15 per cent employed in agriculture.

This differential variation in swing has been reinforced by the pattern of the rise in 1974 of the Liberals and SNP, who both took votes from the weaker of the two main parties in each constituency (usually Labour) where the performance of Liberals or SNP improved. In 1979, Labour failed to win back this support, so that in many constituencies in the South of England it enjoys less support than in 1959 or 1970.

Curtice and Steed, who were the first to draw attention to these changes, have summarised their combined effects as being 'that between 1970 and

1979, Conservative-held seats have swing 5.0% to Conservative, while Labour seats have swung 0.1% to Labour'. This has undermined an 'essential assumption behind the "cube law"', namely 'that such non-uniform behaviour as exists would be randomly distributed'.

There have been three important political effects of these psephological changes. The first is a reduction in the number of marginal constituencies. This can be seen from the accompanying table.

No. of marginal seats, 1955–1979

Year	No. of marginal seats	No. of seats fought in Great Britain by both Conservative and Labour and won by either of them
1955	166	610
1959	157	610
1964	166	609
1966	155	605
1970	149	608
1974 February	119	598
1974 October	98	596
1979	108	607

Source: John Curtice and Michael Steed, *ibid.*
Note: Marginal seats are defined as those where the Conservative share of the two-party vote less the difference between 50 per cent and their share of the total (UK) two-party vote at that election was between 45 and 55 per cent.

Because there are less marginal seats, fewer seats will change hands on any given percentage swing. The result is that, whereas in 1964 and 1966, approximately 18 seats changed hands for every 1 per cent swing, in 1979 the equivalent figure was 12 seats. Even if support for minor parties remains at its 1979 level, to win a majority Labour would need a greater swing against the Conservative Government than in, say, 1955. Indeed, any swing against the Government of between 1.4 per cent and 4.0 per cent would produce a hung parliament, and since the war only two elections (1970 and 1979) have shown a swing above 4 per cent, and only three (1951, 1959 and February 1974) swings below 1.4 per cent. The swing needed to produce an overall majority would, of course, have to be greater if the Liberals or Nationalists did better than in 1979.[7]

A second consequence follows. For the plurality system discriminates unequally against third parties. It discriminates more against a third party like the Liberals whose support is evenly spread across the country, than against a party such as the SNP or Plaid Cymru, whose support is relatively concentrated. In February 1974, the Liberals secured only 14 seats on 19.3 per cent of the vote, while the Ulster Unionists, with 1.3 per cent of the total UK vote, gained 11 seats; and in October 1974, the Liberals, with

18.3 per cent of the vote, gained 13 seats, while the SNP, with only 2.9 per cent, secured 11 seats. Thus in a hung parliament the SNP and Ulster Unionist parties will wield as much bargaining power as the Liberals, although they command less support. In the 1974–9 Parliament, the SNP committed the Labour Government to a directly elected Scottish Assembly, and two parliamentary sessions were needed to steer the legislation through the Commons: the Ulster Unionists were able to press the Government to increase the number of parliamentary constituencies in Northern Ireland from 12 to 17. These were far more substantial gains than the Liberals achieved under the Lib–Lab Pact. Since the SNP is committed to the break-up of the United Kingdom, and the Ulster Unionists reject power-sharing in Ulster, which all three Westminster parties support, it is clear that a hung parliament produced by the plurality system could constitute a danger to the unity of the country.

There has been a third political consequence of the cumulative variation in swing between Conservative-held and Labour-held seats since 1979. Each of the two major parties is better represented in the areas of the country where it is comparatively popular, and worse in those where it is not. Comparison of the regional distribution of party strengths in 1955, when Sir Anthony Eden gained an overall majority of 60, and in 1979, when Mrs Thatcher won an overall majority of 44, is shown in the accompanying table.

	North 1955			South 1955			Great Britain 1955		
	Con.	Lab.	Other	Con.	Lab.	Other	Con.	Lab.	Other
Large city	29	34	0	29	54	0	58	88	0
Remainder	82	92	3	194	97	4	276	189	7
	111	126	3	223	151	4	334	277	7
	North 1979			**South 1979**			**Great Britain 1979**		
	Con.	Lab.	Other	Con.	Lab.	Other	Con.	Lab.	Other
Large city	12	49	1	20	52	0	32	101	1
Remainder	66	102	8	241	66	6	307	168	14
	78	151	9	261	118	6	339	269	15

Source: *Economist*, 12 May 1979.
Note: North: Scotland and three northernmost English standard regions
South: Wales and five southernmost English standard regions

In 1955, 111 Conservative MPs came from north of the Trent, and 223 from south of it; in 1979, 78 and 261 respectively. By contrast, Labour in 1955 held 151 seats in the south and 126 in the north but by 1979, only 118 seats in the south while it had 151 in the north. The parties have been pushed back into their safe seats in their safe regions, Labour in the larger cities, the North and Scotland, the Conservatives in rural areas and the South.

There has been a significant change in the regional distribution of party support, but it is smaller than the number of seats won suggests; for the electoral system exaggerates regional disparities by giving a large bonus to the party with most votes in a region. In Figure 1, for example, it will be seen that Labour managed to secure only four seats in 1979 in the South-east region (excluding the GLC area) although winning over 25 per cent of the vote. In the North-west (Lancashire and Cheshire as before the 1974 local government reorganisation, Cumberland and Westmorland) an anomalous result was produced. The Conservatives succeeded in winning more votes than Labour, but because these votes were piled up in safe constituencies, Labour won many more seats.

The electoral system thus discriminates not only against third parties but also against second parties in particular regions. It overstates the true regional discrepancy in popular support. For, although there is a real difference between North and South, the two main parties can still call upon the support of voters in every region. What they cannot do is win seats in every region. This has fundamental consequences for the attitudes of the electorate, the strategies of the parties and the policies of governments.

Because Conservative voters in the large cities of the north and Labour voters in the rural areas of the South of England are under-represented in the Commons, governments will fail to take full account of their aspirations. If the country were socially and geographically homogeneous a Labour voter in Bournemouth might be just as well represented by a Labour MP in Manchester as by one in Bournemouth; and similarly, a Conservative voter in Manchester by a Conservative MP in Bournemouth.

But the regional variations in swing in recent elections indicate that Britain is no longer as socially and geographically homogeneous as it was in the 1950s. Thus the need for proper local representation is greater while the means of securing it is less; and the inability of local minorities in different parts of the country to gain full representation could easily lead to alienation from politics.

The parties will themselves adjust to this new condition. Their campaign strategies and policy proposals will be geared to the areas in which they can win votes, not to areas where they have no chance of winning. Thus Labour policy will be excessively influenced by the interests of the large cities in the North, the home of the declining industries. They will be comparatively insensitive to the needs of commuter suburbs, agricultural areas or areas of new industry. The Conservatives, on the other hand, are liable to be insensitive to the economic and human problems resulting from the decay of traditional industries, and the run-down of the inner

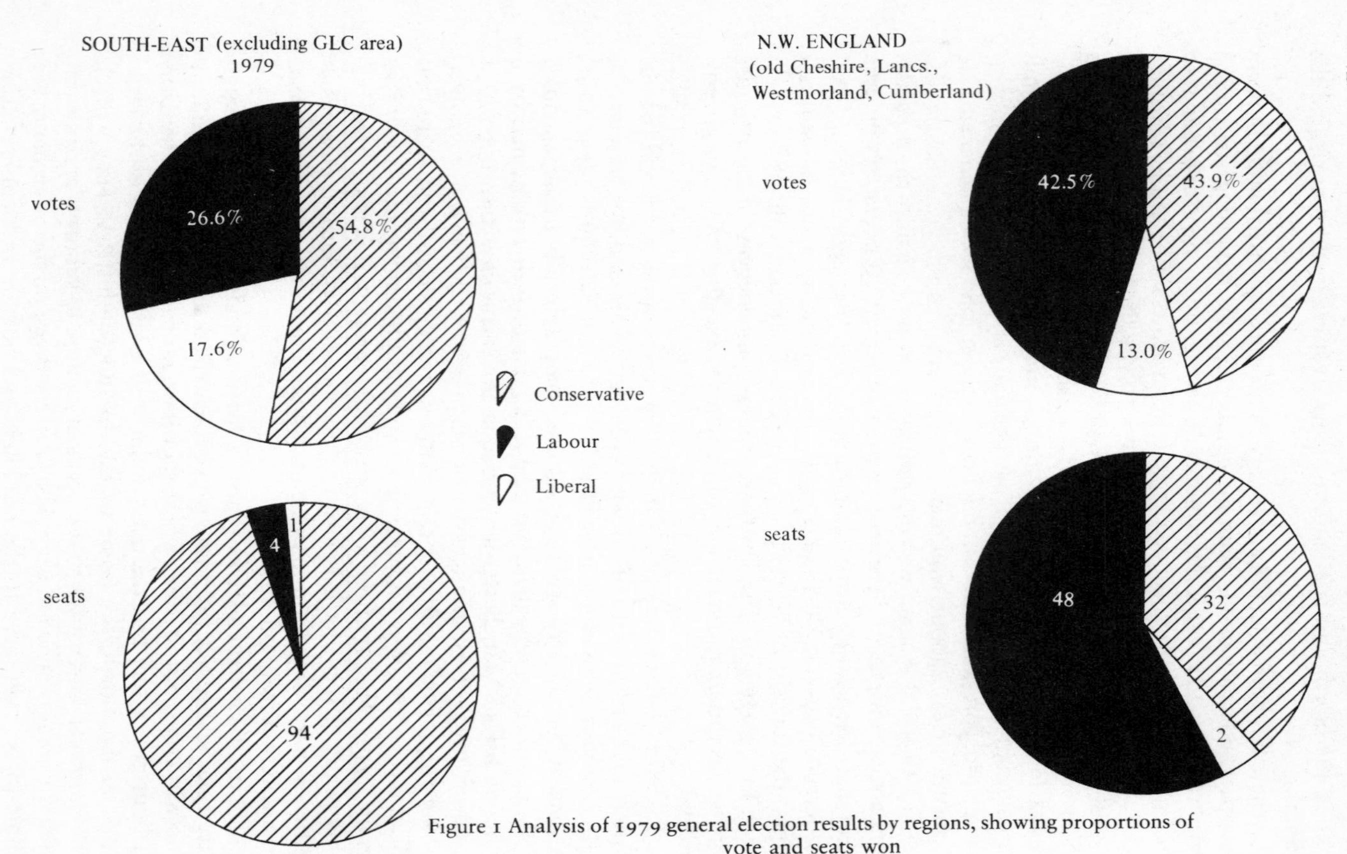

Figure 1 Analysis of 1979 general election results by regions, showing proportions of vote and seats won

cities. The 1979 Conservative Government is often accused of a lack of awareness of industrial problems and of the human costs of unemployment. This is hardly surprising since it holds only eight out of the 51 seats in Bradford, Glasgow, Hull, Leeds, Liverpool, Manchester, Newcastle and Sheffield.

Such a regional distribution of party support tempts each party when in office to 'reward' its supporters through a favourable distribution of inter-regional benefits. Thus the Conservative Governments of 1970 and 1979 altered the needs element of the rate support grant (the block grant paid by the government to local authorities to assist in the financing of local authority expenditure), so as to benefit the rural areas. The 1974 Labour Government reversed this decision, channelling more back to the metropolitan councils. The effect[8] was that rates in Oxfordshire and Cumbria would rise 25 per cent, in West Sussex by 24 per cent, but in Manchester by only 8 per cent and in Liverpool 4 per cent. When ratepayers believe that governments are being over-sensitive to the feelings of their own supporters, the motives of government become suspect and its legitimacy weakened.

Since the regional distribution of party support largely coincides with the social class distribution of the population, the electoral system encourages the parties to define political issues in class terms, which are thus given more salience than the feelings of the electorate warrant, while issues which cannot easily be fitted into the class alignment of politics will be underplayed or even ignored.

This tendency is strengthened by the impact of the electoral system on parties whose appeal is not a socio-economic one directed at particular social groups. The Liberal Party is seen by its supporters

> as reflecting a dimension of individualism versus collectivism which the class-based conflict of the two main parties obscures. . . . The Liberal Party does not represent a class, or section, nor a developed ideology; it is quintessentially a vehicle of certain ideas, and a certain style of politics.[9]

There is some sociological justification for this view in that support for the Liberal Party is more evenly divided amongst the social classes than support for the Conservatives and Labour parties which draw disproportionately from particular classes, professional, managerial and non-manual workers in the case of the Conservative Party, and manual and unskilled workers and the poor in the case of the Labour Party.

Its even distribution of support makes it far more difficult for the Liberal Party to win as many seats as its rivals on a given percentage of the vote. For the electoral system is biassed in two different ways against the Liberal Party; as a small party and also as one whose support is evenly distributed rather than geographically clustered. Steed and Faull have attempted to estimate the extent of this second bias in the general election of 1979.[10] They have done so by taking the voting figures in the election and 'assuming a switch of the total vote evenly from each of the other two parties to the Liberals such as to give the Liberals the average of these parties' votes'.[11] They have then applied this switch of votes to the result in each individual constituency (assuming 1979 constituency boundaries). The result is quite startling.

May 1979 general election	Votes (%)	Seats (%)
Conservatives	43.87	339 (53.39)
Labour	36.94	269 (42.36)
Liberals	13.82	11 (1.73)

Steed and Faull simulation	Votes (%)	Seats (%)
Conservatives	35.01	299 (47.09)
Labour	28.08	265 (41.73)
Liberals	31.54	47 (7.41)

The Liberals, securing precisely the average of the votes of the two major parties, gain less than one-twelfth of the seats, while the Conservative and Labour hegemony is almost unchallenged, since they retain almost 90 per cent of the seats.

Steed and Faull then go on to explore various projections of the Liberal vote, confining themselves to England and assuming a swing which makes support for the Conservative and Labour Parties equal. When all three parties are equal with 33 per cent of the vote, the Liberals would still gain only 56 seats as compared to 207 for the Conservatives and 253 for Labour (assuming that there is no tactical voting). If the Liberals secured 35 per cent of the vote, as compared with 32 per cent each for the Labour and Conservative parties, they would still have only 85 seats as compared to 179 for the Conservatives and 252 for Labour; while if the Liberals secured 37.5 per cent of the vote compared to 30.75 per cent each for Labour and the Conservatives, the Liberals with 149 seats would gain more than the Conservatives who would fall back to 123, but less than Labour who would have 244. Only when the Liberals had secured 40 per cent of the popular vote would they become the largest party in terms of seats. It is little wonder that Steed and Faull conclude that 'The unfair bias against Liberals at any level of support below about 39% . . . is enormous. It is built into the electoral system and the non-class character of Liberal support. No whistling in the dark by optimistic Liberals will make it disappear; only electoral reform can do that.'[12]

The same bias will of course operate against the new Social Democratic Party to the extent that its electoral support is evenly distributed across the country. The prospect of such a new party in February 1981 aroused considerable interest amongst the electorate, and various opinion polls published at the time seemed to show that it could win a significant share of Conservative as well as Labour votes. In the *Economist*, a calculation was made of the likely share of the new party's vote if it secured an alliance with the Liberals. Three assumptions were made; that the alliance gained the whole of the 1979 Liberal vote, that it gained in each constituency 30 per cent of the 1979 Labour vote, and that there was a straight 10 per cent swing from the Conservatives to the new alliance. The result in terms of voting shares is shown in the accompanying table.

	% share of vote
Liberal–Social Democratic Alliance	34.9
Conservative	33.9
Labour	25.9

But the number of seats won would be

	Seats
Liberal–Social Democratic Alliance	142
Conservative	295
Labour	183

If, as was more likely, the new alliance secured less of the vote, its allocation of seats would be very considerably reduced. If, for example, its vote fell to 25.9 per cent, it would secure only 20 seats.[13] It is clear, therefore, that the new alliance would be unlikely to find itself in the position of being able to form a government without a reform of the electoral system.

The plurality system exerts a profound influence upon the way in which the political system is perceived by both the electors and the parties. It conditions their approach to political issues and to political reality. It plays a major role in entrenching class conflict at the centre of the British political system.

The electoral system is now much less likely to fulfil its function of bringing about a one-party government with a working majority. It is more likely to produce hung parliaments, in which territorially concentrated parties such as the SNP and Ulster Unionists will wield disproportionate power. Moreover, recent changes in the distribution of party support have made parties more likely to resort to a sectional rather than a national appeal, since the electoral system gives an advantage to a party with class-based support against one whose support is evenly distributed amongst social classes. The electoral system thus makes the country – as reflected in Parliament – look more divided than it actually is; it overemphasises the divisive factors in British society, and under-plays the strong feelings of national unity which still exist. It thus militates against the ideal of 'One Nation' to which politicians of all parties pay lip-service.

THE ELECTORAL SYSTEM AND THE PARTIES

The defence of the plurality system rests on another assumption, that it encourages the alternation of two parties in office so providing for stable and effective government.

But in the last fifty years of British politics, the alternation of two parties in office has not been the invariable pattern. Indeed, between 1929 and 1964 there was only one complete change of personnel in government, in 1951 when Winston Churchill replaced Clement Attlee. Since 1964, on the other hand, there have been no less than four complete changes of government, and each has been progressively more destabilising.

During the interwar period, government appeared stable because one party – the Conservatives – were in office most of the time, facing as they did a divided Left which was prevented, in part by the electoral system, in part by ideological preconceptions, from co-operating to form a lasting alternative government. The post Second World War consensus was a product not of the party system, but, as Paul Addison has shown,[14] of the war itself. Many of the policies pursued by the postwar Labour Government – the introduction of the National Health Service, the National Insurance Acts, the nationalisation of public utilities – were the product of wartime investigation and broad political agreement, although this agreement was masked by the highly rhetorical way in which political differences were expressed. But because the Labour Government's proposals were the product of broad agreement, they have, on the whole, stood the test of time and (with the exception of the nationalisation of iron and steel, and road haulage) they were not reversed by the Churchill Government which succeeded it in 1951. Having participated in a wartime coalition with Attlee, Morrison, and Bevin, Churchill could not but regard them as politicians whose aspirations had a good deal in common with his own. Indeed, upon regaining office in 1951, he characteristically expressed the hope that 'Now perhaps there may be a lull in our party strife which will enable us to understand more what is good in our opponents, and not to be so very clever at all their shortcomings.'[15] For this reason, the change of government did not impair political stability.

The alternation of parties in office since 1964 need not have been destabilising and could easily have been accommodated by the political system but for three recent changes in the character of party politics: the decline in electoral support for the two major parties, the growing centrifugal tendencies within the parties and the ossification of the party system.

Support for the two major parties fall from a high point of 96.8 per cent in 1951, to 75.0 per cent in October 1974. In 1979, when the Conservative and Labour parties between them won 80.8 per cent of the total national vote, this was still the lowest figure at any postwar general election except for those of 1974. One consequence, as we have seen, is the greater likelihood of a hung parliament in which no party has an overall majority. But even when a party does win an overall majority, it is likely to do so on a lower percentage of the popular vote than in the past. Labour's percentage of the vote in October 1974 was the lowest won by any government with an overall majority this century, while that of the Conservatives in 1979 was the smallest of any government with an overall majority since 1922, with the exception of October 1974, and below Labour's percentage in 1959, its heaviest postwar defeat.

If a party wins power with the support of less than 50 per cent of the electorate, it ought, lacking the support of a majority in the country, to proceed cautiously in implementing the more controversial items in its manifesto. Yet, as their support narrows, governments have become more insistent on implementing their programmes, drawn up by party activists whose enthusiasms are hardly shared by the ordinary voter. Mrs Thatcher enjoyed far less popular support in 1979 than Winston Churchill in 1951. Yet whereas Churchill strove for conciliation with his political opponents, and especially with the trades unions, Mrs Thatcher interpreted her election victory as an endorsement of the complete Conservative programme and a mandate for implementing it. 'Those who voted Conservative', she declared at the 1979 Conservative Conference, 'know the principles we stand for. We have every right to carry them out and we shall.'[16] Voters are deemed to agree with every item on the party manifesto, and the plurality system encourages party leaders to believe that their policies enjoy wide support in the country even when, as in 1979, the party wins office with the support of one-third of the electorate.

Contrary to the assumptions once made by defenders of the plurality system, parties can win general elections even if not led from the political centre. When in 1959 Hugh Gaitskell urged Labour to reform itself, he argued that Labour could not hope to gain power unless it deleted Clause 4 of its Constitution which laid it open to constant misrepresentation. Labour has since succeeded only once, in 1966, in winning a higher percentage of the vote than in 1959. But it still won the elections of 1964 and February 1974. By contrast, the SPD in West Germany knew that it could not, under a proportional representation system, hold power on a minority vote, but would either have to gain (nearly) 50 per cent of the vote or make itself acceptable as a coalition partner. For this reason it had a greater incentive than the Labour Party to modernise its constitution, which it did at Bad Godesberg in 1959, since when its share of the popular vote has risen at each election, except that of 1976.

The power of the centre in British politics, contrary to the assumption made by the defenders of the plurality system, is negative rather than

positive. The elector, as in 1974 and 1979, can vote against policies he does not like, but he cannot, because of the limited effect of his vote under the plurality system, exert any positive influence upon the political colour of the government which he is electing. He can only choose the lesser evil. The result is that governments lack the authority to mobilise consent in support of their policies.

Those who have led the two major parties in a centrifugal direction have sought to substitute fundamental change for the pursuit of arid consensus. Yet, it is remarkable how little fundamental change there has been since 1964, as the favourite measures of each party are repealed by the other upon assuming office. Each party needs at least two full terms in office if its most cherished reforms are to prove permanent, but the last time the electorate allowed that length of time to any party was Harold Macmillan's victory in 1959. The last period of fundamental change in British politics was during the years 1940–51, and the reforms of that period have lasted precisely because, in contrast to more recent measures, they rested upon more than the support of one wing of a political party, and succeeded in capturing ground common to the supporters of both major parties. Since 1964, there has been not fundamental change but an abrupt series of policy jerks inhibiting progress in many areas of public policy, and rendering more difficult the industrial success which politicians of both major parties have looked to as a solvent of the country's difficulties.

Viewing the history of British party politics over the last hundred years, one is struck by the remarkable loss of elasticity in the party system and the rigidity of current party alignments. Until the early twentieth century, fluidity came from periodic realignments as new issues stimulated alternative political cleavages: in 1886, following the Home Rule crisis; in 1904 when a group of Free Trade Unionists led by Churchill crossed the floor; and in 1916–31, following the Liberal split and decline and the rise of Labour. But the realignment following the 1931 political crisis was to be the last for fifty years since the trauma it induced in the Labour Party made the very mention of a peacetime coalition or rearrangement of forces anathema. Realignment, however, had brought new blood and new ideas into the parties, and served to moderate the more doctrinaire aspects of their outlook. Harold Macmillan, indeed, was fond of declaring that

> the last purely Conservative Government was formed by Mr Disraeli in 1874 . . . it is the fact that we have attracted moderate people of Liberal tradition and thought into our ranks which makes it possible to maintain a Conservative Government today. A successful party of the Right must continue to recruit its strength from the centre, and even from the Left Centre. Once it begins to shrink into itself like a snail it will be doomed.[17]

The end of realignment would not matter if there were a real unity of feeling and purpose in the political parties. But since 1945 the party system has become frozen, and it hardly corresponds with the main divisions of opinion amongst the electorate as a whole. The two major parties held together until 1981 even though the schism between the two wings of the Labour Party and the conflict between monetarists and moderates in the Conservative Party became far wider than the comparatively small gap separating the beliefs of Social Democrats and supporters of the Tory Reform Group. The warring elements within each party have come to resemble nothing so much as partners to a loveless marriage. Indeed, the manufacture of disagreement with the other side in the Commons becomes the only way of diverting attention from the more fundamental divisions in one's own ranks.

So divided, indeed, are the parties in their views on basic policy issues that office has become almost a precondition of party unity. Only a few weeks after its defeat in the 1979 general election, the Labour Party was shown to be so bitterly in disagreement on almost every issue of public policy that commentators began to ask whether the Party could ever hold office again as a united party. A similar conflict would have arisen, as it did after the 1974 elections, within the Conservative Party if, as had at one time seemed likely, it had failed to win the 1979 election. The desire to win elections, not agreement on policy, is the basis of party unity in Britain today. The result is that the division between the parties no longer corresponds with the main differences of opinion amongst the electorate. Many of the crucial lines of division lie within the parties, not between them. Perhaps for this very reason, the parties concentrate their fire with exaggerated vehemence at the other side, and the style of politics which results is profoundly inimical to the achievement of national objectives.

Chapter 2

Political consequences

INDUSTRY AND THE ELECTORAL SYSTEM

It is not difficult to find examples of ways in which the alternation of parties in office under the plurality system has harmed Britain's chances of industrial progress. Industrialists plan investment projects over a considerable period of time, usually longer than the life-span of any one government. Current industrial conditions make co-operation between industry and government particularly important, as the greater capital intensity of industrial projects, and the new aspirations of those who work in industry, have contrived to make it more difficult for industry to respond to unexpected policy changes. What industry seeks from government is not so much specific policies, such as lower direct taxation and investment incentives, as a climate of stability within which investment plans can be made with confidence. Many industrialists believe, however, that whereas 'changes in markets and technology come relatively slowly and can usually be anticipated by efficient forecasting, and plans made accordingly',[1] political changes are not so easy to anticipate.

Because the two main parties differ so radically in their approach to the ownership of industry, it has proved impossible to reach agreement on a common framework for government assistance. In 1970, the Heath Government abolished the Industrial Reorganisation Corporation as inconsistent with its policies of free competition, only to resurrect it in 1972 as an agency under the Department of Trade and Industry. In 1974, the new Labour Government established in its place the National Enterprise Board, originally conceived as a body through which large-scale nationalisation could take place. In 1979, the Conservative Government weakened the authority of the NEB, and yet found itself forced to grant government assistance to industry in much the same fashion as its predecessor.

Industrialists find themselves dependent upon a stable framework of company taxation, investment incentives, pay policy and industrial relations law, yet the political system seems to prevent these aspirations from being realised. Every administration since Harold Macmillan's in 1962 has adopted an incomes policy in government, having in opposition excoriated its predecessor for attempting the same. This has meant that incomes policies have lasted for, at most, two or three years, to be followed by a period of free collective bargaining before a new incomes policy is again reimposed. Industrial relations law has been subject to similar uncertainty since the Wilson Government produced its 'In Place of Strife' proposals in 1969.

Other areas of policy where needless changes have caused instability have been investment incentives and company taxation. In 1979, the Hansard Society published the report of an independent committee chaired by Sir Richard Marsh, *Politics and Industry – The Great Mismatch*. This committee made a comparison of political and industrial lead-times, that is, the time-scales involved in making political and industrial decisions. It found that broadly projects in manufacturing industry took between two-and-a-half years and four years to complete, while larger projects such as the construction of power stations, could take between five and fifteen years from initial planning to normal working. The political time-scale, on the other hand, is far shorter than this. In the case of investment incentives, for example, there have not only been five major policy changes since 1945, but even when the same policy operated, rates of investment grant or allowance changed with bewildering frequency. During the sixteen years when initial allowances were paid (1945–51, 1953–4, 1956–62 and 1970–2), the rate changed no less than eight times, and varied by an average of 20 per cent for expenditure on plant and machinery. Similarly in the case of regional policy, there have been, since 1945, twelve changes in the form, content or coverage of the various incentives. Industry has suffered just as much from changes in the structure of taxation. Between 1958 and 1974, for example, corporate taxation changed on average once every two years; and between 1958 and 1977, the rate of indirect taxation levied on domestic appliances changed twelve times, creating an atmosphere within industry of uncertainty and instability. With such frequent changes, incentives become less important in influencing industrial decisions, and the benefits from them come to be discounted. Perhaps the worst example of the effects of adversary politics upon industry has been in nationalisation in aerospace, shipbuilding and steel. 'Steel', in the words of Lord Caldecote,

> has been a political shuttlecock for a quarter of a century. Threatened with nationalisation, nationalised, denationalised, renationalised, now reduced through lack of coherent long-term investment policy to a shambles. In no other country has so much waste and human misery been caused by fundamental changes of government policy resulting from our two-party adversary electoral system.[2]

These continual policy changes would be understandable if the British parties or the electorate were in reality divided by deep ideological differences. But the Hansard Society's Committee did not believe this to be the case.

> It is tempting, but the committee firmly believed it would be incorrect, to ascribe a

leading role to ideological considerations as causes of mutual incomprehension and distrust. There is, on the contrary, far more in the way of practical agreement between parties on economic objectives, and even on ways of achieving those objectives, than is commonly recognised, or even admitted by politicians whose natural instinct is to heighten differences and emphasise distinctions for reasons connected with the need to present a clear-cut image to their public. . . . We believe that all the major British parties at the present time hold sufficient ground in common to make it possible to avoid ideological clashes between Government and industry.[3]

It was not deep-seated ideological disagreement which caused industrial instability, but rather the practice of adversary politics, one which 'The committee fully recognised . . . is deeply embedded in British constitutional convention; we concluded, however, that this practice is now producing increasingly pernicious effects so far as industry is concerned.' For this reason, the committee concluded that, although electoral reform lay outside its term of reference, the problems raised by the mismatch between government and industry 'could not be adequately treated without reference to issues of national economic and constitutional organisation'. The committee urged the need for a modicum of consensus on industrial policy, and if electoral reform could help to produce this 'by tending to produce govenments of the centre rather than either political extreme', then 'we would support the view that it deserves serious consideration'. It is difficult to see how else a programme designed to improve the industrial environment can be effective, since industrialists are likely to be sceptical as to the permanence of policies which can be easily reversed. Indeed the Conservative Government elected in 1979 faced the problem that, however favourably disposed industrialists might have been towards it, many were bound to feel that the accession to power at the next election of a Labour government, elected on a minority of the popular vote, would inflict major damage upon their investment plans: therefore they would not respond to economic incentives. It is for this reason that the British electoral system is profoundly inimical to the country's chances of industrial recovery.

THE ELECTORAL SYSTEM AND LOCAL GOVERNMENT

Another area of British life where the plurality system exaggerates and gives disproportionate power to the forces of conflict and strife is local government. Since local government plays an increasingly important role in the development of public services, and in policy areas such as housing, education and the social services, governments, if they wish to fulfil their policy objectives, must attempt to secure the confidence of local authorities who will have to implement them. If each side insists upon its statutory rights or its own interpretation of social priorities, reversals in policy on issues such as the distribution of rate support grant or the structure of secondary education will prevent the smooth development of public services. Co-operation between central and local government, therefore, is crucial if progress is to be achieved.

Moreover, local authorities today play a vital role in the management of the economy. Governments of both major parties have believed that the control of inflation must mean the control of public expenditure, and, since local authorities are now responsible for one-quarter of current public expenditure, this must mean control of local government expenditure. Yet local authorities enjoy the right to raise their own taxation in the form of rates, and central government has no statutory authority to control this method of financing additional public expenditure. Here, too, co-operation rather than collision between central government and local authorities is more likely to secure the satisfaction of conflicting objectives.

Most fundamentally, if perhaps a little more intangibly, local government is for many people an important focus of political participation. Admittedly turnout in local elections is far lower than in national elections, but it is nevertheless easier to gain access to a councillor or Chief Education Officer than to an MP or civil servant in a Whitehall Department. Indeed, many of the pressure groups which have burgeoned in Britain in recent years have been focussed on essentially local government issues such as education and housing, rather than on matters which are the prime responsibility of central government. Thus a well-functioning system of local government is not merely an agency for the provision of services but an essential element of a democratic society.

Unfortunately local government in Britain today falls sadly short of this ideal. Turnout in local elections is low, and local councils suffer from considerable unpopularity, being charged with arrogance, extravagance, excessive bureaucracy and failure to protect essential services. Without necessarily conceding the justice of these accusations, it is worth asking whether the lack of representativeness of so many local authorities has not contributed to their unpopularity.

Different types of local authorities are elected in different ways. The plurality system with single-member wards is used in elections to county councils, metropolitan districts and some non-metropolitan districts, whereas in the rest of the non-metropolitan districts, the London boroughs and parish councils, elections are conducted by a variant of the plurality system known as the block vote. The block vote gives each elector one vote for each vacancy to be filled in a multi-member ward; thus in a ward returning three members, each elector will have three votes (which he is not allowed to cumulate on one candidate). This system was introduced into local government in the Municipal Corporations Act of 1835, long before parties were organised to fight local elections. Where the candidates are all independents, the block vote generally results simply in the election of the most popular candidates, but if elections are fought on party lines, as almost all local government elections are, and electors vote the straight party ticket, as the vast majority do, then the block vote produces distortions even greater than those of the plurality system. The result in the Greater London Council election in 1970 in Waltham Forest is a good example.

	Con.	Lab.	Lib.	Communist	Union Movement
	31,190	28,847	2,472	1,016	436
	30,833	28,645	2,433		
	30,780	28,207	2,117		
	92,803	85,699	7,042		
Seats	3	0	0	0	0

Source: Enid Lakeman, *How Democracies Vote: A Study of Electoral Systems* (4th edn., Faber, 1974), p. 38.

The Conservatives, with 49.63 per cent of the vote, won three seats, while Labour, with 45.83 per cent, gained none.

It is thus not surprising that the block vote can lead to a clean sweep whereby one party gains almost all of the seats on a council without its vote approaching anywhere near 100 per cent. In the 1978 London borough elections, there were eight authorities where there was an almost complete sweep for one party.[4]

London borough elections, 1978

		Conservative		Labour		Liberal		Others	
Borough	No. of members	% Vote	Seats	% Vote	Seats	% Vote	Seats	% Vote	Seats
Barking	48	26.1	3 (6.25%)	57.2	42 (87.5%)	7.2	–	9.5	3 (6.25%)
Hackney	60	28.4	1 (1.7%)	57.9	59 (98.3%)	3.0	–	10.7	–
Islington	52	38.2	2 (3.8%)	49.0	50 (96.2%)	2.8	–	10.0	–
Kingston	50	61.0	44 (88.0%)	24.2	6 (12.0%)	14.2	–	0.6	–
Newham	60	15.5	–	64.1	57 (95.0%)	–	–	20.4	3 (5.0%)
Southwark	64	36.1	8 (12.5%)	58.0	56 (87.5%)	3.7	–	2.2	–
Sutton	56	59.5	47 (83.9%)	23.8	7 (12.5%)	15.9	2 (3.6%)	0.8	–
Tower Hamlets	50	14.8	–	55.6	43 (86.0%)	10.5	7 (14.0%)	19.1	–

It can be seen that in all these authorities, a majority of the vote (and in Islington not even that) sufficed to give one party – the Conservatives in Kingston and Sutton, Labour elsewhere – nearly complete control of the council. Between 35 and 50 per cent of the voters find themselves nearly totally unrepresented, and so entirely unable to influence the operations of their local council except through the grace and favour of the ruling group. In Islington, the Conservatives, although commanding the support of nearly 40 per cent of the electorate, secured only two out of the 52 seats on the council, a number wholly insufficient to provide proper representation on the crucial committees which make spending decisions. In Tower Hamlets, the Conservatives, with nearly 15 per cent of the vote, secured no seats at all, while the Liberals, with 10 per cent, gained seven. The anomalies are even greater when the low turnout at these elections is taken into account. For in Tower Hamlets, only 27 per cent of the electorate bothered to vote, and so Labour's 43 seats out of 50 is based upon the support of only 15.1 per cent of the electorate.

The clean sweep can also occur in authorities where, as in parliamentary elections, the plurality system is used. In Barnsley, for example, in 1980, Labour won 20 out of 22 vacancies on the local council for just over 60 per cent of the vote which, on a turnout of under 50 per cent, was equal to 26 per cent of the electorate. In the county council elections in Oxfordshire in 1977, the Conservatives secured 57 out of the 63 contested seats on just under 60 per cent of the vote, while Labour, with just over 25 per cent of the vote, secured only three seats; and in Gloucestershire, the Conservatives, with 47 per cent of the vote, won 35 out of the 50 contested seats, while Labour, with 17.5 per cent of the vote, had to be content with only two.

But the clean sweep is not the only kind of anomaly that can occur. In contrast to national elections, there are a large number of local authorities where the party which gains control of the council wins fewer votes than its main competitor. In 1978, this occurred in no less than ten of the 36 metropolitan districts, including Birmingham, Coventry, Liverpool and Sunderland. In other authorities, a narrow victory for one party is translated by the electoral system into a large majority on the council. In Lambeth, for example, in the London borough elections in 1978, Labour gained 48.5 per cent of the vote to the Conservatives' 46.8 per cent, but this was sufficient to give them 42 seats to the Conservatives' 22. In many of these cases, of course, a small swing to the opposition would produce an equally disproportional result in the other direction, thus contributing to upheavals in policy which may well not be desired by the local electorate.

It is therefore clear that neither the plurality system in single-member wards nor the block vote can offer the elector any assurance that his opinions will be reflected in the composition of his local council. This might not perhaps be a matter of great concern if it led to good government at the local level, but in fact the political consequences of these anomalies in representation are pernicious.

For the electoral system is one of the factors preventing effective co-operation between central government and local authorities by exaggerating the swing against the government of the day. It produces a conflict between local authorities and central government. When a Conservative government is in power, Labour local authorities are unlikely to implement its expenditure cuts, and so the Conservatives are unable to carry out their policy of retrenchment in public spending; while when Labour is in office, Conservative authorities will resist implementing policies which they dislike in areas such as the provision of comprehensive education.

Moreover, because the anomalies resulting from the electoral system benefit the Conservatives in rural areas and Labour in the cities, they exaggerate instead of mitigating social and geographical divisions. As with the inter-regional distribution of seats in the Commons, Britain is made to appear a more divided country than in fact it is, because the electoral system deprives the Labour minority in rural areas, and Conservative minority in the cities, of an effective political voice.

No democrat, of course, could object to conflict between central government and local authorities if that truly reflected the wishes of the electors. If voters in, say, Lambeth or Hackney, wished their local council to withhold all co-operation from a Conservative government, or Conservatives in Buckinghamshire wished to do the same vis-à-vis a Labour government, then conflict would be an understandable, if perhaps regrettable, result. But there is no reason to believe that the majority of voters wish their local authority to be in a state of perpetual conflict with a government of another political colour. In the summer of 1980, Michael Heseltine, the Secretary of State for the Environment, naming 23 local authorities who had flouted his requests to contain expenditure, proposed to punish them by withdrawing grant. (Later 15 authorities were reprieved.) The local authorities concerned all pleaded in aid local autonomy and accused the minister of wishing to destroy local democracy. Of the 23 authorities in Heseltine's list, 14 were London boroughs, and 10 of them constituted good examples of how the electoral system artificially intensified central/local conflicts. In two – Hounslow and Waltham Forest – the party with the most votes in the last London borough elections in 1978 had fewer seats than its main rival. In five others – Brent, Camden, Greenwich, Lambeth and Lewisham – a narrow victory for Labour was translated by the electoral system into a large Labour majority on the council; while in the other three authorities – Hackney, Islington and Tower Hamlets – as we have seen, the clean sweep was in operation, giving Labour nearly all the seats for 60 per cent or less of the vote, and, taking into account the low turnout, a minority of the electorate. It is because governments know that they will be unable to secure co-operation from local authorities dominated by unrepresentative caucuses that they resort to legal instruments and administrative devices to secure their ends; and in this way the values of local self-government come to be undermined.

Thus the electoral systems used in local authority elections stand condemned not only on theoretical grounds as producing grossly unrepresentative local councils, but as a direct cause of bad government and the growth of centralised control.

The case for electoral reform is even stronger and more pressing at local than at national level. One of the arguments used against altering the system for elections to the Commons is that it would lead to 'weak' government. Whether this is a good argument or not, it cannot possibly be applied to local government, since in local authorities there is no Cabinet system or separate executive, but the council as a whole is constitutionally supposed to take the key decisions, even though, of course, it delegates much of its work to committees. Moreover, there has been only one Parliament in living memory in which the opposition was almost totally obliterated – in 1931 when the Government held 554 out of the 615 seats – and that is generally held to have been the worst Parliament this century. Yet, in many local councils such election results are commonplace, and party control will never change whatever the result at national level. The Salmon Commission on Standards of Conduct in Public Life noticed that in such circumstances the possibility of corruption is always present, for

> The local authorities most vulnerable to corruption have tended to be those in which one political party has unchallenged dominance. Not only are such authorities at particular risk because of absence of an effective opposition which can scrutinise their decisions, but investigations and the making of complaints in such areas may also be inhibited by the feeling that there is no way round the 'party' machine.[5]

At local government level, it would be natural to adopt the single transferable vote method of proportional representation. This would not only provide a more accurate reflection of opinion in terms of the representation of political parties. It would also, because it allows for the recording of preferences, give the voter the opportunity to discriminate between councillors. Under the present electoral systems, the voter lacks this power since good and bad councillors alike become the victim of an adverse swing against their party, usually as a result of its unpopularity at national rather than local level. In giving the elector this power to discriminate, the single transferable vote would also strike a powerful blow at the party caucus which would have an incentive to offer a balanced selection of candidates to the voters. In addition, voters who favoured the election of independent candidates would no longer be virtually disfranchised, and indeed many of them might welcome the chance to reduce the prominence of party politics in local government.

Electoral reform might lead to there being more councils with no one party in overall control, which could be led only by someone able to secure support from other parties to construct a majority. That would compel the major parties to elect local leaders who might appeal less to the party faithful but would be better at conciliating the other groups on the council.

Reform could also encourage co-operation between local authorities and central government by ensuring that the opposition was strongly represented on every council, and that the council itself would be unable to refuse co-operation to the government of the day unless that was the settled wish of the majority of voters as reflected in local elections. Under a system of proportional representation there will, of course, still be councils with a majority opposed to the government, but conflict may be lessened because there will be adequate minority representation, and because, under the single transferable vote, the elector will be able to choose between moderate and extremist candidates. If the mood and temper of the British people favours co-operation between different levels of government, then the reform of the electoral system would be a preferable means of securing control of public expenditure to further restrictions on local autonomy.

Local government, therefore, where there are already many multi-member wards, would be an ideal arena to evaluate the consequences of electoral reform – as was done in the Irish Republic, and elsewhere. Of course, if a limited experiment was tried at local level and failed, that would cast doubt on the value of proportional representation at national level. Those who oppose such an experiment as a dangerous precedent seem therefore to be committed to the view that proportional representation might work so well in local government as to make the case for introducing it at national level irresistible.

POLITICAL RECRUITMENT

The final effect of the plurality system which must be considered is the influence which it exerts upon political recruitment. For it is arguable that the single-member constituency system makes it more difficult for either minorities or women to enter politics. While women are not a minority numerically,

> their characterisation as a minority has a well-documented history in sociological writings. Many of the criteria used to characterise minorities – from cultural

differentiation and social and economic insecurity, to restricted legal and property rights – have until very recently applied to women.[6]

Certainly they are a political minority in national legislatures. But the extent to which women are represented differs in countries with different electoral systems, as the table shows.

Percentage of women elected to national legislatures under different systems

Plurality systems	% women members	List systems	% women members
Britain, October 1974	4.25	Norway, Storting 1977	22.50
Britain, 1979	2.99	Sweden, Riksdag, 1979	27.50
US Senate, 1978	1.00	Denmark, Folketing, 1979	23.40
US House of Representatives, 1978	3.68	Finland, Eduskunta, 1977	23.50
Canada, House of Commons, 1979	6.15	Netherlands, Second Chamber, 1974	13.30
W. Germany constituency members of *Bundestag*, 1976	2.82	Italy, Chamber of Deputies, 1977	8.40
		W. Germany, members of *Bundestag* elected from *Land* list, 1976	11.69

Source: These figures are derived from Elizabeth Vallance, *Women in the House* (Athlone Press, 1979), ch. IX; Walter S. G. Kohn, *Women in National Legislatures* (Praeger, 1980), pp. 20, 51, 93, 127; letter from Gwyneth George to *The Times*, 26 Nov. 1980; Caroline Moorehead, 'Why not 300 women in the Commons?', *The Times*, 24 Nov. 1980. The Irish figure has been calculated from the official publication, *Election Results and Transfer of Votes* for the 1977 general election (Stationery Office, Dublin, 1978).

In the Republic of Ireland, under the single transferable vote, the percentage of women elected to the Dáil in 1977 was 4.9 per cent, a figure comparable with that of Britain, but of course cultural attitudes in the Republic are far less favourable than in Britain to the participation of women in public life.

It might be suggested that the different levels of female participation in politics in Britain and the Scandinavian countries could be explained by differences in cultural attitudes, but this would not explain why the representation of women in Scandinavian legislatures was so high compared with, for example, the comparatively low proportion of doctors in Finland and Norway – 8 per cent and 12 per cent respectively (as compared to 22 per cent in Britain) – and of university professors – 2.3 per cent and 1.7 per cent respectively.

Even allowing for differences in cultural attitudes, therefore, the figures above are a striking illustration of the effects of the electoral system upon representation. Particularly striking is the disparity between the percentage of women in the *Bundestag* elected from constituencies, and elected through nomination on the *Land* list. This disparity has been a striking feature of elections in the Federal Republic since its inception.[7]

Year	No. of women elected from constituencies	No. of women elected from *Land* list
1949	12	15
1953	9	31
1957	9	35
1961	7	33
1965	8	25
1969	5	27
1972	4	24
1976	7	29

It would seem that in the single-member constituency selection committees are less willing to take the risk of adopting a woman as the sole candidate, whether because they are themselves prejudiced, or believe that the electorate is prejudiced against women candidates. In a list system, on the other hand, the parties have an incentive to present a balanced list, for in a multi-member constituency 'the pressure is in the opposite direction – not to offend either sex by excluding it but to include both so as to widen the party's appeal'.[8] Women therefore fare much better on the list in West Germany than in the constituencies. While, under the single transferable vote, if women demanded a chance to vote for a female candidate, parties would be under pressure to present one in each constituency.

The same factors which handicap women in Britain and in other countries using single-member constituencies also make it more difficult for immigrants and other minorities to secure representation. Here too, selection committees may well be loth to adopt coloured candidates in winnable seats, claiming that prejudice exists amongst the electorate. But in a multi-member constituency, where an immigrant population creates a demand for a coloured representative in the Commons, there will be an incentive to adopt one. Lord Pitt, at present the only West Indian member of the House of Lords, found it difficult to secure a winnable parliamentary seat, but was a candidate for the GLC when its elections were held in multi-member wards, and went on to become its Chairman.

The absence of coloured MPs from the House of Commons undoubtedly deprives it of the knowledge and experience of an increasingly important minority, deeply affected by legislation passed by Parliament – which, in discussing immigration rules or relationships between immigrants and the police, is an inadequate forum of the nation without representatives of those most directly concerned with the issues. Parliament, therefore, is prevented from being what Burke thought it ought to be, 'the express image of the feelings of the nation'.

THE DEFECTS OF THE PLURALITY SYSTEM

The claims made for the plurality system, therefore, can no longer be sustained. It is now less likely than it ever was to provide for strong majority government, but even if it did, that would not necessarily ensure good government. To defenders of the plurality system a majority government is 'strong' if it has a majority in the House of Commons. But if this does not correspond to broad popular support in the country, it will lack the authority necessary to implement its policies successfully. In theory, the plurality system should encourage the parties to broaden the basis of their support by seeking consensus, but there is no mechanism to prevent parties moving away from the centre, or misrepresenting the opinions of those who vote for them.

Moreover, the system positively incites sectional appeals and highlights areas of conflict rather than reconciliation. In industry and in local government, it makes problems intractable by manufacturing disagreements beyond the real differences of opinion felt by the electorate. Indeed, by putting unrealistic alternatives before the electorate, it paradoxically obscures the very real choices which need to be made in an advanced industrial society. It therefore provides neither stability nor effective choice. And it handicaps two groups – minorities and women – whose growing desire for self-expression is an important feature of life in contemporary Britain.

The plurality system thus frustrates rather than fulfils the aspirations of the British electorate which, although increasingly alienated from the two main political parties, remains thoroughly wedded to moderate constitutional government and is distrustful of doctrinaires. Class and regional divisions in political attitudes are still important, but by no means as important as the electoral system makes them appear. The electoral system makes it difficult for the parties to co-operate, although numerous surveys have shown that the voter is sceptical of party shibboleths and would like politicians to operate on a broader basis of agreement. The voter seeks a consensus which the electoral system prevents him from achieving. That is the nub of the criticism of the plurality system. It is difficult, therefore, not to conclude that the balance of the argument lies conclusively in favour of reform; for, whatever services the plurality system may have performed for the country in the past, today it forms an obstacle to both national unity and social progress.

Part V

Alternative electoral systems

Now, the distributive justice to be realized in representation is first and foremost to the electors and not to the parties.

OSTROGORSKI

INTRODUCTION

In 1918, J. Fischer Williams claimed that there were over 300 alternative electoral systems in existence.[1] Human ingenuity being what it is, there are probably many more today. Amongst so wide a diversity of systems, it is improbable that one perfect system is to be found, a system suitable for every country no matter what stage of social development it has reached. For electoral systems must be judged by a number of different criteria, and these are unlikely to prove totally compatible with each other.

High priority amongst conflicting criteria would generally be given to such considerations as the extent to which a particular system promoted stable and effective government, fairness of representation, a wide choice of representatives, and contact between the electorate and its chosen representatives. But there will be disagreement on the relative priorities to be attached to each of these aims. Frequently a balance will have to be struck between them. Fair representation is a valuable aspiration, but not perhaps at the expense of encouraging the growth of too many splinter groups which could weaken the effectiveness of government. On the other hand, it would be foolish to pursue the aim of strong government so single-mindedly as to prevent the natural diversity of opinion amongst the electorate from being reflected in the composition of the legislature.

The precise balance to be sought between different objectives cannot be decided in the abstract without paying attention to the requirements imposed by a country's geographical situation and its historical experience. It will be struck differently at different times and in different places. What is appropriate for a developing country which has recently gained independence will not necessarily be suitable for a country with long experience of the working of democratic institutions. What is suitable for a country which is ethnically homogeneous would not necessarily work in a country such as Belgium or Switzerland where linguistic and religious differences are such that a majority vote will not secure legitimacy unless it is a concurrent majority, that is, a majority not just in one community but in all of the major communities. An electoral system suitable for a period such as the nineteenth century when the major issues were constitutional and political may not be equally suitable for a period when the dominant issues are economic and social; for the methods needed to resolve them may require parliamentary institutions to display new and very different virtues.

Since every electoral system that has been seriously analysed has been found to contain anomalies or inconveniences of one kind or another, a search for the perfect system would resemble the search for the philosopher's stone. Instead, we must look for a system whose virtues in the context of a particular time and place – Britain at the end of the twentieth century – outweigh its defects; and so it is wise to conduct this search in a spirit of relativism and scepticism. For in judging between electoral systems, the theological convictions of the true believer are, or should be, entirely out of place.

The precise nature of the influence exerted by the electoral system upon a country's political arrangements has long been disputed by political scientists. They used to believe that the electoral system exerted a crucial influence upon the number of parties. In his classic work, *Political Parties* (1954), Maurice Duverger claimed that a plurality system of election would produce a two-party system while proportional representation would lead to fragmentation and the creation of a multi-party system. In what follows it will be shown that such a simplistic view can no longer be sustained. But, in attacking Duverger, contemporary political scientists have gone too far in seeming to deny the influence of the electoral system upon the character of a country's politics. For the electoral system is bound to play a major role in shaping the political system, by influencing the attitudes of the parties to government, of legislators to their parties and to the electorate, and of the voters to those who represent them. Such effects may be long-term and not easily susceptible to the statistical analysis of the behavioural scientist, but they are none the less important for that.

It is in these terms that the examination of alternative electoral systems should be conducted. It would obviously be impracticable to examine every electoral system, but in practice they reduce to a few main types. Our purpose is to analyse only those systems which have been seriously considered for adoption in Britain, omitting technical details unnecessary for the appraisal of their political effects.

PROPORTIONAL REPRESENTATION

Electoral systems can be divided into two main types – plurality and majority systems, and proportional systems of various kinds. The British system is of course an example of the plurality system in the single-member constituency. There are two majority systems – the alternative vote and the second-ballot – which aim to overcome one of the alleged weaknesses of the plurality system, namely that it allows a candidate to win a seat on a minority vote. The second-ballot system as used in elections to the French

Presidency provides that if no candidate succeeds in gaining an absolute majority on the first ballot, the leading two candidates compete again in a second ballot.* The alternative vote, used in elections to the Australian Lower House, requires the voter to record his preferences for the various candidates. If no candidate gains an absolute majority of the vote, then the candidate with the fewest votes is eliminated and his second preferences taken into consideration. This process continues until one candidate gains an absolute majority.

The various proportional systems are more difficult to explain. For 'proportional representation' is a generic term covering a number of different systems each with very different properties and political consequences, but each seeking to conform to an idea – which is as old as the idea of popular sovereignty itself – that the purpose of an election is to bring about the representation of voters in proportion to their numbers. This notion seems first to have been expressed by Mirabeau who in 1789 argued that a representative body should be to the people as a map to the country it represents.[2] The history of proportional representation consists of attempts to give concrete embodiment to Mirabeau's conception.

Proportional systems can in turn be subdivided into two main types – party list systems and the single transferable vote – according to what it is they seek to represent proportionally. These two types rely for their justification upon different conceptions of representation. Party list systems aim to represent *parties* in proportion to their popular support; the single transferable vote, elaborated before organised parties arrived on the British political scene, aims at representing *individual opinions* proportionately to their popular support. For party list systems, parties are the basic units of representation; for the single transferable vote, the individual elector is regarded as sovereign.

The single transferable vote has been adopted (with the exception of Denmark in the mid-nineteenth century) only in countries which have fallen under British influence – Ireland, Malta and Australia (elections for the Senate since 1949; elections to the Tasmanian legislature since 1907). It has not been seriously considered for adoption in any Continental country in the twentieth century.

The democracies of Western Europe, on the other hand, with the exception of France, all conduct their elections with a version of the list system. But, until the Hansard Society's Commission reported in 1976 in favour of the additional member system, there was very little advocacy of any such system in Britain. Until then, almost everyone who advocated proportional representation in Britain sought the adoption of the single transferable vote.

*Variants of the second ballot do allow a candidate to win on a minority vote, but the intention is to encourage the search for a majority.

The reasons for this remarkable geographical division are partly accidental, partly rooted in divergent interpretations of the role of political parties. In Britain, as Stein Rokkan noticed, there was 'a strong tradition of direct territorial representation through individual representatives. The early English advocates of proportionality were profoundly indifferent to the survival of organised parties; they wanted to equalise the influence of individual voters.'[3] During the years between 1885 and 1905, when opinion in many Continental countries was moving towards proportional representation, the Proportional Representation Society in Britain, which always equated proportional representation with the single transferable vote, was inactive and so unable to exert any influence upon the Continental debate. In 1959 it changed its name to the Electoral Reform Society so as to avoid any confusion with Continental variants of proportional representation.

European countries saw proportionality in terms of the accurate representation of political parties, and the individualistic liberalism of Hare and Mill never exerted as much influence there as in Britain. On the Continent the primacy was often underlined by giving political parties legal recognition in contrast to Britain where, although the parties are mentioned in various statutes and party labels (since 1969) appear on ballot papers, the law on the whole takes little cognisance of their activities. List systems are appropriate to countries where political allegiance is seen as fundamentally doctrinal in nature and where representation is seen as representation of party; while the single transferable vote is more appropriate to a country where representation is seen as representation of individuals, with the individual regarded as conceptually prior to party.

So firmly ingrained on the Continent is the idea that proportional representation relates to parties that in Continental countries students of elections sometimes refuse to grant the single transferable vote the title of a proportional system at all. For example, the European Parliament's Subcommittee on a Uniform Electoral Procedure referred to the single transferable vote as 'a special system closely related to the majority system. The other seven Member States used systems of proportional representation.'[4]

In the simplest form of list system – the national list as used in Israel – there is one national constituency, and the elector cannot vote for an individual candidate, only for a complete and unalterable party list drawn up by the party before the election. There is no element of personal choice of candidate or local representation in the system, and therefore no link between the elector and his representative in the legislature. The party decides which of its members are to be elected, and the vote is still considered by many to be a vote for a doctrine, for 'The political parties in Israel were established as parties of principle, each with a definite ideology and a particular *Weltanschauung*.'[5]

The central weakness of such a system is the power which it yields to the party organisation to decide which candidates are to appear on the list and in what order. The voter cannot change the order of the candidates on the list, nor eliminate candidates; he can play no part in either the construction of the list, or the process of coalition formation following the election; and every Israeli government since the foundation of the state has been a coalition. According to Duverger, 'The internal oligarchy reigns supreme in the Proportional Representation system with fixed lists and the ranking of candidates in a strict order which determines their election, for here the parliamentary representatives are chosen by the inner circle; the party in this case is a closed circuit.'[6] This is nearer to the truth in Israel than in any other country with a proportional representation system.

The rigidity of the Israeli list system obliges a party rebel who finds himself in a minority in his party to leave it, and, with his followers, found another party whose symbol will appear on the ballot paper; this is not particularly difficult since the threshold needed for a party or independent candidate to qualify for a seat is only 1 per cent of the national vote. Many prominent leaders have found the party organisations too inelastic for them. Ben Gurion, the former Prime Minister, Moshe Dayan and Shimon Peres left the Mapai party in 1965, and in 1981 Moshe Dayan formed a separate party when his policies were rejected by the governing Likud party. Thus the system tends to the proliferations of parties, and in the last election in 1977 no less than 14 parties secured representation in the Knesset.

These parties can, however, be divided into four main blocs – Labour, the Right wing, the religious parties and the reformist Democratic Movement for Change, which between them secured 102 out of the 120 seats in 1977, and 78.8 per cent of the vote. For this reason the proliferation of parties has not prevented Israel from remaining a stable and, despite blemishes, reasonably tolerant democracy. Nevertheless, the system has not been copied elsewhere and, even in Israel, there have been pressures for change from those dissatisfied with the role of the party oligarchies.

In all other countries which use list systems the voter is offered some choice of candidate. The vote thus assumes a double aspect, being cast both for an individual candidate and for the party to which he belongs. Since all votes for a particular party list count towards the number of members of that party who qualify for a seat in the legislature, it follows that a vote for one candidate may help to elect another candidate from the same party of whom the voter may disapprove. This is a weakness of all list systems, especially where a party suffers from ideological divisions, since, if one faction wishes to prevent its party opponents from benefiting from votes cast for its own candidates, it may have no alternative but to leave the party and establish a separate list. To prevent a proliferation of parties, the threshold for representation in list systems is, with the exception of the

Netherlands, higher than 1 per cent, the figure in Israel: in West Germany, for example, it is 5 per cent, and in Sweden 4 per cent. This acts as an effective barrier to small parties and splinter groups.

There are, broadly, four different types of list system in addition to the national list used in Israel. In the first, used in countries such as Belgium, Denmark, Italy and the Netherlands, the party decides the order of candidates in the list but the elector is allowed to vote for one or more candidates in a different order if he so chooses, rather than 'voting the ticket' in the order decided by his party. In general, however, few electors take advantage of this opportunity (except in Belgium), and most decide to vote for the list as presented by their party; so the provision for choice of candidate is of little effect.

The second type of list system, as used in Switzerland and Luxembourg, offers the elector as many votes as there are candidates to be elected, and allows him to vote for individual candidates as he pleases. He may distribute his votes amongst candidates on different lists, if he so chooses, or cumulate two votes on one particular candidate. The parties, therefore, lose their power of deciding which of their candidates should be elected.

Thirdly, there is the 'regional list' system as used in Finland, where the parties do not order their lists at all, but allow the voter to decide which candidates of his party are to be elected. The elector is given one vote in a multi-member constituency, and he votes by endorsing one candidate presented in one party list. The number of seats which each party receives in the legislature is proportional to the number of votes received by the party; and the individual candidates elected for each party are those who have proved most popular with the voters. The ordering of the list is, in effect, determined by the voters themselves.

The fourth type of list system is the West German mixed system according to which half of the members of the legislature are elected in single-member constituencies by plurality voting, as in Britain, whilst the other half are elected from ordered party lists, with no choice of candidate, so as to give overall party proportionality. This system, although in appearance a hybrid, is fundamentally a proportional one, in that it ensures proportional representation of the political parties. The list element is, moreover, of the 'rigid' type in that it offers the voter no choice of candidate. A variant on this system is the additional member system recommended by the Hansard Society's Commission on Electoral Reform in 1976, whereby in place of a list drawn up by the political parties the additional members who provide the 'topping-up' element to secure party proportionality are chosen from the 'best losers', that is, losing candidates who have secured the highest percentage of votes in their constituencies.

It may prove helpful to schematise these various electoral systems in diagrammatic form (see Figure 2).

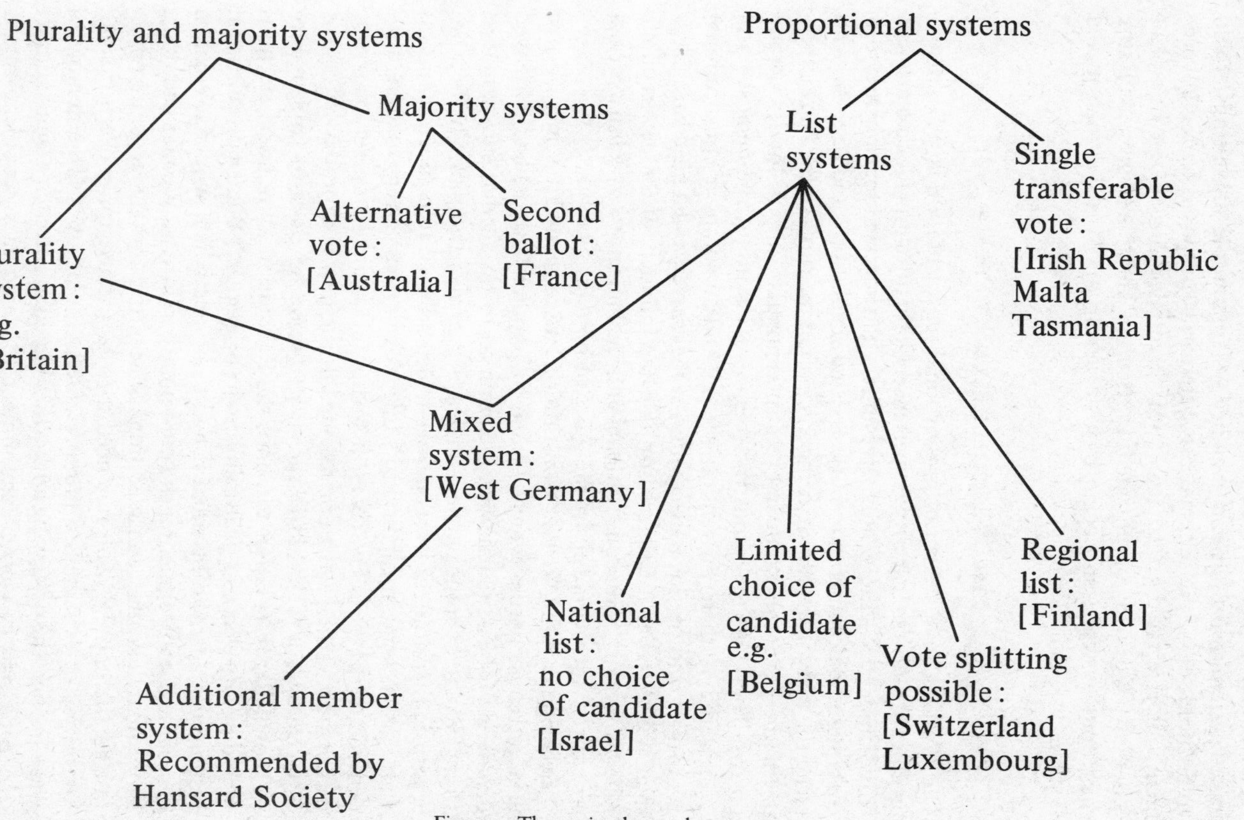

Figure 2 The main electoral systems

Of the various proportional systems, three have been advocated at various times for use in British parliamentary elections – the West German mixed system, the additional member system and the single transferable vote. In addition, the regional list system was proposed by the government but rejected by Parliament for direct elections to the European Assembly. We shall concentrate our attention, therefore, upon analysing these four systems; and begin by considering the West German mixed system.

THE WEST GERMAN SYSTEM

The West German system of proportional representation is very much a product of German historical experience. Germany's previous experiment with democracy – the Weimar Republic – had survived for only fourteen years before succumbing to Hitler's 'legal revolution', and so those who faced the task of rebuilding democracy upon the ruins of the Nazi experiment knew that they could not rely upon popular support for democratic norms. They had to 'reconstruct democracy without the demos';[7] and 'considered it their mission to set up and maintain a constitutional democracy without the participation of the masses, and if need be, against their will'.[8] It was for this reason that the founders of the new republic relied so heavily upon constitutional and legal norms to establish a formal structure which could resist the gusts of popular passion.

Believing that the Weimar Constitution had facilitated the emergence of new extremist parties which, fuelled by popular hatreds, had destroyed democracy, the founders were determined to do all that they could to strengthen democratic parties and discourage new groupings. In the Constitution, therefore, political parties which adhered to democratic norms were given legal recognition, while power was given to ban anti-democratic parties. This bias in favour of a small number of strong democratic parties was to be retained in the new electoral law.

'Germany', it was said in the 1930s, was 'the classical land of Proportional Representation for since the Revolution all political elections including city elections have followed its principles.'[9] But if a proportional system was again to be tried, it had to be one which would strengthen democracy, not fragment it. It could not, therefore, as Weimar had done, subordinate all other considerations to securing a totally accurate reflection of the popular will; nor need it to be a cause for concern if small minority parties remained unrepresented. In place of a large number of weak parties, the occupying authorities hoped to entrench a small number of strong parties whose commitment to democracy would be totally reliable; and they insisted that the new electoral system should not repeat the errors of Weimar in giving excessive power to centralised and rigid party machines which had come to assume a more important role in the life of parliamentarians than the interests of their constituents.

In the occupation zones, it appears that the Americans and the French were prepared to leave the choice of election system to the Germans themselves, but the British favoured the plurality system because it allowed for constituency contact and would therefore lessen the influence of both demagogic leaders, and party managers.[10] The Christian Democrats – CDU/CSU – were at this time the strongest party in West Germany, and were alone in favouring the plurality system. The Social Democrats – SPD – had been committed to proportional representation since the days of the Wilhelmine Empire. They feared that the British system would discriminate against them since many SPD votes were 'wasted' in large urban constituencies; under a plurality system, therefore, they might be condemned to permanent opposition. The minor parties, too, were in favour of proportional representation. Eventually a compromise between the plurality system and the Weimar system of list proportional representation was worked out, and this mixed system of 'personalised Proportional Representation' as it came to be called, was adopted. It has remained in essence unchanged from the time it was used in the first elections of the new republic in 1949.

The electoral system is based upon three principles. The first is that the elector has two votes, one for a constituency representative, as in Britain, and the second for a party list. Half of the West German lower house – the *Bundestag* – consists of constituency members, while the other half comprises members from the party lists. These lists are presented by each party on a regional (*Land*) basis, but list seats are allocated on a national basis according to the total national votes secured by the parties. A sample ballot paper is shown on p. 218.

The second principle is that the list seats are distributed between the parties so as to make their total representation in the *Bundestag* proportional to their respective second votes. This is done by 'topping up' each *Land* (regional) delegation to the *Bundestag* with candidates from the party lists. But the principle of proportionality is qualified by the third principle which provides that no party which fails to secure 5 per cent of the national vote or to win three constituencies can be represented in the *Bundestag*. This gives those parties which succeed in securing representation a slight bonus of seats in proportion to votes. There are no by-elections, and all vacancies are filled by co-opting the next candidate on the party's *Land* list.

Although there are two classes of MP in the *Bundestag*, there appears to be surprisingly little difference in the role or status of the two types of member. 'Once in the Bundestag they perform identical functions with no differentiation on grounds of election.'[11] The majority of candidates both

Voting Slip

for the Parliamentary Election in the Constituency of
110 Wanne-Eickel-Wattenscheid on 3 October 1976

You have 2 votes

1 vote here for the election of a Constituency Representative (First vote)	**1 vote here** for the election of a Regional List (Party) (Second vote)

No.	Candidate	Party	First vote	Second vote	Party	Regional List	No.
1	**Westphal, Heinz** Flugmotorenschiosser Bonn Am Zinnbruch 23 **SPD**	Sozialdemokratische Partei Deutschlands	◯	◯	**SPD**	**Sozialdemokratische Partei Deutschlands** Brandt, Arendt, Frau Renger, Schmidt, Frau Dr. Focke.	1
2	**Krampe, Wilh.** gen. Brügger, Diözesansekr. Hamm 1 Am Pilsholz 2a **CDU**	Christlich Demokratische Union Deutschlands	◯	◯	**CDU**	**Christlich Demokratische Union Deutschlands** Prof. Dr. Biedenkopf. Dr. Barzel, Katzer, Frau Dr. Wex, Windelen.	2
3	**Stoltmann, Reinhold** Student Bochum 6 Wacholderweg 24a **F.D.P.**	Freie Demokratische Partei	◯	◯	**F.D.P.**	**Freie Demokratische Partei** Genscher, Frau Funcke, Prof. Dr. Maihofer Ollesch, Dr. Graf Lambsdorff.	3
				◯	**AUD**	**Aktionsgemeinschaft Unabhängiger Deutscher** Prof. Dr. Beuys, Frau Degen, Eifers, Frau Horstmann, Fastabend.	4
5	**Dr. Hirsch, Hans** Universitats-Professor Aachen-Walheim Am Schaafweg 3 **AVP**	Aktionsgemeinschaft Vierte Partei	◯	◯	**AVP**	**Aktionsgemeinschaft Vierte Partei** Meyer, Kasper, Frau Müller, Prof. Dr. Hirsch, Willger.	5
6	**Farle, Robert** Journalist Bochum 6 Sachsenring 65 **DKP**	Deutsche Kommunistische Partei	◯	◯	**DKP**	**Deutsche Kommunistische Partei** Mies, Kapluck, Lang, Tummers, Frau Richter.	6
				◯	**EAP**	**Europäische Arbeiterpartei** Frau Zepp, Cramer, Frau Hortighott, Kampert, von Scheibner.	7
				◯	**GIM**	**Gruppe Internationale Marxisten** Hulsberg, Liebs, Frau Queiser, Meuffels, Latz.	8
				◯	**KPD**	**Kommunistische Partei Deutschlands** Hutter, Luczak, Beste, Zoller, Redereit.	9
				◯	**KBW**	**Kommunistischer Bund Westdeutschland** Hager, Frau Schmidt, Heinemann, Schulze, Wieland.	10
11	**Scharpwinkel, Walter** Schießmeister a. D. Herne 2 Eickeler Bruch 89 **NPD**	Nationaldemokratische Partei Deutschlands	◯	◯	**NPD**	**Nationaldemokratische Partei Deutschlands** **Seetzen, Gertach, Rumping,** Frau Koletzko, Muller.	11
12	**Pajonk, Ernst** Vorzeichner Essen 11 Haus-Berge-Straße 101 **UAP**	Unabhangige Arbeiter-Partei (Deutsche Sozialisten)	◯	◯	**UAP**	**Unabhängige Arbeiter-Partei (Deutsche Sozialisten)** Kliese Buhlow, Koesling, Pajonk, Villmow.	12
				◯	**VL**	**Vereinigte Linke** Schnieber, Peuker, Hanstein, von Schuckmann, Frau Schauenberg.	13

Figure 3 Voting slip for the parliamentary election in the constituency of 110 Wanne-Eickel-Wattenscheid, October 1976

stand for a constituency seat and are given a place on the list, and indeed a good performance in a constituency election increases a candidate's chances of securing a favourable position on the party list.

The working of the system can be illustrated by the most recent general election held in West Germany in 1980. The result in terms of constituency and list votes is shown in the table.

	% Constituency votes	Constituency seats	% List votes
SPD	44.5	127	42.9
CDU/CSU	46.0	121	44.5
FDP	7.2	0	10.6
Others	2.3	0	2.0
	100.0	248	100.0

The overall result, based on list votes, and excluding parties which failed to surmount the 5 per cent threshold, entitled the SPD to a total of 218 seats in the *Bundestag*, the CDU/CSU to 226 seats and the FDP to 53 seats. For the SPD, therefore, subtracting the 127 constituency seats which it had won from the 218 to which it was entitled, gave it 91 list seats, for the CDU/CSU subtracting 121 from 226 gave it 105 list seats, while all of the FDP's 53 seats came from the list. Thus the final composition of the *Bundestag* was as follows:

	Constituency seats	List seats	Total
SPD	127	91	218
CDU/CSU	121	105	226
FDP	0	53	53
Totals	248	249	497*

(There are also 22 members of the *Bundestag* with limited voting rights representing West Berlin.)

The relationship between seats and votes in the West German system is highly proportional as the accompanying table shows.

	% Share of list votes	% Share of seats
SPD	42.9	43.9
CDU/CSU	44.5	45.5
FDP	10.6	10.6

At first sight, it may seem that the West German system is a variant of the British electoral system modified by a proportional element. But this is

*For the *Bundestag* elected in 1980 there was an extra list seat, since in Schleswig–Holstein, the SPD had succeeded in winning more constituency seats than it had a right to on a strictly proportional basis, gaining all 11 seats on a vote of 49.7 per cent. In such – very rare – circumstances, it is allowed to keep the extra seat, and the *Bundestag* is correspondingly enlarged.

a misconception. It is the proportional element expressed in the list vote which is fundamental, while the constituency element is very much subordinate. For the constituency vote offers the elector no more than an opportunity to indicate the personal popularity of a particular candidate, while using his list vote for his favoured party. But, as the small difference between the constituency and list votes shows, few West Germans avail themselves of this opportunity, and in 1980 no consituency seat changed hands as a result of vote splitting.

In 1976, by far the largest personal vote had gone to an FDP candidate, Liselotte Funcke, whose constituency votes were equal to 140.4 per cent of the FDP's list vote in the constituency. She was, nevertheless, third in her constituency owing her election to her place on the party list, and she would of course have been elected even if she had received no constituency votes at all. The main function of the constituency vote, therefore, is simply to elect a constituency representative who is invariably chosen on party lines.

Although the West German system secures a nearly perfect proportionality of party representation, it does not avoid the geographical distortions characteristic of the plurality system. As in Britain, the left-wing party – the SPD – is under-represented in rural areas while the CDU/CSU is under-represented in the cities. In 1972, for example, the SPD secured all eight seats in Hamburg on 54.4 per cent of the vote, while the CDU with 33.3 per cent was unrepresented. Indeed, had it not been for the list vote, West Germany's four largest cities would have returned only one CDU representative from 47 constituencies.[12] In Munich, on the other hand, an SPD sweep in 1972 was transformed in 1976 into a CSU sweep on a relatively small change in the vote.

	1972		1976	
	% Constituency votes	seats	% Constituency votes	seats
SPD	51.0	5	42.3	1
CSU	41.0	0	47.4	4
FDP	6.6	0	8.9	0
Others	1.4	0	1.4	0

These distortions could have, as in Britain, important effects upon the campaigning strategies and policies of the parties, giving them an incentive to be especially responsive to certain socio-economic and regional interests at the expense of others. But the effects of such distortions are probably not too serious in West Germany since they can be modified through the selection of suitable list candidates.

The selection of candidates for both constituency and list seats is regulated by the Basic Law, Article 21 of which declares of the political parties that 'Their internal organisation must conform to democratic principles.'

Candidates must be chosen by party members either directly or indirectly and by secret ballot. In practice, selection committees are usually established to decide upon constituency candidates and upon the order of the *Land* list. There is considerable stress on federalism and decentralisation in West Germany and because the lists are drawn up by the *Land* organisations of the party, in consultation with the constituencies, it is impossible for the central party organisation to dictate candidatures. Nevertheless the list system can serve to protect unpopular candidates from the electorate, so that, whereas in Britain a candidate sitting in a marginal seat may lose it if he fails to attract a personal vote, in West Germany there is always security in the list. Because nomination for a high place on the party list offers a safe seat for life, it must act as a disincentive to independence of mind and discourage criticism of the party leadership. In West Germany, the party mediates between the elector and his choice since the list system offers an insurance to any candidate who appears before the electorate. This was in part the deliberate intention of the framers of the Constitution who, in the absence of popular support for democracy, relied upon the strength of democratic parties, and it has led 'to what German critics of the Basic Law have called the "mediatisation of the people" through political parties'.[13]

Although the West German system is fundamentally a proportional one, its results have been very far removed from those conventionally attributed to 'proportional representation': the proliferation of parties, weak coalition governments, and the rise of extremism.

Thanks largely to the 5 per cent clause, there has been an elimination rather than a proliferation of new parties. In the first *Bundestag* there were ten parties (counting the CDU and its Bavarian sister the CSU as one party), but since 1961 only three parties have been able to secure parliamentary representation; and no party which has once been eliminated by the 5 per cent hurdle has been able to surmount it on any later occasion.

West Germany has experienced coalition government continuously since 1949, for even in 1957 when the CDU/CSU succeeded in gaining an absolute majority in the *Bundestag*, it offered Cabinet posts to members of a small party. Yet these governments have been anything but weak. They have generally been able to rely upon a stable two-party majority in parliament, and have pursued clear policies with a considerable degree of consistency. Every coalition government except for the 'Grand Coalition' between 1966 and 1969 has involved the FDP – the German equivalent of the Liberal Party – and the FDP has become the pivot party of the German system, drawing the other parties to the centre and weakening the attraction of the extremes. The philosophy of the FDP is broadly relativist, and its liberalism is marked by a distaste for absolutes, such as state socialism and laissez-faire; liberalism is not, in the view of the FDP, itself a specific social state, but a critique of absolute conceptions of politics. The FDP has become a self-consciously anti-ideological party, and its conception of politics has helped to wean the German electorate away from its preoccupation with doctrines and *Weltanschauungen*.[14]

Moreover, the German system offers to the electorate the opportunity to indicate through its votes that it seeks a particular type of coalition arrangement. In 1969, for example, the FDP had made it clear by its support for the SDP's candidate for the Presidency, Gustav Heinemann, that it would enter into coalition with the SPD if the opportunity arose. Analysis of the FDP vote in the 1969 election shows that the majority of its supporters, though by no means all, approved of this strategy.

Constituency votes of FDP list voters, 1965 and 1969 (%)

	1965	1969
SPD	6.7	24.8
CDU/CSU	20.9	10.6
FDP	70.3	62.0
Others/invalid votes	2.1	2.6

Over one-third of FDP voters split their vote, so helping the SPD, for the first time in the Federal Republic, to gain more constituency seats – 127 – than the CDU/CSU – 121.[15]

In 1972 the leaders of the coalition government, Willy Brandt and Walter Scheel, asked voters to support the coalition by giving their constituency votes to the SPD but their list votes to the FDP. FDP voters were asked to vote tactically and to ensure that constituency seats were won by the SPD rather than by the CDU/CSU; for the FDP is in a hopeless position in most constituencies, and indeed has not won a constituency seat since 1957, its representation in the *Bundestag* since then being composed entirely of list members. For SPD supporters the strategy would not seem to promise such obvious gains, since any list votes given to the FDP would detract from the overall SPD total and therefore from the number of seats to which it was entitled. But SPD supporters feared that the FDP might fail to clear the 5 per cent hurdle – in 1969 it had secured only 5.8 per cent of list votes (and 4.8 per cent of constituency votes). If that happened, the FDP would secure no parliamentary representation at all, and the CDU/CSU might be able to form a government.

But the 1972 election proved to be the only one in the Federal Republic's history in which the SPD succeeded in gaining more seats than the CDU/CSU; and the FDP surmounted the 5 per cent hurdle without difficulty.

1972 election: List votes

SPD	46.1%
CDU/CSU	44.9%
FDP	8.4%
Others	0.9%

In constituency votes, however, the FDP secured only 4.8 per cent, the same percentage as in 1969, and it is clear that many voters must have followed the advice of Brandt and Scheel and 'lent' their constituency vote to the SPD while placing their list vote for the FPD. The constituency votes of list FDP voters were as follows:

SPD	52.9%
CDU/CSU	7.9%
FDP	38.2%
Others/invalid votes	1.0%

This pattern of voting constituted a clear mandate for the continuation of the coalition.

West German experience, therefore, serves to cast doubt upon the generalisation frequently put forward that proportional representation makes for coalitions formed in 'smoke-filled rooms' after the ballots have been counted. For by their voting behaviour, West German electors can indicate which combination of parties they would like to see acting together in government, and a party which ignored the signals of the electorate would be in danger of losing support. In fact, the FDP lost support from some of its more Right-wing adherents when it joined with the SPD in 1969 and 1972, but it would have lost a great deal more support if it had formed a coalition with the CDU/CSU, or if, by refusing to enter a coalition with the SPD, it had allowed the CDU/CSU to form a minority government.

Since the establishment of the Federal Republic, there has been no complete change of government in West Germany. Change occurs through a shifting of coalition partners. Until 1966, the CDU/CSU governed, except for the years 1957 to 1961, in coalition with the FDP (and in 1949 with two other small parties which have now disappeared). In 1966 the 'Grand Coalition' between the CDU/CSU and the SPD was formed, and since 1969 an SPD/FDP government has been in power in Bonn. This shifting of coalition partners gives stability to the political system, at the cost of 'a narrower range of acceptable opinion than is usual in Western Europe, with Schmidt, Kohl and Genscher crowding the political centre'.[16] In contrast to Britain, where the upsurge of Liberals and Nationalists in 1974 created uncertainty and confusion, it has not proved difficult to agree on arrangements for a coalition. The West German model, therefore, shows that coalition government can be responsible government, and can reconcile choice and stability. It encourages the parties to make themselves acceptable to voters in the centre of the political spectrum.

The successful working of the West German political system must also be credited to strong political leadership – Adenauer, Brandt, Schmidt – and to the economic prosperity which has become associated with democracy and moderate government. It is significant that it was during the one period when economic progress was threatened – the years 1966–9 when West Germany was affected by a mild recession and governed by a Grand Coalition comprising the CDU/CSU and SDP – that extremist movements gathered strength and the neo-Nazi National Democratic Party – the NPD – nearly secured representation in the *Bundestag*.

The results of the 1969 election were as follows:

List votes	
SPD	42.7%
CDU/CSU	46.1%
FDP	5.8%
NPD	4.3%
Others	0.2%

If the FDP had received 0.8 per cent less of the vote – 270,000 fewer votes – it would have failed to surmount the 5 per cent threshold. If these votes had gone to minor parties with the SPD and CDU/CSU percentage unchanged, the CDU/CSU would have gained 52 per cent of the seats and formed a majority government.

Even more serious would have been the situation if the NPD had succeeded in gaining the extra 0.7 per cent of the vote – 230,000 more votes – needed to surmount the threshold while the FDP had fallen below it. The only possible governments would then have been a renewal of the Grand Coalition between the SPD and CDU/CSU, with the NPD as the sole opposition party; or a CDU/CSU government dependent upon NPD support. Neither of these alternatives offered a very appetising prospect, and there is no doubt that West Germany's international reputation, which men such as Konrad Adenauer had laboured so hard to build, would have been seriously undermined.

It can be seen, therefore, that the reputation of the West German electoral system as a bulwark of moderation and stability only narrowly survived the 1969 election. It may well be that with deepening economic difficulties the West German electorate once more begins to feel the attraction of extremism. We may well ask whether a West Germany which had faced the economic difficulties and failures which Britain has endured in the postwar period would still have remained as democratic and tolerant a society as Britain has been.

Moreover, it cannot be denied that there is less contact between members of the *Bundestag* and their constituents than would be acceptable in Britain today. German attitudes to parliament put far less stress upon its representative functions than is customary in Britain, and, writing in 1966, one authority on the West German Parliament was complaining that there was 'no sense of participation in government, or a commitment to the political system which goes beyond satisfaction with the day-to-day results it produces'.[17] Members of the *Bundestag* give less time to routine constituency matters than their British counterparts, and the main emphasis of their work is upon scrutinising legislation. However, if the German voter finds himself rather less well represented in terms of his constituency needs than his British counterpart, this is perhaps compensated for by the existence of strong provincial and local layers of government. It would be difficult, therefore, to argue that the West German voter *feels* badly represented, or that there is a great dissatisfaction with the working of the political system. It would therefore be ungenerous to conclude without recognising that West Germany's political system has made a considerable contribution to the postwar stability both of Germany and of Europe; and her electoral system has been an important factor in creating that stability.

THE ADDITIONAL MEMBER SYSTEM

When the Commission on Electoral Reform, established by the Hansard Society and chaired by Lord Blake, surveyed various alternative electoral systems, it devoted only three paragraphs to the West German system, and came to the conclusion that 'as it stands', it was not 'suitable for adoption in Britain'.[18] For, if Britain were to adopt the West German system either the size of constituencies or of the House of Commons would have to be doubled: and candidates could appear on a party list who had never presented themselves to the electorate at all. The Commission thought that this would be unacceptable in Britain. Indeed, the list system might not work as smoothly in Britain as it has worked in the very different conditions of West Germany: it could lead to central domination of party candidatures with the battle for selection being fought out behind closed doors in Smith Square or Walworth Road.

The Commission therefore worked out an adaptation of the West German system – the additional member system – which ensured that no one could be elected to the Commons without having fought a constituency contest. The Commission proposed that the House of Commons be enlarged to 640 members, and that three-quarters of the MPs be elected in single-member constituencies as at present. This would of course necessitate an increase in the size of constituencies, but only by one-third, rather than a doubling, as in the West German model. The remaining one quarter of the Commons MPs would be chosen, not from a list, but on a regional basis from defeated constituency candidates. They would be allocated to each party in proportion to its share of the vote in each region, and to those candidates of each party who, not having won a constituency seat, secured the highest percentage of the vote within the region. There would be a regional threshold of 5 per cent, and any party which failed to surmount this would be ineligible for additional seats in that region.

The Commission believed that the additional member system was more in accord with British traditions than either the West German system or the single transferable vote, since it retained the single-member constituency and did away with the need for a party list. The elector would not be required to give a double vote or to master a complex new system, and so he could be introduced gradually to the concepts of proportional representation. Moreover the electoral system could be gradually changed if it proved to be successful, so as to secure a higher degree of proportionality, and the one quarter of additional members could be raised to one-third or even a half in due course. The additional member system, therefore, respected British traditions, but attempted to supplement them so as to overcome the grosser distortions in the electoral system by adding a new more equitable element to it.

But in attempting to make the West German system more palatable to the British voter, the system of election proposed by the Hansard Society incurred new objections. The West German system by providing for a double vote allowed the elector to dissociate his preference for a particular candidate from his choice of a political party. With only one vote, as in the additional member system, a vote for a particular candidate in one constituency is at the same time a vote for another candidate from the same party in another constituency. Yet the voter may well not support this second candidate who secures election as a 'best loser'. Indeed, he cannot know when he votes who his choice will benefit. He cannot predict in advance how his vote will be used, and this sharply differentiates the additional member variant from the West German system where the voter at least can see the ordering on the list. The voter himself has not supported the defeated candidate who gains election as a 'best loser', and he may be bitterly hostile to him if he represents a faction of his party which he opposes. For example, a Conservative elector in Greater London voting for Edward Heath in Sidcup might not be pleased to see his vote used to help Margaret Thatcher in Finchley. Indeed, he might well prefer to support a Liberal rather than Margaret Thatcher. But the additional member system, like many list systems, assumes that party differences are sharply defined, and that there is little meeting-point between supporters of different parties.

Thus, the choice of candidates seemingly offered by the additional member system is entirely illusory, for the 'topping-up' to secure proportionality is not from candidates chosen by the voter himself but from those candidates who have secured their party nomination for constituencies in which the party polls well.

Further defects in the additional member system were noticed when it was proposed in the Commons in January 1977 for use in the new Scottish and Welsh Assemblies. An all-party amendment sponsored by a Labour MP, John Mackintosh, and a Conservative, Anthony Kershaw, provided that, in addition to the 71 directly elected members of the Scottish Assembly, there would be 29 additional members; and in addition to the 36 directly elected members of the Welsh Assembly, there would be 14 additional members.

On the basis of the October 1974 general election results, this would have produced Assemblies composed in the following way:

Scotland	Lab.	SNP	Con.	Lib.
Constituency members	41	11	16	3
No. of additional members	0	18	7	4
% votes	36.0	30.4	24.7	8.3
Total no. of seats	41	29	23	7

Wales	Lab.	Plaid Cymru	Con.	Lib.
Constituency members	23	3	8	2
No. of additional members	2	2	4	6
% votes	49.5	10.8	23.9	15.0
Total no. of seats	25	5	12	8

This proposal was rejected by the Commons, and serious criticisms of it were raised during the debate and in an article in the *Economist* which appeared shortly before the debate.[19]

The first objection was that the number of topping-up members would not be large enough to secure proportionality. Labour in the October 1974 election had won 41 out of the 71 Scottish seats on 36 per cent of the vote. With 41 out of the 100 seats, Labour would still be over-represented, although less so than under the plurality system. But there would have been more serious anomalies. In Wales the 14 additional members would have come from the following constituencies.

6 Liberals (defeated candidates from Denbigh, West Flint, Wrexham, Cardiff S.E., Cardiff N.W. and Cardiff N)
4 Conservatives (defeated candidates from Swansea West, Brecon and Radnor, Cardiff West and East Flint)
2 Labour (defeated candidates from Pembroke and Monmouth)
2 Plaid Cymru (defeated candidates from Caerphilly and Aberdare)

Thus Cardiff N. and Cardiff N.W., with electorates of 44,000, would gain additional members while Newport, with an electorate of 75,000, and Barry and Pontypridd, each with electorates of 75,000, would gain no additional members.

Clwyd would have gained four additional members, whilst Gwynedd would have gained none. Cardiff would have gained four, and Gwent, Mid-Glamorgan and West Glamorgan only four between them. The additional members would have altered unreasonably the geographical balance of the proposed Welsh Assembly. A similar anomaly would occur in Scotland, where all seven of the Conservative additional members would come from the rural periphery, with none from Clydeside, thus exacerbating the geographical imbalance of Conservative representation in the Scottish Assembly.

Moreover, the system would be unfair as between defeated candidates. In Cardiff S.E., the Liberal candidate in October 1974 came over 2,000 votes behind the Conservative candidate, yet the former would become an additional member while the latter would not. The Labour candidate in Carmarthen with over 38 per cent of the vote and the Conservative in Newport with nearly 29 per cent of the vote would not become additional members but three Liberals in Cardiff would succeed with less than 20 per cent of the vote and a Plaid Cymru candidate in Aberdare would with 21.2 per cent. Altogether nine defeated Labour candidates (in Carmarthen, Barry, Cardiff N., Cardigan, Carnaervon, Cardiff N.W., Conway, W. Flint and Merioneth) who would not become additional members, had higher shares of the vote than the most successful defeated Liberal (in Denbigh). Of the six Liberal additional members, three would be from Cardiff constituencies where they had come third, while the Liberal who had come second in Llanelli would not qualify.

Moreover the percentage of the vote which a candidate receives is not solely, or even mainly, a function of his personal popularity. A candidate in a three- or four-cornered fight has less chance of securing a high percentage of the poll than a candidate in a straight fight. For this reason the Conservative candidate in E. Dumbarton who lost to the SNP in October 1974 by 32 votes in a four-cornered contest would not have been an additional member.

If the 'topping-up' exercise is carried out for the 1979 general election results, the geographical distortions are not so extreme, and the degree of proportionality nearer to that of full party proportionality. Yet in Scotland and Wales there are still many Labour candidates who would fail to become additional members although polling a higher percentage than a Liberal or Nationalist candidate who would succeed.

The additional member system would encourage parties to put up candidates in hopeless seats so as to secure the 5 per cent of the vote in the region to beat the threshold. The National Front, for example, would put up a candidate in every constituency in the Greater London Council area so as to surmount the threshold: so would extremist Left-wing groups. With more candidates, more MPs would be elected on a minority vote, and by a smaller percentage of their constituents. With more scope for tactical voting, the vote would be a less reliable indicator of personal preference. Nor does the additional member system allow for 'ticket-splitting' which in West Germany can be used to signal a desire for coalition.

The additional member system, even if an improvement on the plurality system, is too full of distortions and anomalies to be acceptable in Britain.

It is inferior to the West German system and the single transferable vote. It is doubtful whether it should remain as a serious alternative for adoption in this country.

THE REGIONAL LIST SYSTEM

The regional list system proposed by the government in 1977 for elections to the European Assembly, but rejected by the Commons, is basically the Finnish electoral system transposed for British use. As it has not been proposed for elections to the House of Commons, we shall consider it only in the European context.

The essence of the system is that the voter himself rather than the party organisation determines the order of the list and therefore the order in which the candidates are elected. Since it offers the voter a choice of candidates, it is, some would argue, superior to either the West German or additional member systems.

As proposed for the European elections, the regional list system provided for the division of the United Kingdom into 12 electoral regions. These would comprise the South-East, which would be divided into two – Greater London, and the rest – the other seven English standard regions; Scotland; Wales; and Northern Ireland. Each region would form a multi-member constituency returning from three (East Anglia and Northern Ireland) to 14 (South-East England excluding London) members to the European Assembly.

The ballot paper for the election would be of the form shown in Figure 4. Each voter would put a cross against the name of one candidate and the votes for each candidate and each party would be calculated. Each party would then be entitled to a number of seats in proportion to the number of votes received, and these seats would be distributed to the candidates who had gained the most votes within their respective parties. In the ballot paper indicated, suppose that five candidates were to be elected, and the result of the vote was as follows:

						Totals
Conservative Party	Jones	Knott	Parker-Pattison	Philips	Swift	
	50,000	75,000	75,000	300,000	100,000	600,000
Independent	Lawton					
	5,000					5,000
Labour Party	Black (D.R.)	Black (P.T.)	Jackson	Robinson	Simpson	
	100,000	50,000	200,000	150,000	100,000	600,000
Liberal Party	Benson-Harrison	Clark	Green	Masters	Williams	
	20,000	80,000	50,000	140,000	10,000	300,000
						1,505,000

FORM OF BALLOT PAPER

Form of front of ballot paper

You have only ONE vote.

Place an X in the box UNDER the name of the candidate for whom you wish to vote.

CONSERVATIVE PARTY

JONES (William David Jones, of High Elms, Barlington, Grayshire.)	KNOTT (Henry Richard Knott, of The Lodge, High Road, Eastchester, Loamshire.)	PARKER-PATTISON (Samuel Brian Parker-Pattison, of 3, Bagshot Row, Exborough.)	PHILLIPS (Anne Elizabeth Phillips, of 67, Morningside Crescent, Christminster.)	SWIFT (Katharine Emma Swift, of 53, Stokes Road, Barchester.)
☐	☐	☐	☐	☐

INDEPENDENT

LAWTON, (George Langley, Viscount Lawton, of Castle Scarlet, Blankshire.)
☐

LABOUR PARTY

BLACK (DAVID RICHARD Black, of 90, Bath Road, Westchester.)	BLACK (PHILIP THOMAS Black, of 36, Hillside Road, Wellbridge, Blankshire.)	JACKSON (Mary Sarah Jackson, of Flat 3, Duke's Mansions, Casterbridge, Grayshire.)	ROBINSON (James Leonard Robinson, of 91, Old Terrace, Anglebury, Greenshire.)	SIMPSON (Beryl Harriet Simpson, of 36, Firs Drive, Cranford, Loamshire.)
☐	☐	☐	☐	☐

LIBERAL PARTY

BENSON-HARRISON (Barbara Dorothy Benson-Harrison, of 2, Low Road, Stourcastle, Barsetshire.)	CLARK (Frederick John Clark, of 77, Roman Road, Northchester, Greenshire.)	GREEN (Timothy Frederick Green, of 110, Poole Road, Sandbourne, Blankshire.)	MASTERS (Matthew Michael Masters, of 13, Leamington Avenue, Havenpool, Grayshire.)	WILLIAMS (Rosemary Williams, of 32, Parkside Avenue, Overcombe, Loamshire.)
☐	☐	☐	☐	☐

Form of back of ballot paper

No. ....

Election for the Electoral Region of , day of , 19 .

Note.—The number on the Ballot Paper is to correspond with that on the counterfoil.

Figure 4 Form of ballot paper proposed for the European Assembly elections under the regional list system

The Conservative and Labour Parties, with nearly 40 per cent of the vote, would be entitled to two each of the five seats – these would go to Phillips and Swift for the Conservatives, and Jackson and Robinson for the Labour Party. The Liberals, with 20 per cent of the vote, would secure one seat which would go to Masters. Of course this is a highly artificial example, and in practice the allocation would not work out as neatly as this, but the fundamental principle remains the same, and for our purpose it is not necessary to enter into technical details.

The regional list system as it has worked in Finland has provided a very high degree of party proportionality combined with a choice of candidate for the voter. Since 1975, the parties have been required by law to hold internal primaries to decide which candidates appear on the ballot paper, and this mitigates to some extent the power of the party machine in this particular type of list system. The system, however, encourages fragmentation and a proliferation of parties, since if one faction in a party finds itself in a minority, it would do better to establish a list of its own, so that votes cast for the faction cannot be used to help elect members of the opposing faction. There is, admittedly, a threshold in Finland varying from 4 per cent to 12 per cent with the size of the constituency, but it has failed to inhibit the growth of new parties.

The system would work oddly in a country such as Britain where the parties are coalitions of widely differing views and not held together by adherence to any single doctrine. On the European issue, where party allegiances are not congruent with attitudes to the European Community, it could make for some strange results. For the central defect of the regional list system is that, as with the additional member system, votes cast for one candidate can be used to help elect another whose views on Europe might well be wholly opposed to those of either the candidate for whom the votes were given, or the voter who gave them. Suppose, for example, that both Roy Hattersley and Barbara Castle were candidates in a regional list Euro-constituency. The Labour voter who supported the EEC and voted for Roy Hattersley might help elect Barbara Castle; and vice versa. For, as with the additional member system, the voter cannot know beforehand how his vote will be used. In Finland, this does not matter too much since the parties are much more ideologically cohesive, and there are more of them. In Britain, however, the section of the Labour Party with the most support in the country, say the anti-EEC faction, could easily gain fewer seats than the pro-EEC faction if the votes were heavily concentrated upon one popular anti-EEC candidate, or spread over too many anti-EEC candidates; and there is no way in which the individual voter can so place his vote as to prevent this happening. Such an outcome would surely cause considerable disillusionment.

Moreover, the regional list system would have to be combined with primary elections to prevent excessive power being concentrated in the party machine. Without primaries, a member of the European Assembly would have too great an incentive to remain a good party man even when party interests conflict with constituency interests. It might, therefore, lead to the voter feeling less well represented under the regional list system than under the plurality system where an MP can revolt against his party line provided that he can carry his constituency association with him.

One eventual consequence of the regional list system might therefore be separate Labour and Conservative Party pro and anti lists; and indeed Michael Steed, who recommended the regional list system to the government, later claimed that it could have led to the emergence of an anti-Common Market list as in Denmark.[20] For there is greater hostility to the EEC in Britain than in Denmark, or indeed any other EEC country. The regional list system, therefore, could fulfil its purpose of indicating the state of public opinion on Common Market questions only by profoundly altering the configuration of parties for the elections to the European Assembly. It would be likely, moreover, for such changes to spill over into domestic politics. With the present party configuration, the regional list system is particularly inappropriate in elections where the main division of opinion lies within rather than between the parties, and therefore, unsuitable for elections to the European Assembly.

THE SINGLE TRANSFERABLE VOTE

The single transferable vote is a modification of the system developed by Thomas Hare, whereby voting takes place in multi-member constituencies rather than the single nationwide constituency he originally advocated. It stems, as we have seen, from a liberal conception of representation according to which the task of the representative is to represent the opinions of electors rather than the community in which they live, as in the plurality system, or their party allegiance, as in the list systems. According to this conception, an elector is not properly represented unless there is a member of the legislature to speak for him. For this reason, many early advocates of the single transferable vote referred to it as providing for 'personal' or 'real' representation.

Although its working may seem complex, the fundamental principle of the single transferable vote was said by Thomas Hare's son to be 'simplicity itself – nearly all great ideas are extremely simple when you see them. It was merely this: if you want to be represented by a member of your choice you must first of all *express* your choice.'[21] To be represented by a candidate of one's choice is only possible in a multi-member constituency where the elector is offered a choice of candidates both between and within the parties. He is presented not with a list but with a number of candidates from each party whom he can support in order of preference. The fundamental aim is to minimise the influence of party organisation in the interests of securing individual choice; and the nineteenth-century advocates of the system thought this would ensure that the parties were represented in Parliament 'by their ablest and most trusted members',[22] rather than by party delegates.

The single transferable vote would ensure the proportional representation of political opinion, so that a majority in the legislature must have the support of a majority of the electorate. But this majority would not dominate the legislature, for minorities too would be represented in their true proportion. The system, therefore, would 'secure that the majority of electors shall *rule* and all considerable minorities shall be *heard*'.[23]

Only two countries retain this system for the election of the lower chamber of their legislatures – the Irish Republic and Malta. But it has also been used for elections to the lower house of the Tasmanian legislature since 1907, to the Australian Senate since 1949, and to all bodies in Northern Ireland since 1973. It has thus not been used in any large advanced industrial society. This is of some importance since, requiring multi-member constituencies, it may work better with a small electorate than with a large one. There is a great contrast between electing five candidates in an Irish constituency with a population between 100,000 and 150,000 and a British one where the population would approach half a million. It might have very different political effects in a congested and bustling industrial centre from those apparent so far in rural and semi-rural societies. Nevertheless, evaluation of the single transferable vote must perforce content itself with the limited evidence available.

The single transferable vote may seem complex to describe, but it operates perfectly successfully in a number of societies whose population is not more sophisticated than the British, and in one, Malta, where there is much illiteracy. The elector merely chooses an order of preference for the candidates on the ballot paper, and he need not understand the operation of the system to be able to cast his vote effectively. In the last three general elections in the Irish Republic the percentage of invalid votes was 1.20 per cent, 1.17 per cent and 0.85 per cent.

The single transferable vote is designed to ensure that as many electors as possible succeed in voting for a candidate of their choice and in being represented by him. It therefore seeks to do away with the wasted vote, one which cannot be used to elect a candidate either because he has too few votes to be able to secure election, or because he is so popular that he enjoys a surplus and could have won the seat with a smaller number of votes. For example, in the general election in Britain in 1979, the result in the Liverpool, Walton constituency won by Eric Heffer was as follows:

Labour	20,231
Conservative	12,673
Liberal	3,479
National Front	254

Of the 36,637 electors who voted in the constituency, the votes of those who voted for the Conservative, Liberal and National Front candidates – equal to 16,406 votes – were wasted in the sense that they did not help to elect a candidate. So also were the 7,557 surplus votes accumulated by Eric Heffer over and above the 12,674 which he needed for victory. Thus a total of 65.4 per cent of the votes cast – 16,405 plus 7,557 – did not help elect a candidate.

The single transferable vote allows votes which cannot be used for the election of a first choice candidate, either because they are not needed or because he has no chance of victory, to be transferred to another candidate who is able to use the vote.

The ballot paper in this system is in fact perfectly straightforward, and is illustrated in Figure 5 in the form prescribed by law in the Irish Republic. The elector is asked to express his preferences for the various candidates by marking a '1' by his first choice, a '2' by his second, and so on until all his preferences are exhausted. In Ireland, he may, but need not, express a preference for every candidate on the ballot paper; and he may if he so wishes 'plump' by expressing a preference only for candidates of his own preferred party. The ballot paper will be judged invalid only if there is no unambiguously marked first preference; ambiguity in expressing later preferences will not render it invalid.

The expression of preferences is in effect a direction to the returning officer to transfer a vote if it cannot be used to elect a candidate who is the voter's first choice. For example, in the ballot paper shown, if the first preference is for Ahern and the second for Fennessy, the returning officer is directed to transfer the vote to Fennessy if Ahern cannot use it, either because he has a surplus of votes above what is needed for election, or because he has so few votes that he cannot possibly be elected and must be eliminated from the contest.

It is now possible to see this system in operation in an Irish constituency, Sligo–Leitrim, the results for which in the general elections of 1969 and 1973 are shown on pp. 236–7. Sligo–Leitrim is a three-member constituency which, both in 1969 and 1973, was contested by the three main parties in the Irish Republic – Fianna Fáil, Fine Gael and Labour. Politics in the Republic is less influenced by ideology than politics in Britain, and Fianna Fáil and Fine Gael are both broadly conservative parties whose origins lie in different attitudes to the 1921 Treaty with Britain. Fianna Fáil, the party of De Valera, repudiated the Treaty and has always been the most republican of the parties, while Fine Gael was in an earlier form the party of W. T.

Marcáil ord do rogha sna spáis seo síos. Mark order of prefer- ence in spaces below.	Marc Oifigiúil Official Mark.
	AHERN—FIANNA FAIL (Liam Ahern of Dungourney, Co. Cork. Farmer and Public Representative).
	BARRY—FINE GAEL (Richard Barry of 26, Patrick Street, Fermoy, Co. Cork. Auctioneer and Publican).
	BRODERICK—FINE GAEL (Michael Broderick of Walshestown, Churchtown, Mallow, Co. Cork. Farmer and Co. Councillor).
	BROSNAN—FIANNA FAIL (Sean Brosnan of Claycastle, Youghal, Co. Cork. Barrister-at-Law).
	COLLINS— (Noel Collins of 60, St. Mary's Road, Midleton, Co. Cork. Office Clerk).
	CRONIN—FIANNA FAIL (Jerry Cronin of 71, Main Street, Mallow, Co. Cork. Public Representative).
	FENNESSY—THE LABOUR PARTY (Billy Fennessy of 3. Patrick Street, Fermoy, Co. Cork. Auctioneer and Farmer).
	HEGARTY—FINE GAEL (Patrick Hegarty of Ballinvoher, Cloyne, Co. Cork. Farmer).
	KELLY— (Cuthbert J. Kelly of The West End Stores, Cobh, Co. Cork. Businessman).
	SHERLOCK—SINN FEIN (Joseph Sherlock of 20, Blackwater Drive, Mallow, Co. Cork. Factory Worker).

Figure 5 Voting slip for the North-East Cork constituency

Results for the Sligo–Leitrim constituency in the Irish general elections of 1969 and 1973

June 1969

Candidates by parties	Stage I	Stage II O'Rourke's votes	Stage III Mrs Gallagher's votes	Stage IV Fallon's votes	Stage V Higgins' votes	Stage VI Mooney's votes	Stage VII McLoughlin's surplus	Result
Fianna Fáil								
Gallagher J.	6124	11 6135	70 6205	135 6340	96 6436	645 7081	132 7213	Third
MacSharry R.	5616	18 5634	189 5823	162 5985	424 6409	912 7321	111 7432	Second
Mooney J. M.	2267	203 2470	40 2510	11 2521	41 2562	2562		Eliminated
	14007	14239	14538	14846	15407	14402	14645	
Fine Gael								
McLoughlin J.	6053	158 6211	100 6311	527 6838	455 7293	718 8011	517 7494	First
Gilhawley E.	5858	8 5866	111 5977	373 6350	210 6560	48 6608	69 6677	Runner Up
Fallon J.	1332	3 1335	44 1379	1379				Lost Deposit
	13243	13412	13667	13188	13853	14619	14171	
Labour								
Higgins T. J.	1251	29 1280	410 1690	122 1812	1812			Lost Deposit
Gallagher Mrs J.	967	51 1018	1018					Lost Deposit
O'Rourke P. V.	506	506						Lost Deposit
	2724	2298	1690	1812				
Non-transferable votes		25 25	54 79	49 128	586 714	239 953	205 1158	
Total	29974	29974	29974	29974	29974	29974	29974	

February 1973

Candidates by parties	Stage I	Stage II MacSharry's surplus	Stage III Higgins' votes	Stage IV Mooney's votes	Result
Fianna Fáil					
MacSharry R.	7535	234 7301	7301	7301	First
Brennan B.	4922	144 5066	162 5228	1438 6666	Runner Up
Mooney J. M.	2325	40 2365	56 2421	2421	Lost Deposit
	14782	14732	14950	13967	
Fine Gael					
Gilhawley E.	6520	13 6533	649 7182	43 7225	Third
McLoughlin J.	5743	22 5765	1208 6973	743 7716	Second
	12263	12298	14155	14941	
Labour					
Higgins T. J.	2158	15 2173	2173		Lost Deposit
Non-transferable votes			98 98	197 295	
Total	29203	29203	29203	29203	

Source: James Knight and Nicolas Baxter-Moore: *Republic of Ireland: The General Elections of 1969 and 1973* (Arthur McDougall Fund, 1973), p. 154.

Cosgrave who accepted the Treaty. The parties appeal to different social groups in the Republic, but they are not fundamentally divided by class. The Labour Party, the third party in the system, although the oldest of the Irish political parties, has never been able to overcome its minority status in the Republic. Because of this it can enjoy power only through a coalition with one of the two main parties, and this, together with the deeply conservative and Catholic culture of Ireland, compels it to offer only a very much modified form of socialism. In the election of 1969, however, the Labour Party decided not to enter into any coalition agreement with another party, but to fight the election entirely independently. In Sligo–Leitrim, therefore, it put up three candidates in the rather forlorn hope that it might gain sufficient first preference votes to secure one or even two seats.

The stages of the election are shown on pp. 236–7. The first task of the returning officer is to add up the total of validly cast first preferences given to the candidate. He then has to compute a quota. This is the minimum number of votes a candidate needs to secure election. It might, at first sight, seem that the quota will be equal to one-third of the total number of first preference votes cast, that is, 29,974 divided by three equals 9,991. But in fact if a candidate can secure one more than one-quarter of the votes, then the three other candidates cannot overtake him, and he can be sure of election. This is the lowest possible number of votes needed to ensure election. The formula for the quota, then, is always equal to $\frac{V}{S+1}+1$ where V is the total number of valid votes and S is the total number of seats. The justification for this method of calculating the quota can be most clearly seen by imagining a single-member constituency. Here any candidate with just over 50 per cent of the vote must be sure of election. In the example given, the quota is equal to $\frac{29{,}974}{4}+1$ equals 7,494 (disregarding fractional numbers). Any candidate who secures 7,494 votes, therefore, has won the election.

Looking at the total of first preference votes in the chart, we can see that no candidate has secured the quota by virtue of his first preference votes. The returning officer therefore eliminates the candidate with the least votes, O'Rourke, who has lost his deposit by failing to secure one-third of the quota, and his votes are transferred as shown. As there is still no candidate who has secured the quota, the returning officer then eliminates the candidate still remaining with the fewest votes, Mrs Gallagher. Then Fallon, Higgins and Mooney are eliminated in turn, and one candidate, McLoughlin, has at last reached the quota. Indeed he has exceeded the quota by 8,011 − 7,494 votes, equals 517. These must be redistributed, in accordance with the wishes of voters, to other candidates who can thereby be helped to reach the quota.

But we cannot, of course, redistribute *all* of McLoughlin's votes to other candidates; we must redistribute only the surplus, those votes not needed to elect him. We have no means of telling which of the 8,011 votes are in fact surplus, and therefore the returning officer gives to each of McLoughlin's votes a value equal to the ratio of the surplus to the number of transferable votes cast for McLoughlin. This can be made clear by following through the transfer of McLoughlin's preferences to Gilhawley. We first calculate McLoughlin's surplus: this is equal to 8,011 minus the quota, 7,494, equals 517. Next we calculate the total number of McLoughlin's transferable votes which is 8,011 minus his non-transferable votes, 205, equals 7,806. Then we divide the surplus by the total of transferable votes, that is, 517 divided by 7,806, equals $\frac{33}{500}$. This means that each continuing candidate receives $\frac{33}{500}$ of those papers showing next preference papers for him. Thus we are to assume that Gilhawley received 1,046 next available preferences out of McLoughlin's total of 8,011; for 1,046 multiplied by $\frac{33}{500}$ equals 69. This same operation is carried out for transfers to the other continuing candidates, the formula being:

$$\frac{\text{Number of surplus votes}}{\text{Number of transferable votes}} \times \text{Number of votes for continuing candidate}$$

It will be noted that there is a difference of procedure in the transfer of surplus votes and the transfer of votes from eliminated candidates. In the case of candidates being eliminated, *all* of his votes are transferred since, *ex hypothesi*, none of them can be used to assist in his election; while in the case of a candidate whose surplus is being redistributed only a proportion of his votes are transferred since some have already been used to assist in his election.

After the transfer of McLoughlin's surplus, there are three candidates left – Gallagher, MacSharry and Gilhawley – competing for the two remaining seats. None of these candidates has reached the quota, but further transfer of surpluses would be pointless. MacSharry and Gallagher are therefore declared elected and Gilhawley is the runner-up. At this last stage of the count, it is possible to gain election without reaching the quota. That is because there are a total of 1,158 votes which are non-transferable, that is, no further preferences have been marked upon them and therefore they cannot be redistributed after the candidate whom they have been used to support has been eliminated or has been elected with a surplus of votes. If enough of those 1,158 votes had been transferred to Gilhawley, they could have helped him secure the quota and defeat Gallagher for the third seat. As it is, the non-transferable votes of those eliminated and those cast for the runner-up, Gilhawley, are the only votes which have not been used to help select a winning candidate, and they are equal to only 7,835 votes, 26 per cent of the total. Even so, those who voted for Gilhawley have at least the consolation that amongst the elected members there is one, McLoughlin, who belongs to a party which they support; while those whose votes are non-transferable have deliberately chosen to abstain if their favoured candidate or candidates does not need their vote. The remaining 22,139, 74 per cent of the total, have been used to assist in the election of a candidate of the voter's choice. Each party secures one seat for polling the number of votes indicated in the quota. Therefore, the single transferable vote will secure a rough proportionality of seats to votes. Moreover, each party will be represented in the legislature by its most popular candidates.

One may contrast this with the result in Liverpool, Walton in 1979 where 65 per cent of the votes were wasted in that they did not assist in electing any candidate and where, in any case, the candidate was chosen by the party organisation and the elector had to accept him unless he wished to vote for the opposition. Eric Heffer is a prominent figure on the Left wing of the Labour Party and there must be many Right-wing Labour supporters for whom he can have little appeal, yet they had no alternative but to vote for him if they wished to avoid a Conservative victory in the constituency. In effect, therefore, the candidate was chosen not by the voters but by the selection committee, and the electorate was unable to express an opinion on the type of Labour candidate which it wanted.

Under the single transferable vote, however – as in other multi-member systems – the elector can choose between different members of the same party, and need not be forced to accept a candidate whose political tendencies he does not like. Indeed, it is not uncommon for sitting members to be defeated by other candidates from the same party and this fate was suffered by 13 out of the 32 defeated members in the 1977 election. Thus each party comes to be represented by the candidates whom the voters, rather than the selection committee, most favour.

The system, therefore, allows a particularly popular candidate to escape an adverse swing against his party. In 1977, for example, Fianna Fáil won a seat from Fine Gael in Dun Laoghaire, the constituency of the outgoing Taoiseach (Prime Minister), Liam Cosgrave, to give Fianna Fáil two seats in the constituency compared with one each to Fine Gael and Labour. Yet Cosgrave was still able to win the largest number of first preference votes – 11,024 – over two thousand more than any other candidate, and so it was his Fine Gael colleague with only 1,472 first preference votes, who lost his seat. Thus the electorate was able to show its support for Cosgrave while still voting against his party. By contrast, the swing against Labour in Britain in 1979 cost Shirley Williams her seat even though she was alleged to be a popular and effective constituency member. Under the single transferable vote, the electors of Hertford and Stevenage (which would be part of a multi-member constituency comprising one-half of Hertfordshire), would be able to vote against Labour while still retaining Shirley Williams as one of the MPs for Hertfordshire, if they wished to do so.

Thus one of the central features of the single transferable vote is that it combines a primary election with a general election. It avoids the expense of carrying out separate primaries which are generally characterised by lower turnout than general elections. Moreover, the victor in a primary becomes the party's *sole* nominee, and those party members and supporters who happen to favour an alternative candidate are compelled to vote for a candidate who is not to their taste. The single transferable vote, on the other hand, offers a primary in which *all* electors, not merely paid-up members of a political party, can participate. It allows the elector rather than the party to choose which candidates he wishes to represent him. It puts the elector face to face with the candidates without interposing the party machine between them.

The 1973 general election in Sligo–Leitrim showed very remarkable differences from 1969. Shortly before the 1973 election, Labour decided to abandon its futile policy of independence and to enter into a coalition agreement with Fine Gael in order to oust Fianna Fáil, the majority party in Ireland which had been in power for the previous sixteen years. Labour and Fine Gael therefore drew up a common programme and asked their supporters to treat the two parties as electoral allies and transfer their votes from one party to the other in a disciplined way when the candidates of their preferred party – Labour or Fine Gael – were eliminated. In Sligo–Leitrim, Labour put up only one candidate in 1973, and he was soon eliminated. But the pattern of transfers from Labour was very different from what it had been in 1969. For in that year, when Higgins, the last Labour candidate, was eliminated, 561 of his 1,812 votes – 31 per cent – went to Fianna Fáil candidates, and 586 – 32 per cent – were non-transferable, leaving only 665 – 37 per cent – to be transferred to Fine Gael. The transfer of the 586 non-transferable votes to Gilhawley would have elected him in place of Gallagher for the third seat.

In 1973, however, because of the coalition agreement, all but 316 – 15 per cent – of Higgins's votes went to Fine Gael candidates, and they played an essential role in ensuring that Fine Gael won the third seat. The single transferable vote thus allows even those voters supporting a hopeless candidate to assist in the election of another candidate of their choice and so avoid wasting their votes.

A further interesting feature of the 1973 election was the transfer of votes of Mooney, the eliminated Fianna Fáil candidate. At each election roughly 30 per cent of his votes went not to his Fianna Fáil colleagues but to McLoughlin of Fine Gael. In 1973, 1,438 of his 2,421 votes went to his party colleague, Brennan, while 786 votes went to Fine Gael candidates, which if used to support Brennan, could have ensured his election. Why did voters choose to break party ranks at this point?

Sligo–Leitrim comprises two counties, Sligo and one-third of Leitrim. In 1969 and 1973, Fianna Fáil put up two candidates, two from Sligo and one, Mooney, from Leitrim. The Fianna Fáil voters of Leitrim, too few to elect a deputy of their own, used their later preferences to elect a candidate from Leitrim of the opposition party, Fine Gael, rather than a Fianna Fáil candidate from Sligo. McLoughlin as the Fine Gael candidate from Leitrim benefited from the transfer of votes from Mooney both in 1969 and in 1973. In 1973, this gave Fine Gael two seats, while in 1969 it ensured that he rather than Gilhawley from Sligo would be the Fine Gael deputy elected to represent the constituency.

The combination of these two influences – the transferability of votes between Labour and Fine Gael, and the desire for a local candidate which benefited Fine Gael – allowed Fine Gael to win two seats in 1973, even though Fianna Fáil secured over 50 per cent of first preferences, a better result than in 1969. It will be evident, therefore, that the single transferable vote may not ensure perfect proportionality of seats to first preference votes.

Percentage share of first preference votes, in Sligo–Leitrim

	1969	1973
Fianna Fáil	46.7	50.6
Fine Gael	44.2	42.0
Labour	9.1	7.4

The same phenomenon can be noticed in Ireland as a whole. In 1973, Fianna Fáil secured a higher percentage of the vote than in 1969, and the total percentage vote of Fine Gael and Labour was lower than in 1969 (although the percentage share of the vote for Labour exaggerates the decline in its vote since it fought only 35 constituencies in 1973 as compared to 42 constituencies in 1969). Nevertheless Fine Gael and Labour succeeded in winning more seats than Fianna Fáil and ousting it from government.

All constituencies

	1969 % share of first preference votes	Seats	% seats	1973 % share of first preference votes	Seats	% seats
Fianna Fáil	45.7	74	51.7	46.2	68	47.6
Fine Gael	34.1	50	35.0	35.1	54	37.8
Labour	17.0	18	12.6	13.7	19	13.3
(Fine Gael & Labour)	51.1	68	47.6	48.8	73	51.1
Inds. and others	3.2	1	0.7	5.0	2	1.4

The explanation for this at first sight anomalous result lies in the more effective use of transfers between Fine Gael and Labour in 1973 following the coalition agreement. In 1969, seven seats (including Sligo–Leitrim) won by Fianna Fáil would have been vulnerable to Fine Gael or Labour had there been co-operation over vote transfers. Had these seven been won by Fine Gael or Labour, Fianna Fáil would have lost its majority in the Dáil.

In 1973, six of these seven seats were won by Fine Gael or Labour; only two other seats were gained by the allies from Fianna Fáil. In these eight seats, the fall in the percentage of non-transferable votes shows how the coalition agreement facilitated transfers between the two component parties of the coalition.

Average percentage of non-transferable votes in the eight seats won by Fianna Fáil in 1969, but by Fine Gael or Labour in 1973 (Laois–Offaly, Sligo–Leitrim, Longford–Westmeath, Roscommon–Leitrim, West Mayo, Waterford, Kildare, and North Tipperary).

1969	1973
6.39%	1.83%

Thus, in 1969, Fine Gael and Labour failed to secure the percentage of seats to which their first preference votes entitled them since they refused to co-operate by calling for transfers to assist each other's candidates; while in 1973, effectiveness of transfer gave them a bonus in terms of seats.

In general, the single transferable vote deviates a little more from party proportionality than list-type systems but it secures a far higher degree of proportionality than plurality and majority systems. Like nearly all electoral systems, the single transferable vote gives a bonus to the largest party and generally to the second largest party while handicapping minor parties. In the Irish Republic, the largest party has always secured a bonus, and the second largest party has usually secured a bonus, while the third party – Labour – has usually secured less seats than the number to which it would be proportionately entitled.

Because the bonus is smaller under the single transferable vote, it is more difficult for a party with less than 50 per cent of the vote to secure a working majority in the Dáil than in the House of Commons. But, since independence, Ireland has been ruled by nine single-party majority governments lasting for 34½ years, seven minority governments lasting 14 years (four of which lasted less than a year) and three coalition governments lasting 10 years and 5 months. The single-party governments have generally lacked large majorities; in 1965 Fianna Fáil won only 72 out of 143 seats, and in 1969 74 out of 143: in 1973, the Coalition enjoyed a precarious overall majority of only three seats. In spite of this, however, governments have generally been able to rely upon their majority in the Dáil and to choose their own time for dissolution without being forced out of office. The Irish parliamentarian displays strong party loyalty, and small majorities have not led to unstable government. Indeed, with one party, Fianna Fáil, having enjoyed two unbroken periods of sixteen years in office in the last fifty years (1932–48, 1957–73) it has been suggested that stagnant would be a better description of the state of Irish politics.[24]

Coalition governments, moreover, function very much as a single-party government with comparatively little strain between the coalition partners. The leading opposition party sets up a shadow administration and acts much as Her Majesty's Opposition does in Britain, with the leader of the opposition being paid a salary like his British counterpart. Thus the Dáil, like the House of Commons, is an arena in which government confronts opposition; there is a fusion of powers as in Britain, and not a separation as in most Continental countries where the legislature can act as a genuine check on government. The single transferable vote seems, therefore, to be in general compatible with British parliamentary norms and procedures, and there is certainly no reason to believe that it need result in weak or unstable government.

Nor need the single transferable vote necessarily lead to a proliferation of parties. It is less favourable to smaller parties than list systems of proportional representation because it imposes a higher threshold, a local threshold of between 12½ per cent in a seven-member constituency to 25 per cent in a three-member constituency, rather than a national one as in most list systems. Indeed a smaller party must secure a larger number of votes to win a seat under the single transferable vote, albeit over a wider geographical area, than it would need to win under the plurality system. Therefore small parties can only win seats if they can secure a broad measure of support.

However, because the single transferable vote encourages the parties to present a balanced slate of candidates, including representatives of all the various factions in the party, it may serve to discourage party fragmentation. The system offers a premium to large parties and to parties which can work together, and therefore there is an incentive for different factions within a party to coalesce since a splinter group might well fail to surmount the quota. In the Irish Republic, the three main parties have between them monopolised over 96 per cent of the seats in the Dáil and over 92 per cent of first preference votes at every election since 1965. Even the controversy within Fianna Fáil in 1970 over the supply of arms to Northern Ireland, when four cabinet ministers resigned within a week, did not serve to disrupt the party. One of the ministers established a new republican party, Aontacht Éireann, but it did not succeed in winning any seats; two others were expelled from Fianna Fáil and stood as Independent Fianna Fáil candidates, with one securing election; while the fourth, Charles Haughey, worked his way back into favour, and became Taoiseach (Prime Minister) upon the resignation of Jack Lynch in 1979.

Malta and Tasmania also have only two parties represented in the legislature. Indeed, Tasmania is the only province of Australia where the two-party system has succeeded in beating off challengers to its hegemony.

There is no Country Party in Tasmania, and, in the 1950s, the right-wing breakaway from the Australian Labour Party, the Democratic Labour Party, was unable to win seats since the Australian Labour Party used to put up a right-wing candidate in its slate of candidates. In Northern Ireland, on the other hand, as we shall see, adoption of the single transferable vote has not led to a two-party system, but has intensified party fragmentation.

Smaller parties are offered reinsurance under the single transferable vote since, even if they are too small to win representation, votes cast for them are not wasted but transferred to other parties. A vote for a smaller party cannot let another party win the seat on a split vote. It is therefore possible even for supporters of parties which cannot reach the threshold to secure representation. But a small party can exert influence upon the political system only if it is prepared, as Labour was in 1973, to enter into a coalition agreement with another party so that its transfers may be made in a disciplined way. The system facilitates agreement between the parties because it does not require, as in Britain, an electoral pact involving the withdrawal of candidates to secure co-operation. Evey elector can still vote for the party and candidate of his first choice so long as he transfers in accordance with the coalition agreement. But he cannot, of course, be compelled to transfer. If, in 1973, Labour or Fine Gael voters had objected to the coalition agreement, they could have shown their feelings simply by making their votes non-transferable after having indicated preferences for their own party candidates. Thus, the single transferable vote prevents coalitions being constructed in the proverbial smoke-filled rooms; voters have to endorse it if it is to prove effective. In 1977, although Fine Gael and Labour again appealed jointly to the electorate for support, there was a significant decrease in Labour transfers to Fine Gael and an increase in transfers to Fianna Fáil; and this helped Fianna Fáil win 84 out of 147 seats in the Dáil, the largest number gained by any single party in the history of the state, on 50.63 per cent of first preference votes, giving it a 'bonus' of 6.13 per cent in seats won above those to which it would be entitled in terms of party proportionality.

Transfers from Labour, with Fianna Fáil and Fine Gael (and possibly others) still competing

To	1973	1977
Fianna Fáil	9.68%	13.93%
Fine Gael	71.47%	58.53%
Others	4.06%	14.98%
Non-transferable	14.79%	12.55%

Source: Richard Sinnott, 'The electorate' in Howard R. Penniman (ed.), *Ireland at the Polls: The Dáil Elections of 1977* (American Enterprise Institute, 1978), p. 63.

The Irish electorate generally has the opportunity of choosing between a one-party Fianna Fáil government and a coalition, and it usually, though not invariably, prefers a single-party government. It would be difficult to argue, however, that coalition governments in Ireland have been less effective than Fianna Fáil governments, and the stereotyped arguments against coalition cannot find much support in Irish political experience.

It would, however, be foolish to claim that the single transferable vote achieves all that its supporters claim for it. Some early advocates claimed that it might do away with organised political parties entirely, and all hoped that it would replace the power of the party machine with the sovereignty of the voter. But, wherever the single transferable vote is in operation, politics is still party politics. Indeed the Irish Republic, Tasmania and Malta are closer to two-party systems than Britain or Canada.

Nor is party organisation irrelevant under the single transferable vote. It still has a role to play, although it is an attenuated role as compared with the experience of countries using plurality or list systems. The party organisation must attempt so to divide the constituency amongst first preference voters as to secure even first preference support for all of its candidates. Otherwise there is a danger of less favoured candidates being eliminated at an early stage of the count, and not being available to receive transfers from popular candidates. In Ireland it is customary for candidates to divide the constituency between them, and the Unionist parties in Northern Ireland have also learnt to manipulate the system in this way. To the extent that this occurs, the choice offered to the voter may seem illusory; but of course he is not compelled to accept the advice of his party and may use his first preference vote for whichever candidate he pleases.

Moreover, it is in the interest of the party although not of the voter, to ensure that its own favoured candidates are elected. In Ireland, 'dummy' candidates are occasionally put up for this purpose, so that an incumbent may be re-elected without danger; and in elections for the Australian Senate, voters are handed 'how to vote' cards telling them the order in which they should place their preferences. So far the voter has always followed these instructions, but in Ireland they would be counter-productive because of the strongly localist political culture and the electorate would be likely to resent dictation.

If a party can persuade its supporters to 'plump' as the Unionists in Northern Ireland have done, that is, vote only for candidates of their own party with the rest of their preferences non-transferable, this may be of considerable assistance to it. For the party will be receiving transfers from other parties without contributing any to them; and a party with a more solid vote will always perform better under the single transferable vote than a party whose preferences are not solid but 'leaky'.

Finally, Irish governments have been able to subvert the purposes of the single transferable vote by implementing partisan boundary revisions transforming three-member constituencies into four-member constituencies where they are weak, since two seats can occasionally be won on $37\frac{1}{2}$ per cent of the vote, and can usually be won on a vote of 42 per cent; and transforming four-member constituencies into three-member constituencies where they are strong, since 47 per cent of the vote will normally secure two out of the three seats unless the vote of the opposition is completely solid.[25] Such attempts at gerrymandering, however, are vulnerable to unexpected swings in electoral opinion, and in 1977, they backfired against the coalition, causing it to lose seats rather than gain them.

In the Irish Republic, the dominant form of political organisation in rural areas is not the national but the local political machine, a complex network of individuals bound by promises and favours to a particular candidate, and working to secure his election. Politics is marked by an absence of deep ideological divisions, and political allegiance has been based as much upon traditional loyalties as upon issues. Where personal loyalty rather than partisan commitment is the basis for party organisation, the local machines have 'inhibited political recruitment, stifled debate and competition, and contributed to perpetuating the local status quo'.[26] Members of the Dáil are seen not as representatives of ideologies or policy-makers, but as brokers between the electorate and the administration. Their central task is to assist their constituents in dealing with public authorities. When asked in 1977 what was the most important criterion determining their vote, a representative sample of the Irish electorate gave the following answers:

Quality of the Taoiseach	8%
Quality of the ministers who will form the government	18%
Party policies	21%
Confidence that the candidate will look after the needs of the constituency	46%
Don't know	7%

Source: Sinnott, 'The electorate' in Penniman (ed.), *Ireland at the Polls*, p. 62.

Politics, therefore, is strongly localist, even parochial, and a candidate can easily lose his seat if, by concentrating upon the grand political issues, he neglects to cultivate his constituency. In 1977, 86 per cent of the members of the Dáil had been born either in the constituency which they represented or in an adjacent constituency, and 93 per cent lived in their constituency or one adjacent to it. Membership of a local authority is both a useful stepping-stone to the Dáil and valuable to a member already elected since it increases his ability to deal with the problems of constituents most of which have to be resolved at local level. It serves also to maintain a politician's local connections, and to prevent potential competitors from building up an alternative power-base. In 1977, 78 per cent of Dáil members were serving or had served as members of local authorities, and 17 per cent had begun local government service *after* their election to the Dáil.

In contrast to the hopes of Hare and Mill, the single transferable vote has not resulted in the election of a superior class of legislator. In the Irish Republic, there are frequent complaints of the low level of talent of members of the Dáil, and of their limited and parochial outlook. Nor has the system resulted in a legislature which is independent-minded. For because of the spirit of loyalty which lies so deeply rooted in Irish cultural life, 'a loyalty to institutions and especially persons rather than ideas',[27] party rebellion is even less frequent in the Republic than in the House of Commons; and because members of the Dáil are so preoccupied with constituency business, the Irish parliament 'has never been much more than a rubber stamp for the executive, to a degree which leaves the level of government accountability to the people's representatives well below what might be expected in a democratic governmental system'.[28] Paradoxically, the emphasis laid upon the member's role as an intermediary between the citizen and the administration has led to a divorce between local and national issues. The result has been a government and an administration comparatively free from the processes of parliamentary inquiry and scrutiny common in most other democracies.

In Ireland, as in Malta, it could be argued that the single transferable vote is 'ideally suited to the needs of the traditional patron–politician with his own localized, semi-private political organization of canvassers, mock candidates and clients'.[29] It does not, however, follow that the system must necessarily work in the same way in countries with very different political cultures, based less upon face-to-face relationships and particularistic attitudes, and with a greater interest in political programmes and issues.

In Northern Ireland, for example, the introduction of the single transferable vote for all elections other than those to Westminster has not so far encouraged the development of similar political patterns. Instead, it has permitted the electorate to display very clearly its views upon the future of the province. These have proved to be very different from those expected by policy-makers in London when the single transferable vote was introduced in 1973 following the demise of Stormont.

For the belief then was that the sectarianism of the political parties in Northern Ireland did not reflect the real attitudes of its citizens. The electorate, it was thought, was tired of a politics which polarised the province into two irreconcilable communities. If given the opportunity through reform of the electoral system, it would support non-sectarian parties such as Alliance rather than the Catholic or Unionist parties. Moreover, since the single transferable vote would allow voters to support new parties without letting the opposition win seats on a split vote, the Unionist monolith would crumble, electors would support moderate Unionists who believed in power-sharing and the intransigent Unionists would fall by the wayside.

The reality has been very different. Admittedly, candidates advocating violence have been on the whole unsuccessful in Northern Ireland's electoral politics; but the forces of the 'centre', Alliance and the Unionist Party of Northern Ireland (UPNI), have been no more successful under the single transferable vote than under the plurality system. Alliance, for example, has fought six elections, three under the single transferable vote and three under the plurality system, as shown in the accompanying table.

		Alliance: % of votes
June 1973	To Northern Ireland Assembly (STV)	12
February 1974	To Westminster (plurality)	6
October 1974	To Westminster (plurality)	8
May 1975	To Northern Ireland Convention (STV)	11
May 1979	To Westminster (plurality)	11.8
June 1979	To European Assembly (STV)	6.8

The figures for the two general elections of 1974 understate the extent of support for Alliance, since it contested only five seats on each occasion. In contested seats, its average vote was 12 per cent. The Unionist Party has as predicted splintered, but the main beneficiary has been not the moderates, but Ian Paisley's Democratic Unionist Party.

There has been hardly any transfer of votes from parties representing one community to parties representing the other, except in the Northern Ireland Convention Elections of 1975. Then in S. Belfast and S. Antrim, there were transfers of about 90 per cent of the votes, first of the last SDLP candidate to Alliance, and then from Alliance to the UPNI. For those seeking the breakdown of sectarianism in Northern Ireland, such a voting pattern offers a small glimmer of hope.[30]

The main effect of the single transferable vote in Northern Ireland has been, not to erode, but to heighten sectarian loyalties by reflecting them more accurately. The old Unionist Party was in some respects a moderating force in that, dominated by businessmen and the landed gentry, it forswore the crude populism of a Paisley which, no doubt, represents all too accurately the feelings of the less sophisticated section of the Northern Ireland electorate. The single transferable vote in Northern Ireland has proved to be a mirror which reflects the face of the electorate; if British liberals find the reflection unattractive, they must seek an explanation for it in the historical experience of the province and the relations between the two communities. They should not blame the electoral system.

For the single transferable vote is in essence a *transparent* electoral system. It reflects the cleavages already existing in a society accurately enough to ensure that the legislature is a true representation of the feelings of the community. Where, as in the Irish Republic and Tasmania, political issues tend to be subordinate to other loyalties, the legislature will reflect this condition. The single transferable vote will intensify localist feelings, the legislature will tend to be dominated by the parish pump, but the result will probably be a highly stable if not stagnant political structure resistant to extremist views. But in a society, such as Northern Ireland, dominated by the one central issue of the relationship between the two communities, the electoral system will reflect the polarisation. It is unfortunate for the political scientist that there is no example of its working in a society such as Britain where localism is weak and where voting behaviour is based upon social and economic patterns and upon attitudes to political issues.

Nevertheless, if the main criterion for the choice of an electoral system is that it accurately represents the opinions of the electorate without giving excessive weight to the party machine, then the single transferable vote is the best of the systems which we have examined. It is easy for the voter to understand, and he can use it to elect the government and candidates of his choice. The Irish electorate has twice voted to retain it in referendums and rejected proposals to adopt the British plurality system. Opponents, claiming that it raises insuperable technical difficulties and is incomprehensible to the ordinary voter, have been conclusively refuted by experience. The central issue for Britain, therefore, is not whether the system is a practical one, but whether it is desirable. That issue will now be examined.

ELECTORAL REFORM AND COALITION GOVERNMENT

We have seen that the shortcomings of the plurality system are its failure to produce a government which is either representative or strong in any other sense than that of enjoying a majority in the House of Commons. These shortcomings can only be remedied by electoral reform.

In the light of our discussion of alternative electoral systems, many of the conventional objections to proportional representation seem to lack substance. Electoral reform would be unlikely to encourage extremist parties. Indeed, both the West German system and the single transferable vote would make it difficult for extremists to gain power unless they enjoyed considerable popular support. The West German system, if adopted in Britain, would require a regional threshold of 5 per cent.* Under the single transferable vote, the threshold would be higher, being one-sixth plus 1 vote in a five-member constituency. In no recent election

*The threshold would have to be regional rather than national so as not to handicap the nationalist parties or the parties which contest elections only in Northern Ireland.

in Britain would the National Front, the Communist Party or any other extremist party have won a parliamentary seat under either system.

Nor would the adoption of either of these two systems lead to a proliferation of parties. In West Germany, the threshold has proved a disincentive to small parties. The single transferable vote, by making the parties more elastic, might lessen the need for new protest parties – as it has done in the Irish Republic and Tasmania which have fewer parties represented in their legislatures than Britain. Indeed, insofar as the Liberal vote is a protest vote directed against specific policy positions of the main parties, the single transferable vote might not help them;[31] for if it made the Conservative and Labour parties broader in their appeal, Liberals might lose the benefit of that protest vote. Similarly, Scots voters might desert the SNP if they could choose candidates within the major parties committed to greater autonomy for Scotland. If the single transferable vote allowed changes in public sentiment to be better reflected within the existing party structure, new parties and protest movements would be less necessary.

However, indisputably proportional representation in Britain would make it more difficult (unless voting patterns changed radically) for one party to win a majority in the Commons: coalition or minority governments would become more likely and majority government less likely. This, in the view of its critics, would make for weak government.

Coalitions, it is argued, will be dependent for support upon varying, precarious and uncertain majorities. Each measure would have to be fought for in Parliament not as part of an agreed programme, but by offering potential waverers whatever price is necessary for their support. Coalition government, therefore, blurs the lines of responsibility in the Commons, and makes it more difficult for the electorate to hold governments accountable for their policies and to vote for a genuine alternative government. If electoral reform led to more frequent coalition governments, then, it would deprive the elector of his sovereignty rather than enhance it since the policies of a government would be decided not through clear endorsement at a general election but by dubious bargaining in the Commons.

To meet this argument, it is first necessary to distinguish between two different kinds of coalition – a 'grand coalition' comprising leaders of all the main parties, and a more limited coalition of two (or more) parties co-operating together, but opposed by another party or parties in the legislature. The former is really only suitable in wartime when, as between 1940 and 1945, there is a clear and agreed objective. When formed in peacetime, it can endanger democratic government, since if all the main streams of parliamentary opinion unite, they leave the electorate no alternative but to support extremist groups if they seek a change of government. Thus the grand coalition in Germany between 1928 and 1930 was blamed for the depression, and voters turned to the Communists and Nazis; while in the years of the Grand Coalition between the CDU/CSU and the SPD from 1966 to 1969, the New Left gained in strength and the neo-Nazi NPD nearly succeeded in surmounting the 5 per cent threshold.

Coalitions of the second type, on the other hand, can be a natural response to a situation in which no single party enjoys a majority of the seats in Parliament. In this situation, a coalition government will almost certainly have a vigorous opposition championing alternative policies, and it can provide stronger government than could be offered by any one party. For example, in the 1920s or the mid-1970s, a coalition of the Left would have enjoyed stronger support in Parliament and the country than weak minority governments. They would have reshaped political conflict, but would not have abolished it.

In West Germany and Ireland, the electorate has been able to vote for coalition – in West Germany since 1969, and Ireland in 1973 – and against it – in Ireland in 1977. Both the West German and the Irish systems give the electors the opportunity to vote for a particular combination of parties, and they have taken advantage of this opportunity. Since 1969, FDP voters have indicated by their constituency votes that they favour a coalition with the SDP, and in Ireland Labour voters in 1973 indicated that they endorsed coalition with Fine Gael, while in 1969 the high percentage of Labour non-transferable votes, and in 1977 the increase in Labour votes which transferred to Fianna Fáil, were an indication that Labour voters were hostile to coalition. There is no reason, therefore, why coalitions formed under a system of proportional representation should not be specifically endorsed or rejected by the electorate.

An electoral system which allows the voter to make a positive choice for coalition widens the sovereignty of the elector, rather than diminishing it. By contrast, the plurality system denies the voter this opportunity. For the plurality system, as we have seen, exaggerates majorities and enables one party to form a majority government even if it receives less than 40 per cent of the vote, and that party can then claim, however spuriously, a mandate for the whole of its programme.

The system does not allow the elector to signal his desire for a coalition; it does not enable him to say that he would like to see co-operation between a specific combination of parties. Nor can a coalition, formed under the plurality system, easily appeal to the country without there being serious effects on constituency parties in a general election campaign. For, to avoid splitting the vote, there must be reciprocal withdrawal of candidates; this will usually involve a bitter dispute between the parties at constituency level as to which candidate should stand down, and even if agreement is reached, the elector may lose his opportunity of voting for the party of his choice.

Coalitions in Britain, therefore, have been restricted to wartime and to what Gladstone called 'a great and palpable emergency of state'.[32] They are departures from the political norm and not genuine attempts at power-sharing by parties which, lacking sufficient support in the country to implement their policies, wish to co-operate in putting through, on an agreed basis, only those elements of their programmes capable of commanding public support.

Under proportional representation, the elector is not deprived of his right to elect a majority government if he wishes to do so; and this right has been exercised in Ireland in 1977 and in West Germany in 1957. What it prevents is an overall majority in the Commons for any party gaining significantly less than 50 per cent of the popular vote. The issue then is not whether coalition government is preferable to majority government, but whether, in a situation in which no party can claim the allegiance of a majority of the electorate, majority government is preferable to a coalition or to a minority government.

Of course, any political party seeking to exercise the powers of government in a democracy must itself be a coalition bringing together those of different views in a spirit of co-operation. In Britain today, the issue is whether the coalitions which now comprise the main parties are sufficiently in agreement to be held together by anything more than the pursuit of power. When the parties are deeply divided, the policies emerging from an 'intra-party coalition' may be less representative, and reached less publicly than policies thrashed out in bargaining between separate parties. Unless there is more public involvement in the process of policy-making in the political parties, therefore, an 'intra-party coalition' might be less publicly accountable than an 'inter-party coalition'.

Nor need a coalition government be weak. The governments of 1918–22 made many controversial decisions, some of which are now regarded as mistaken, but they could not be accused of weakness. Indeed, the Lloyd George Coalition was rejected by the Conservative Party in 1922 for the opposite reason, that its policies were so controversial that they were in danger of splitting the Party. When Edward Heath sought a coalition government in March 1974, it was because he believed that it could provide stronger leadership than a purely Conservative government. Because a coalition government would enjoy broader public support, it could well be stronger than a single-party government and find it easier to implement policies which are opposed by powerful pressure groups.

Critics of electoral reform have argued that it would lead to parliamentary instability; and indeed, the early advocates of the single transferable vote believed that it would result in a Parliament composed of individualists, with party ties weakening almost to vanishing point. Yet, the examples of West Germany and Ireland show that proportional representation is not incompatible with party loyalty. If the power of Parliament were to increase under proportional representation, therefore, this would not necessarily be because the Commons inflicted more formal defeats on a government, but because the government would be forced to take account of a wider range of views in framing its legislation. Major interest groups would, as now, be consulted on legislation affecting them, but agreement between government and interest groups would be dependent upon whether Parliament, as representative of the electorate, was prepared to ratify it. Moreover, under proportional representation a party might be less able to implement unpopular sectarian legislation, popular with the party activists but less so with the country at large. This would lessen the number of abrupt reversals of policy, and counteract the centrifugal tendencies recently apparent in British government. The consequence, therefore, might well be stronger government co-existing with a House of Commons which, because more representative of the electorate, was also more assertive, and able to counterbalance the power of corporate groups. This too would increase the sovereignty of the elector.

For it is an illusion, and no less an illusion for being so frequently proclaimed, that a pattern of two alternating parties in power gives rise to strong government. Both Edward Heath in 1974, and James Callaghan during the 'winter of discontent' in 1978–9, discovered that it makes for weak government in periods of crisis since government cannot rely upon the broad public support needed to take unpopular measures. In 1918 Lloyd George and the Conservatives favoured coalition precisely because they did not believe that a government dominated by a single party could undertake the ambitious task of postwar reconstruction. In 1931, the National Government was formed because it was thought that a single-party government could not take the harsh measures needed to combat the depression; while in October 1974, Edward Heath proposed coalition because he did not believe that a single-party government could resolve the problem of inflation. In these crises, the model of alternating parties was regarded by many politicians, and in 1918 and 1931 by the majority of the electorate, as inapplicable.

Conversely, in the absence of crisis, it may be that the system of alternating majority party rule offers 'strong' government, that is, government backed by a majority in the Commons, just when it is least needed. For it is difficult to discover what benefits were gained as a result of Labour enjoying an overall Commons majority between 1966 and 1970, or from the Conservatives being immune from parliamentary defeat on major measures of policy since 1979, so that they were able to implement policies which were unpopular in the country. Might not the quality of the decisions made and of the legislation produced have been improved if they had been required to co-operate with other parties in Parliament in order to carry out their programme? There is thus no evidence that majority government has been particularly capable in resolving Britain's social and economic problems; and indeed it may have aggravated them.

More frequent coalition government would have an important effect upon the style of political leadership, requiring the parties to choose leaders able to work with others rather than abrasive leaders intent upon implementing a sectarian programme. Proportional representation, therefore, would be more likely to produce leaders with the cross-bench mind, a quality which, Henry Fairlie has argued, is usually found in the most successful party leaders. Citing Gladstone, Disraeli, Lloyd George and Churchill, Fairlie remarks that 'Even when they have not crossed party boundaries, the greatest politicians have nearly always had minds of their own.' 'The opinions and attitudes of a party can all too easily become rigid, unless it is led by politicians whose minds reach beyond party.'[33]

There is therefore no reason why the electorate should be frightened of coalition government or equate it with weak or vacillating government. On the contrary, it could mean a less rigid structure of party politics, a break with the politics of class conflict and the introduction of a less sectarian approach to the main economic and social issues of the day.

THE MOST SUITABLE SYSTEM

We cannot conclude without specifying which proportional system would be the most suitable for Britain.

We argued that the additional member system recommended by the Hansard Society's Commission was too full of anomalies to be generally acceptable, and that the regional list system could work only at the cost of fragmenting parties; it could not provide a genuine test of popular opinion when the parties contained within themselves as many conflicting currents of opinion as the British parties do, today. This leaves two electoral systems, the West German mixed system and the single transferable vote.

Adoption of either of these systems would do much to cure the shortcomings which we have earlier identified. Either would ensure that no government could secure a majority in the Commons without the support of nearly 50 per cent of the electorate, a larger percentage than has been achieved by any British government in recent years. Either system would therefore encourage the parties to broaden the basis of their appeal, and, if unable to secure sufficient support to govern on their own, to share power in a coalition. Either system, therefore, would exert a centripetal rather than a centrifugal influence upon British politics.

Under either system, each major party would secure representation in all parts of the country. Under the West German system, this would be secured through the party list. The Conservatives, presumably, would give a high place on the list to candidates from Glasgow and Liverpool, and Labour might do the same with candidates from the South and South-west. In West Germany, as we have seen, no distinction is made in the *Bundestag* between constituency and list members, but in Britain where experience of the single-member constituency system is more deeply rooted, it might be that list members would come to be regarded as second-class MPs. Conservatives from Durham, Labour MPs might say, are in the Commons only because of the electoral system and not because they were positively supported by the electorate. This could detract from their legitimacy as MPs.

Under the single transferable vote, on the other hand, each major party in a five-member constituency would win, at the very least, one seat and probably two. Therefore the two parties would have a greater incentive to replace sectional appeals with a programme capable of attracting voters from different social groups in every part of the country. They would be more likely, therefore, to adopt a broader approach both to policy-making and to the task of government. Finally, either system would enable more women to enter the Commons, and would allow the immigrant community to elect, if it so wished, its own spokesmen in Parliament. This would make the Commons more representative in the sense that the opinions of a wider proportion of the electorate would be heard there.

But the similarities between the West German system and the single transferable vote are less important than the differences between them. Indeed, they differ in their basic aim. The West German system seeks to represent parties in proportion to their support amongst the electorate. Like the plurality system, the West German system makes the assumption that every vote must be a party vote; but, unlike the plurality system, it seeks to secure proportional representation of parties. Such an aim may be adequate if the parties represent the main strands of opinion in the country so that the divisions between parties correspond with those in the country. That is not the case in Britain today.

Under a list system, the right of the voter is equated with his right to support a political party. The voter whose opinions cut across party divisions – such as the Labour supporter who is in favour of Britain's membership of the EEC, or the Conservative who favours an incomes policy – finds his vote for his party is construed as a vote for all of its policies. He finds that he is in a no-man's land of politics, and his influence is at a discount. The West German system does not allow him to support some policies of his party but not others. It secures representation only for party opinions. It insists, in J. S. Mill's words, 'that all the opinions, feelings and interests of all the members of the community should be merged in the single consideration of which party shall predominate . . . We require a House of Commons which shall be a fitting representation of all the feelings of the people and not merely of their party feelings.'[34] Both the West German system and the plurality system, therefore, limit the power of decision of the elector, making it difficult for him to express a view on any issue which cuts across party lines.

The West German system, moreover, is the only proportional system in Western Europe which gives the elector no choice of candidate (unless he is a party member). It makes the assumption that while supporting a particular cause he will not care who represents it in the legislature. Hare criticised the plurality system because it gave parties the right to settle 'not indeed who the voters shall elect, but who alone they shall have the opportunity of electing'.[35] The same objection can be made to the West German system. The power given to the parties to select candidates means that when a party is divided into factions, each faction's representation in the legislature will depend upon the decisions of selection committees and party meetings, and not its support amongst the electorate.

In West Germany, the parties are themselves part of the constitution, and given statutory recognition in electoral law. The party member has a statutory right to choose, either directly or indirectly, his candidate. In Britain, by contrast, the internal workings of the parties are hardly regulated at all by statute law. To require the parties to hold primary elections – a necessary step if the system was not to place an altogether excessive power in the hands of the party machine – would be to abandon that long-held convention. It would be a constitutional innovation in British politics since constituency parties in Britain are separate and broadly autonomous entities, joined with the national parties by affiliation rather than as part of a hierarchical chain of command.

Even if primaries were accepted, they would offer less than the elector could secure under the single transferable vote. For only the paid-up party member would participate in choosing a candidate. The single transferable vote, by contrast, offers to every elector the right to choose a candidate without involving a separate primary election.

The single transferable vote is superior to the West German system because it gives the voter a choice both of policy and of personnel; and it allows the voter whose opinions do not coincide with party divisions an influence equal to that exercised by the party voter. It can, therefore, be used to resolve disputes between factions of a party, and would allow the elector rather than the party activist to resolve the dispute between Left and Right in the Labour Party. For by endorsing candidates from one wing of the party or the other, the voter could give a clear public indication of which tendency within the Party was the more popular. If a party refuses to present a balanced slate of candidates, it would lose support; if, for example, the Labour Party offered five Left-wing candidates in Liverpool, the Right-wing Labour voter could switch to a Liberal or independent candidate without fear of splitting the vote. Not to offer a balanced list, therefore, would be both blatant and counter-productive. The single transferable vote, therefore, would weaken the power of the selection committees to determine which faction of the Party was dominant in the House of Commons. For this power depends upon the safe seat, and under the single transferable vote, there are no safe seats. Thus the parties might become broad churches rather than narrow sects.

Moreover, the single transferable vote would offer better local representation than alternative systems. Under the plurality system, an MP with a safe seat has no particular incentive to be a good constituency member and because by convention one MP does not encroach upon the constituency of another, the elector has no redress if he is ill-served by his MP. With the single transferable vote, more MPs will be local residents, whereas under the plurality system a Conservative living in Durham or a Labour supporter in Bournemouth has no option but to seek a constituency in another part of the country if he wishes to enter the Commons.

By contrast with both the plurality system and the West German system, the single transferable vote allows no candidate the luxury of a safe seat (although there will be seats which are safe for parties). Every MP will be a constituency MP, and more electors would have an MP whose political outlook they could share. If a particular MP offered poor constituency service, he could be replaced by another from the same party. Therefore the personal qualities of the candidate would become a real election issue and would not be merged into the question of party allegiance. In Ireland, the result is, arguably, to give excessive weight to localist considerations, but in Britain, where local ties are considerably weaker, the single transferable vote might act as a countervailing force to excessive centralisation; and if MPs became more effective as intermediaries between the public and government, this could lessen alienation and the feeling of remoteness. For the fundamental difference between the West German system and the single transferable vote is that the former tends to the strengthening of political parties; whereas the single transferable vote tends to make them less rigid, more elastic and more responsive to the opinions of the electorate. The central argument of this book is that the parties need to be made more responsive to popular opinion, and since the single transferable vote is the instrument best designed to secure this aim, it is also the electoral system most suited to Britain's present condition.

Conclusion

This book has argued for wider use of the referendum and for the introduction of the single transferable vote. Both seek to achieve greater popular participation, and to replace the sovereignty of party by the sovereignty of the elector. Their functions are complementary. The referendum would ensure that the electorate was consulted on those major issues where a decision by the government would not be accepted by voters as legitimate. But its value is essentially limited. It could not do much to secure popular involvement on social and economic matters – the most important issues for many voters. In this sphere, decisions are often complex and interconnected, and cannot be separately referred to the voters. Therefore the main instrument of popular participation must remain the choice of government.

The single transferable vote attempts to widen this choice by allowing the electorate in a representative system to indicate which governmental decisions would be most in accordance with its own views. If it is, as we have argued, a transparent system, it would reflect without distortion the attitudes of the electorate. To the extent that it does, it yields what Courtney called 'personal substitution' such as 'makes the person within the actual representative of the people without, expressing the want which they themselves in their full numbers could not possibly with convenience come in to express themselves'.[1] Representative government comes to approach real self-government.

Nineteenth-century liberals believed that the consequences of self-government would be educative. By diffusing amongst the electorate a greater sense of personal responsibility for the actions of government, the decisions of government would acquire greater authority and legitimacy because they would be based upon a wider degree of public support. In this way, governments would have a better chance of resolving national problems.

For in a mature democracy these problems are as much political and psychological as they are economic or technical. They are not capable of mechanical resolution through applications of the social sciences because they depend crucially upon the mobilisation of popular consent. This consent requires that there be in the political system some focus for the public interest, a feeling that the policies of a government reflect more than merely the interests of its supporters. Such a community of interest cannot be assumed, but must be constructed through intelligent political action; but in Britain, the party system militates against the construction of any consensus which rises above class interest. It is for this reason that the attempt to secure agreement on matters such as the role of incomes policy, government intervention in industrial affairs, the reform of taxation and employee participation in industry is so unsuccessful. The political structure, because it entrenches class feeling, actually hinders the search for acceptable solutions and deprives governments of the authority needed to implement them, thereby making social and economic problems more difficult to resolve.

It is the rigidity of party which has prevented the political system from responding to social change – to the breakdown of deference, the growing power of interest groups, and the new status of organised labour. These developments are in themselves perhaps little more than a delayed consequence of universal suffrage, but they pose the question of whether a political system fashioned for a different age can be reformed to meet the needs of a more educated and sophisticated electorate. If it cannot, Britain will continue to endure a period of social disorganisation both extensive and profound.

The problem of refashioning the party system so that it takes account of changed social conditions is therefore as pressing and crucial to Britain's future as the extension of the franchise was in the nineteenth century. The nineteenth-century constitution survived because it was able to accommodate itself to the pressures of reform. The Victorians decided to make a 'leap in the dark' and found that democracy, contrary to the fears of its critics, made for both stability and progress. Cannot we meet the twentieth-century challenge to adapt the constitution in accordance with the new aspirations of the electorate with the same self-confidence and optimism as our Victorian forebears showed over a hundred years ago?

Notes to the text

INTRODUCTION, pp. 1–8

1. J. S. Mill, *Considerations on Representative Government* (1861), ch. 7; H. Maine: *Popular Government* (1885); M. Ostrogorski: *Democracy and the Organisation of Political Parties* (1902).
2. W. E. Gladstone, *Gleanings from Past Years* (1879), vol. 1, p. 236, quoted in A. H. Birch: *Representative and Responsible Government: An Essay on the British Constitution* (Allen and Unwin, 1964), p. 72.
3. H. C. Debs., 3s., vol. 304, col. 1244: 9 April 1886. All references to Parliamentary Debates are to Hansard 5th Series, unless otherwise stated.
4. A. L. Lowell, *The Government of England* (Macmillan, 1908), vol. 1, p. 326, argued 'To say that at present the cabinet legislates with the advice and consent of Parliament would hardly be an exaggeration.'

PART I: THE REFERENDUM 1890–1980, pp. 9–66

1. i.e., Conservatives and Liberal Unionists. The two parties merged in 1912, but were known collectively as Unionists until then.
2. Strachey to Lord Balfour of Burleigh, 3 April 1911, Strachey Papers S/3/5/51.
3. Dicey to Strachey, 1 Dec. 1910, *ibid.*, S/5/5/20.
4. A. V. Dicey, *Introduction to the Study of The Law of the Constitution* (10th edn, Macmillan, 1959), p. 39.
5. Dicey to Bryce, 23 March 1911, Bryce Papers, MS 3, fo. 83.
6. Dicey, *Introduction*, p. 89.
7. A. V. Dicey, 'The referendum', *National Review* (March 1894), p. 66.
8. Bryce to Dicey, 29 Aug. 1919, Bryce Papers, MS 4, fo. 223.
9. A. V. Dicey, 'Ought the referendum to be introduced into England?', *Contemporary Review* (1890), p. 504.
10. Dicey, *National Review* (March 1894), p. 66.
11. Dicey, *Contemporary Review* (1890), p. 498.
12. *ibid.*, p. 503.
13. Dicey to Maxse, 2 Feb. 1894, cited in Richard A. Cosgrove, *The Rule of Law: Albert Venn Dicey, Victorian Jurist* (Macmillan, 1980), p. 107.
14. Dicey, *Contemporary Review* (1890), pp. 505, 507.
15. A. V. Dicey, *A Leap in the Dark* (2nd edn, John Murray, 1911), pp. 189–90.
16. Dicey to Strachey, 6 May 1895, Strachey Papers, S/5/5/2.
17. Joseph Chamberlain, *Imperial Union and Tariff Reform* (Grant Richards, 1903), pp. x–xi.
18. C. W. Boyd (ed.), *Mr Chamberlain's Speeches*, vol. 2 (Constable, 1914), p. 303.
19. Patricia Kelvin, 'The development and use of the concept of the electoral

mandate in British politics, 1867 to 1911' (Ph.D. thesis, University of London, 1977), offers an excellent discussion of this topic.

20. H. C. Debs., 3s., vol. 190, cols 1785–6, 1788:16 March 1868.
21. G. E. Buckle (ed.), *Letters of Queen Victoria*, 2nd Series (John Murray, 1926), vol. 1, p. 516.
22. H. C. Debs., 3s., vol. 191, col. 931: 3 April 1868.
23. H. L. Debs., 3s., vol. 197, col. 84: 17 June 1869.
24. *ibid.*
25. *ibid.*, col. 37.
26. H. C. Debs., 3s., vol. 274, col. 680: 2 Nov. 1882.
27. Lord Salisbury, 'Disintegration', *Quarterly Review* (1883), reprinted in Paul Smith (ed.), *Lord Salisbury on Politics* (Cambridge University Press, 1972), p. 356.
28. Benjamin Disraeli, *Vindication of the English Constitution* (Saunders and Otley, 1835), p. 65.
29. S. Gwynn and G. Tuckwell, *Life of the Right Hon. Charles Dilke* (John Murray, 1917), vol. 1, p. 371. Before the Parliament Act of 1911, the maximum duration of a Parliament was seven years rather than five.
30. Salisbury to Carnarvon, 20 Feb. 1872, cited in Lady G. Cecil, *Life of Robert, Marquess of Salisbury* (Hodder and Stoughton, 1921), vol. 2, p. 26.
31. Balfour Papers, Add. Mss. 49730, fos. 28–9.
32. H. C. Debs., vol. 24, cols 1809ff.: 26 April 1911.
33. Notes of Meetings of the Conference on the Constitutional Question, 11th Sitting, 26 July 1910: Austen Chamberlain Papers, 10.2.45.
34. 18th Sitting, 1 Nov. 1910: *ibid.*, 10.2.52; 19th Sitting, 2 Nov. 1910: *ibid.*, 10.2.53.
35. J. A. Spender and Cyril Asquith: *Life of Herbert Henry Asquith, Lord Oxford and Asquith* (Hutchinson, 1932), vol. 1, p. 291.
36. Beatrice Webb: *Our Partnership* (Longman Green, 1948), p. 466.
37. H. L. Debs., vol. 7, col. 262: 2 March 1911.
38. *ibid.*, col. 266.
39. *ibid.*, col. 727: 29 March 1911.
40. Balfour of Burleigh to Strachey, 31 March 1911: Strachey Papers, S/2/5/50.
41. Strachey to Lansdowne, 27 Nov. 1911: *ibid.*, S/9/7/8.
42. Strachey to Lansdowne, 22 Nov. 1910: *ibid.*, S/9/7/2.
43. H. C. Debs., vol. 25, cols 915ff.: 8 May 1911.
44. *ibid.*, col. 926.
45. H. L. Debs., vol. 9, cols 47ff.: 3 July 1911.
46. Strachey to Lansdowne, 6 Dec. 1910: Strachey Papers, S/9/7/2.
47. Dicey to Strachey, 26 Nov. 1910: *ibid.*, S/5/5/20.
48. H. C. Debs., vol. 21, col. 1748: 21 Feb. 1911.
49. H. L. Debs., 3s., vol. 211, cols 1493–4: 10 June 1872.
50. Lord Sheffield, H. L. Debs., vol. 9, col. 226: 5 July 1911.
51. Curzon MSS, Eur. F 112/39. I am indebted to Dr Brian Harrison for drawing my attention to this reference.
52. Keith Middlemas and John Barnes, *Baldwin* (Weidenfeld and Nicolson, 1969), p. 571.

53. H. C. Debs., 4s., vol. 21, col. 1768: 21 Feb. 1911.
54. Quoted in Philip Goodhart, *Full-Hearted Consent* (Davis–Poynter, 1976), p. 171.
55. Douglas Jay, *Change and Fortune: A Political Record* (Hutchinson, 1980), p. 452.
56. Goodhart, *Full-Hearted Consent*, p. 13.
57. *The Times*, 11 April 1972.
58. Stanley Alderson, *Yea or Nay? Referenda in the United Kingdom* (Cassell, 1975), p. 2.
59. Goodhart, *Full-Hearted Consent*, p. 181.
60. *Financial Times*, 7 June 1975.
61. David Butler and Uwe Kitzinger, *The 1975 Referendum* (Macmillan, 1976), p. 273.
62. *The Times*, 21 February 1975.
63. Butler and Kitzinger, *The 1975 Referendum*, pp. 158–9, 131, 137.
64. *ibid.*, p. 274.
65. Peter Jenkins, quoted in Goodhart, *Full-Hearted Consent*, p. 184.
66. Butler and Kitzinger, p. 271. See also *Economist*, 14 June 1975.
67. *Sunday Times*, 8 June 1975; *Guardian*, 7 June 1975.
68. H. C. Debs., vol. 888, col. 293: 11 March 1975.
69. Butler and Kitzinger, *The 1975 Referendum*, p. 280.
70. *ibid.*
71. *ibid.*, p. 259.
72. Goodhart, *Full-Hearted Consent*, pp. 153, 152, 166, 154.
73. Cmnd. 5925, Feb. 1975, p. 2. My italics.
74. H. C. Debs., vol. 893, col. 37: 9 June 1975.
75. H. C. Debs., vol. 881, cols 1742–3: 22 Nov. 1974.
76. *The Times*, 11 April 1972.
77. My book, *Devolution* (Oxford University Press, 1979), examines the background to the issue, and the subsequent legislation.
78. *Why Devolution* (Labour Party Wales, Sept. 1976), p. 4.
79. H. C. Debs., vol. 944, col. 595: 15 Feb. 1978.
80. See the letter by Nevil Johnson to *The Times*, 24 Dec. 1976.
81. Quoted by Norman Buchan MP, H. C. Debs., vol. 926, col. 329, 15 Feb. 1977.
82. *South Wales Echo*, 21 Feb. 1977.
83. This section is largely based upon my article 'The 40 per cent rule', *Parliamentary Affairs* (Summer 1980).
84. P. Gray and F. A. Gee, *Electoral Registration for Parliamentary Elections* (HMSO, 1967).
85. *The Economist*, 19 Feb. 1979, discussing the research of David Butler and Colin O'Muircheartaigh.
86. 'The two registers', *Scotsman*, 12 Feb. 1979.
87. Letter to the *Scotsman*, 26 Feb. 1979.
88. 'The case for the 40% test', *Scotsman*, 1 Feb. 1978.
89. H. C. Debs., vol. 958, col. 1367: 22 Nov. 1978.
90. Harold Wilson, *Final Term* (Weidenfeld and Nicolson/Michael Joseph, 1979), p. 213n.

91. H. C. Debs., vol. 968, cols 1364, 1452–3: 20 June 1979.
92. *Scotsman*, 3 March 1979.
93. *Scotsman*, 17 April 1979.
94. James Kellas, 'Political science and Scottish politics', *British Journal of Political Science*, vol. 10 (July 1980), p. 375.
95. H. C. Debs., vol. 968, col. 1335: 20 June 1979.
96. *ibid.*, col. 1423.
97. Quoted in Jacques Leruez, 'A Frenchman looks at the Referendum Thistle: a few remarks on the March referendum in Scotland against the background of French experience' (unpublished paper read at PSA Conference, Warwick, 1979).
98. Philip M. Williams and Martin Harrison, *Politics and Society in de Gaulle's Republic* (Longman, 1971), p. 40.
99. *The Referendum and the Constitution*, Old Queen St Paper no. 16, 12 Sept. 1978 (Conservative Research Dept, 1978).
100. H. C. Debs., vol. 833, col. 1862: 24 March 1972.
101. H. C. Debs., vol. 846, col. 1100: 21 Nov. 1972.
102. H. Maine, *Popular Government* (5th edn, John Murray, 1897), p. 28.
103. Dicey to Maxse, 12 Oct. 1909, 2 Feb. 1894, cited in Cosgrove, *The Rule of Law*, pp. 108, 107.

PART II: THE REFERENDUM AND THE CONSTITUTION, pp. 67–93

1. *The Times*, 25 Nov. 1891.
2. Bryce to Dicey, 6 April 1915: Bryce Papers MS 4, fo. 84.
3. *The Referendum and the Constitution*, Old Queen St Paper no. 16, 12 Sept. 1978 (Conservative Research Dept, 1978).
4. Strachey to Balfour of Burleigh, 7 March 1911: Strachey Papers, S/2/5/38.
5. John Locke, *Second Treatise of Government*, para. 141.
6. H. C. Debs., vol. 888, col. 293: 11 March 1975.
7. *ibid.*
8. A. V. Dicey, *Introduction to the Study of the Law of the Constitution* (10th edn, Macmillan, 1959), p. 83.
9. *ibid.*, p. 432.
10. *ibid.*, p. 429.
11. *ibid.*, p. 431.
12. H. L. Debs., vol. 7, col. 255: 2 March 1911.
13. *ibid.*, cols 255–6.
14. H. L. Debs., vol. 9, cols 274–5: 5 July 1911.
15. A. V. Dicey, *A Leap in the Dark* (2nd edn, John Murray, 1911), p. 189.
16. Speech to the Electors of Bristol (1774), reprinted in Edmund Burke, *Speeches and Letters on American Affairs* (Everyman Edition, 1961), pp. 72–3.
17. H. C. Debs., vol. 881, col. 1757: 22 Nov. 1974.
18. Lord Tennyson, H. L. Debs., vol. 7, col. 276: 2 March 1911.
19. R. J. Williams and J. R. Greenaway, 'The referendum in British politics: a dissenting view', *Parliamentary Affairs* (1975), p. 259.

20. Dicey: *Introduction to the Study of the Law of the Constitution* (8th edn, Macmillan 1915), Introduction, p. c.
21. Report of the Royal Commission on the Constitution, vol. 11: *Memorandum of Dissent* (HMSO, 1973), Cmnd. 5460–1, p. 34.
22. David Butler and Austin Ranney (eds.), *Referendums: A Comparative Study of Practice and Theory* (American Enterprise Institute, 1978), pp. 6, 63–4.
23. J. St L. Strachey, *The Referendum* (T. Fisher Unwin, 1924), p. 29.
24. S. E. Finer, *The Changing British Party System 1945–1979* (American Enterprise Institute, 1980), p. 218.
25. *ibid.*, pp. 218, 219.
26. Charles M. Price, cited in Eugene Lee, 'California' in Butler and Ranney (eds.), *Referendums*, p. 119.
27. Kenneth E. Miller, *Government and Politics in Denmark* (Houghton Mifflin, 1968), p. 137.
28. Hugh Bone, in The Senate Judiciary Committee on the Voter Initiative Constitutional Amendment, SJ Res 67, p. 189.
29. James Bryce, *Modern Democracies* (Macmillan, 1921), vol. 2, pp. 476–7.
30. Stanley Alderson, *Yea or Nay? Referenda in the United Kingdom* (Cassell, 1975), p. 113.
31. Sarah Wambaugh, *Plebiscites Since the World War* (Carnegie Institute, Washington, 1933), vol. 1, p. 98.

PART III: PROPORTIONAL REPRESENTATION, 1831–1931

Chapter 1: 1831–1974, pp. 97–143

1. H. C. Debs., 3s., vol. 5, col. 1360: 13 Aug. 1831.
2. *ibid.*, col. 1361.
3. *ibid.*, col. 1362.
4. *ibid.*, col. 1372.
5. Derek Hudson, *A Poet in Parliament* (John Murray, 1939), p. 178.
6. James Garth Marshall, *Minorities and Majorities: Their Relative Rights: A Letter to the Lord John Russell M.P. on Parliamentary Reform* (James Ridgway, 1853), pp. 5, 9.
7. *ibid.*, p. 24.
8. *ibid.*, pp. 25, 26.
9. H. C. Debs., 3s., vol. 188, col. 1074: 5 July 1867.
10. *ibid.*, col. 1102.
11. *ibid.*, col. 1091.
12. *ibid.*, col. 1111.
13. A. Patchett Martin, *Life and Letters of the Rt Hon. Robert Lowe, Viscount Sherbrook* (Longman Green, 1893), vol. 2, p. 324.
14. C. 5485 (1888), p. 234.
15. G. J. Shaw-Lefevre, *The Representation of Minorities* (National Liberal Federation, Birmingham, reprinted from *Contemporary Review* (May 1884)), p. 3.
16. H. C. Debs., 3s., vol. 1189, cols 446, 441, 442: 30 July 1867.
17. H. C. Debs., 3s., vol. 189, col. 1148: 8 Aug. 1867.
18. *ibid.*, cols 1162–3.

19. Compare Enid Lakeman, *How Democracies Vote* (Faber and Faber, 4th edn, 1974), pp. 84–5.
20. M. Ostrogorski, *Democracy and the Organisation of Political Parties* (Macmillan, 1902), vol. 1, pp. 162–3n.
21. Poul Andrae: *Andrae and His Invention: The Proportional Representation Method* (Philadelphia, 1926), p. 69.
22. *Considerations on Representative Government* in *John Stuart Mill: Collected Works*, vol. xix: *Essays on Politics and Society* (University of Toronto Press, 1977), p. 477.
23. *ibid.*, p. 466n.
24. Thomas Hare, *The Election of Representatives* (4th edn), pp. xxxii, xxxiii.
25. Mill, *Representative Government*, pp. 450, 451, 456.
26. Mill, *Recent Writers on Reform*, p. 362; *Representative Government*, p. 460.
27. Thomas Hare, *The Election of Representatives* (4th edn), p. xix.
28. Mill, *Collected Works*, vol. xv, pp. 598–9.
29. H. C. Debs., 3s., vol. 187, col. 1357: 30 May 1867.
30. *ibid.*
31. *ibid.*, col. 1361.
32. *The English Constitution* in *Collected Works*, ed. N. St John-Stevas (The Economist, London 1974), vol. 5, pp. 299–300.
33. Bagehot, review of J. S. Mill: *Representative Government, Collected Works*, vol. 6, pp. 344, 345.
34. *The English Constitution*, p. 303.
35. *ibid.*, p. 304.
36. Minutes of Evidence Taken Before the Royal Commission on Systems of Election: Cd. 5352, para. 1481.
37. *ibid.*, para. 1480.
38. Roy Jenkins, *Sir Charles Dilke: A Victorian Tragedy* (Fontana edn, 1968), p. 189.
39. Lady Gwendolen Cecil, *Life of Lord Salisbury*, III (Hodder and Stoughton, 1931), 123.
40. Cd. 5352, para. 1490.
41. *ibid.*
42. *ibid.*, para. 1487.
43. H. C. Debs., 3s., vol. 294, col. 681: 4 Dec. 1884.
44. *ibid.*, col. 380: 1 Dec. 1884.
45. H. C. Debs., 3s., vol. 294, col. 1928: 3 March 1885.
46. Cd. 5352, para. 1481.
47. *ibid.*, para. 1496.
48. A. J. Balfour, *Chapters of Autobiography* (Cassell, 1930), pp. 220–1.
49. Ostrogorski, *Democracy and the Organisation of Political Parties*, I, 174–5.
50. *Manchester Guardian*, 21 Nov. 1883.
51. Peter Fraser, *Joseph Chamberlain* (Cassell, 1966), p. 56.
52. H. C. Debs., 3s., vol. 286, col. 1566: 3 April 1884.
53. *The Radical Programme* (Chapman and Hall, 1885), pp. 6–7.
54. Cited in Robert McKenzie, *British Political Parties* (2nd edn, Heinemann, 1964), p. 12.

55. Ostrogorski, *Democracy*, vol. 2, p. 536.
56. Andrew Jones, *The Politics of Reform, 1884* (Cambridge University Press, 1972), p. 103.
57. Cited in Minutes, Cd. 5352, p. 13.
58. Jones, *Politics of Reform*, p. 103.
59. *Pall Mall Gazette*, 9 Nov. 1883, quoted *ibid.*, 100n.
60. H. C. Debs., 3s., vol. 294, col. 1839: 2 March 1885.
61. *Letters of Sidney and Beatrice Webb*, ed. Norman Mackenzie (Cambridge University Press, 1978), vol. 1, p. 33.
62. Courtney to Goschen, 4 Nov. 1887: G. P. Gooch, *Life of Lord Courtney* (Macmillan, 1920), p. 278.
63. A. K. Russell, *Liberal Landslide: The General Election of 1906* (David and Charles, 1973), p. 84.
64. Horace G. Hutchinson, *Life of Sir John Lubbock, Lord Avebury* (Macmillan, 1914), II, 276.
65. Gooch, *Life of Lord Courtney*, p. 245.
66. The politics of electoral reform between 1905 and 1918, have been brilliantly illuminated by the work of Martin Pugh in 'The background to the Representation of the People Act of 1918' (Ph.D. thesis, University of Bristol, 1974); *Electoral Reform in War and Peace 1906–1918* (Routledge and Kegan Paul, 1978); 'New light on Edwardian voters: the model elections of 1906–12', *Bulletin of the Institute of Historical Research*, 1978; and 'Political parties and the campaign for proportional representation, 1905–1914', *Parliamentary Affairs*, 1980. The following sections have been considerably influenced by Pugh.
67. A. L. Lowell, *The Government of England* (Macmillan, 1908), I, 195.
68. Contrary to the view of Michael Steed. See *The Evolution of the British Electoral System* in S. E. Finer (ed.), *Adversary Politics and Electoral Reform* (Anthony Wigram, 1975).
69. Minutes, Cd. 5352, paras 981, 849, 940, 836.
70. Grey to Courtney, 23 May 1910. Quoted in Pugh, 'Background to the Representation of the People Act of 1918', p. 59.
71. Report of Royal Commission Appointed to Enquire into Electoral Systems, Cd. 5163, para. 125.
72. *ibid.*, para. 90.
73. Mr R. Clements (Birmingham Labour Representation Committee), Labour Party Conference 1914, p. 104.
74. Labour Party Conference 1914,
75. G. H. Roberts MP and W. C. Anderson, 'The Case for Proportional Representation' in *Proportional Representation and the Alternative Vote* (Labour Party, 1913), p. 7.
76. *ibid.*
77. Roberts and Anderson, 'Case for Proportional Representation', p. 8.
78. Ramsay MacDonald, *Socialism and Society* (1905), quoted in David Marquand, *Ramsay MacDonald* (Cape, 1977), pp. 90, 92.
79. *ibid.*, p. 127.
80. 'The Case Against Proportional Representation', pp. 27, 28 (as n. 75 above).

81. *ibid.*, p. 23.
82. *Representation*, no. 1 (Feb. 1908), p. 2.
83. Quoted in Neal Blewett, *The Peers, The Parties and the People: The General Elections of 1910* (Macmillan, 1972), p. 66.
84. Cecil to Strachey, 10 Nov. 1909; Strachey to Cecil, 11 Nov. 1909: Strachey Papers, S/4/3/17.
85. H. C. Debs., vol. 85, col. 1949: 16 Aug. 1916.
86. Memorandum on The Speaker's Conference on Electoral Reform: Willoughby Dickinson Papers, 1917, 6.
87. Conference on Electoral Reform: Letter from Mr Speaker to the Prime Minister, Cd. 8463 (1917).
88. Willoughby Dickinson Papers, *ibid.*
89. Dickinson, Diary, 4 July 1917, quoted in Hope Costley White, *Willoughby Hyett Dickinson: A Memoir, 1859–1943* (John Bellows Ltd., Gloucester, 1956), p. 147.
90. H. C. Debs., vol. 95, col. 1218: 4 July 1917.
91. Entry for 3 April 1917: Trevor Wilson (ed.), *The Political Diaries of C. P. Scott: 1911–1928* (Collins, 1970), p. 274.
92. H. C. Debs., vol. 95, col. 1186: 4 July 1917.
93. *The Political Diaries of C. P. Scott: 1911–1928*, p. 317: 11–12 December 1917.
94. H. C. Debs., vol. 95, col. 1169: 4 July 1917.
95. H. L. Debs., vol. 27, col. 879: 21 Jan. 1918.
96. Earl Grey to Wilson-Fox, 26 March 1917, cited in Pugh, *Electoral Reform in War and Peace, 1906–1918*, p. 155.
97. Michael Kinnear, *The Fall of Lloyd George* (Macmillan, 1973), p. 141.
98. Desmond MacCarthy (ed.), *H.H.A.: Letters of the Earl of Oxford and Asquith To A Friend*, 2nd Series, *1922–1927* Geoffrey Bles, 1934), p. 107.
99. Burnham to Humphreys, 30 March 1927: Electoral Reform Society Papers.
100. *Daily Chronicle*, 22 Nov. 1922, quoted in J. H. Humphreys, *Practical Aspects of Electoral Reform* (P. S. King and Son, 1923), p. 23.
101. John Campbell, *Lloyd George: The Goat in the Wilderness* (Cape, 1977), p. 43.
102. *The Diaries of C. P. Scott, 1911–1928*, pp. 484–5: 13–14 Nov. 1925.
103. *ibid.*, pp. 460, 461: 15 July 1924.
104. Ross McKibbin, *The Evolution of the Labour Party, 1910–1924* (Oxford University Press, 1974), p. 112.
105. Richard W. Lyman, *The First Labour Government: 1924* (Chapman and Hall, 1957), p. 89.
106. M. I. Cole (ed.), *Beatrice Webb's Diaries, 1912–24* (Longman Green, 1952), p. 256: 8 Dec. 1923.
107. *New Statesman*, 11 Oct. 1924, quoted in Trevor Wilson, *The Downfall of the Liberal Party, 1914–1935* (Collins, 1966), p. 269.
108. H. C. Debs., vol. 229, cols 64–5: 2 July 1929.
109. John Campbell, *Lloyd George: The Goat in the Wilderness*, p. 284.
110. Ramsay Muir, *How Britain is Governed* (4th edn, Constable, 1940), p. 126.

111. *Nation*, May 1920, quoted in Kinnear, *The Fall of Lloyd George*, p. 217.
112. See Robert Skidelsky, *Politicians and the Slump* (Macmillan, 1967).
113. *Liberal Magazine* (April 1931), quoted in Wilson, *Downfall of the Liberal Party*, p. 359.
114. Gooch, *Life of Lord Courtney*, p. 202.
115. Review of J. S. Mill, *Autobiography* in *Westminster Review*, n.s., 1874, p. 150.
116. Graham Wallas, *Human Nature in Politics* (Constable edn, 1948), p. 232.
117. Templewood Papers, VI; 2: 'The Second Labour Government', p. 3.
118. Walter Bagehot, 'Parliamentary Reform', *Collected Works*, ed. N. St John-Stevas, vol. 6 (The Economist, 1974), p. 215.

Chapter 2: 1974–1979, pp. 144–74

1. Henry Pelling, 'Labour and the downfall of Liberalism' in *Popular Politics and Society in Late Victorian Britain* (Macmillan, 1968), p. 120.
2. Aneurin Bevan, *In Place of Fear* (Heinemann, 1952), pp. 1, 2.
3. Samuel H. Beer, *Modern British Politics* (Faber, 1965), p. 71. This discussion is largely based on Beer.
4. *ibid.*, p. 85.
5. *ibid.*, p. 69.
6. Robert Alford, *Party and Society* (John Murray, 1964).
7. *Representation*, vol. 13, no. 51 (April 1973).
8. Cmnd. 5460, para. 787.
9. *Representation*, vol. 13, no. 53 (October 1973), p. 54.
10. Michael Steed, Foreword to Arthur Cyr, *Liberal Party Politics in Britain* (John Calder, 1977), pp. 22ff.
11. Report of the Hansard Society Commission on Electoral Reform (1976), para. 10.
12. S. A. Walkland, 'The report of the Hansard Society Commission on Electoral Reform', *Parliamentary Affairs* (1976), p. 451.
13. Bryan Magee, *The Times*, 25 Oct. 1980.
14. Barbara Castle, *The Castle Diaries 1974–1976* (Weidenfeld and Nicolson, 1980), p. 554.
15. *ibid.*, pp. 69–70, 554.
16. *Daily Telegraph*, 28 Feb. 1976.
17. Message to candidates, October 1974, cited in Trevor Russel, *The Tory Party: Its Policies, Divisions and Future* (Penguin, 1978), p. 144.
18. Jeremy Thorpe to Jack Hayward, 28 Nov. 1974, quoted in Lewis Chester, Magnus Linklater, David May, *Jeremy Thorpe: A Secret Life* (Fontana, 1979), pp. 201–2.
19. Conservative Party Conference Report (1975), p. 75.
20. *Guardian*, 9 Oct. 1975; *The Times*, 9 Oct. 1975.
21. Jo Grimond, *Memoirs* (Heinemann, 1979), pp. 204, 211–12.
22. David Steel, *A House Divided: The Lib–Lab Pact and the Future of British Politics* (Weidenfeld and Nicolson, 1980), p. viii.
23. Grimond, *Memoirs*, p. 250.

24. Steel, *A House Divided*, pp. 125–6, 135, 149, 79.
25. *Labour Weekly*, 17 June 1977.
26. *The Times*, 10 Oct. 1977.
27. Steel, *A House Divided*, pp. 156–7.
28. 'The ABC of the contest for the Euro seats', *Sunday Times*, 3 July 1977.
29. Michael Steed, *Fair Elections or Fiasco?* (National Committee for Electoral Reform, 1977), pp. 9–10.
30. *ibid.*
31. *ibid.*, p. 11.
32. Direct Elections to the European Assembly (Cmnd. 6768, 1977), paras 24, 27.
33. Steed, *Fair Elections or Fiasco?*, p. 23.
34. Mark Hagger, 'The United Kingdom: the reluctant Europeans' in Valentine Herman and Mark Hagger (eds.), *The Legislation of Direct Elections to the European Parliament* (Gower, 1980), p. 218.
35. *ibid.*, p. 220.
36. Steed, *Fair Elections or Fiasco?*, p. 15.
37. George Gardiner, *Daily Telegraph*, 8 March 1977, 5 July 1977.
38. H. C. Debs, vol. 941, col. 319: 13 Dec. 1977.
39. Michael Steed, Twelve into one: the effect of using diverse procedures for the first European Parliamentary Elections, p. 31 (unpublished paper). I am grateful to Michael Steed for allowing me to consult this paper.
40. *Representation*, vol. 19, no. 76 (July 1979).
41. Cmnd. 5460, paras 787–8. My italics.
42. *ibid.*, I, para. 135.
43. Steel, *A House Divided*, p. 101.
44. H. C. Debs., vol. 924, col. 1237: 25 Jan. 1977.
45. H. L. Debs., vol. 390, col. 56: 4 April 1978.

PART IV: THE CASE FOR ELECTORAL REFORM

Chapter 1: The British electoral system, pp. 177–93

1. Sir Goronwy Edwards, 'The emergence of majority rule in English parliamentary elections', *Transactions of the Royal Historical Society* (1964), p. 185 (italics in original).
2. H. J. Hanham, *Elections and Party Management: Politics in the time of Disraeli and Gladstone* (Longman, 1959), p. 197.
3. A. H. Birch, *Representative and Responsible Government* (Allen and Unwin, 1964), p. 121.
4. Kenneth A. Heard, *General Elections in South Africa, 1943–1970* (Oxford University Press, 1974).
5. J. Parker Smith, Royal Commission on Systems of Election (Cd. 5352, 1909), para. 1253; M. G. Kendall and A. Stuart, 'The law of cubic proportions in election results', *British Journal of Sociology* (1950), pp. 185ff.: D. E. Butler, *The Electoral System in Britain Since 1918* (2nd edn, Oxford University Press, 1963), p. 197.

6. E. R. Tufte, 'The relation between seats and votes in two-party systems', *American Political Science Review* (1973), pp. 540ff.
7. These paragraphs have been based on John Curtice and Michael Steed, 'Electoral choice and the production of governments: the changing pattern of the UK electoral system, 1955–79' (unpublished paper, delivered to PSA Conference, 1981); and John Curtice and Michael Steed, Appendix 2, 'An analysis of the voting' in David Butler and Dennis Kavanagh, *The British General Election of 1979* (Macmillan, 1980), pp. 428–30.
8. According to a table circulated to the Consultative Council on Local Government Finance on 22 November 1976.
9. Michael Steed, Introduction to Arthur Cyr, *Liberal Party Politics in Britain* (John Calder, 1977), pp. 12–13.
10. Michael Steed and David Faull, 'First past the post: the Great British class handicap' (Liberal Action Group for Electoral Reform, 1980). What follows is based upon this pamphlet.
11. *ibid.*, p. 3.
12. *ibid.*, pp. 3–6.
13. *Economist*, 7 Feb. 1981.
14. Paul Addison, *The Road to 1945* (Cape, 1975).
15. D. E. Butler, *The British General Election of 1951* (Macmillan, 1952), p. 244.
16. Quoted by Richard Rose in *Do Parties Make a Difference?* (Macmillan, 1980), p. 157.
17. Harold Macmillan, *The Past Masters* (Macmillan, 1975), pp. 18–19.

Chapter 2: Political consequences, pp. 194–205

1. Viscount Caldecote, *Industry Needs Electoral Reform* (Conservative Action for Electoral Reform, 1980).
2. *ibid.*
3. Hansard Society, *Politics and Industry – The Great Mismatch* (1979), pp. 56, 57, 60.
4. Anthony Wigram, *Local Government Elections: The Case for Proportional Representation* (Conservative Action for Electoral Reform, 1978).
5. Cmnd. 6524 (1976), para. 39.
6. Elizabeth Vallance, *Women in the House* (Athlone Press, 1979), p. 59.
7. *ibid.*, pp. 155, 158.
8. Enid Lakeman, 'Political women in their year', *Representation*, vol. 15, no. 60 (July 1975), p. 31.

PART V: ALTERNATIVE ELECTORAL SYSTEMS, pp. 207–58

1. *The Reform of Political Representation* (John Murray, 1918), p. 28.
2. Poul Andrae, *Andrae and his Invention* (Philadelphia, 1926), 28.
3. Stein Rokkan, *Citizens, Elections, Parties* (Universitetsforlaget, Oslo, 1970), p. 162.
4. Note on features of a uniform electoral system by Mr J. Seitlinger, Rapporteur, 1 April 1980, p. 2.
5. Avraham Brichta, '1977 elections and the future of electoral reform in Israel'

in Howard R. Penniman (ed.), *Israel at the Polls: The Knesset Elections of 1977* (American Enterprise Institute, 1979), p. 46.

6. M. Duverger, *Political Parties* (2nd edn, Methuen, 1959), pp. 151–2.
7. Peter H. Merkl: *The Origin of the West German Republic* (Oxford University Press, New York, 1963), p. 176.
8. *ibid.*, p. 81.
9. J. K. Pollock, *German Election Administration* (Columbia University Press, 1934), pp. 51–2.
10. Raymond Ebsworth, *Restoring Democracy in Germany: The British Contribution* (Stevens, 1960), pp. 51–2.
11. Richard Holme, *A Democracy Which Works: An Analysis of the West German Electoral System* (Parliamentary Democracy Trust, n.d.), p. 21. This pamphlet offers an excellent account of the West German system.
12. *Representation*, vol. 13., no. 50, p. 7.
13. Merkl, *Origin of the West German Republic*, p. 176.
14. Heino Kaack, 'The FDP in the German party system' in Cerny (ed.), *Germany at the Polls.*
15. Peter Pulzer, 'The German party system in the sixties', *Political Studies*, (1971), p. 16.
16. Peter Pulzer, 'Responsible party government and stable coalition: the case of the German Federal Republic', *Political Studies* (1978), p. 206.
17. Gerhard Loewenberg: *Parliament in the West German Political System* (Cornell University Press, 1966), p. 437.
18. Hansard Society Commission on Electoral Reform, para. 93.
19. 'Scottish snakes and Welsh ladders', *The Economist*, 22 Jan. 1977.
20. Steed, 'Twelve into one', p. 12.
21. Sir Lancelot Hare, *The Transferable Vote Explained in a Few Words* (P. S. King, n.d.), p. 2.
22. Proportional Representation Society, *Statement of Aims*, No. 5 (1884).
23. Proportional Representation Society, *Statement of Aims*, No. 2.
24. See Basil Chubb, in Howard R. Penniman (ed.), *Ireland at the Polls: The Dáil Elections of 1977* (American Enterprise Institute, 1978) p. 27.
25. Dr Garret FitzGerald, 'How we gerrymander in the Republic', *Representation*, vol. 13, no. 50 (Jan. 1973), p. 10.
26. R. K. Carty, 'Politicians and electoral laws: an anthropology of party competition in Ireland', *Political Studies* (1980), p. 554. This article is an excellent analysis of localist attitudes in the constituency of Kildare.
27. Basil Chubb, *The Government and Politics of Ireland* (Oxford University Press, 1970), pp. 55–6.
28. Michael Gallagher, 'Candidate selection in Ireland: the impact of localism and the electoral system', *British Journal of Political Science* (1980), p. 503.
29. Jeremy Boissevain, *Saints and Fireworks: Religion and Politics in Rural Malta* (Athlone Press, 1969), p. 131.
30. Michael Laver, 'On introducing STV and interpreting the results: the case of Northern Ireland 1973–1975', *Parliamentary Affairs* (1976), pp. 213, 223.
31. See Peter H. Lemieux, 'Political issues and Liberal support in the February

1974 British general election', *Political Studies* (1977), pp. 323ff., who discusses Liberal support in these terms. See especially p. 337.

32. Gladstone to Lord Aberdeen, 18 Dec. 1852, cited in Robert Blake, '1783–1902' in David Butler (ed.), *Coalitions in British Politics* (Macmillan, 1978), p. 6.
33. Henry Fairlie, *The Life of Politics* (Methuen, 1968), p. 69.
34. H. C. Debs., 3s., vol. 187, col. 1351: 30 May 1867.
35. Thomas Hare, *The Machinery of Representation* (W. Maxwell, 1857), p. 6.

CONCLUSION

1. *Proportional Representation: An Address Delivered at the Mechanics Institute, Stockport, 22 March 1907* (PR Pamphlet No. 6), p. 11.

Bibliography

A. MANUSCRIPT COLLECTIONS

The following manuscript collections were consulted in the preparation of this book:

Balfour Papers: British Library
Bryce Papers: Bodleian Library
Austen Chamberlain Papers: University of Birmingham Library
Willoughby Dickinson Papers: Greater London Record Office
Proportional Representation Society (later Electoral Reform Society) correspondence and papers: Electoral Reform Society
St Loe Strachey Papers: House of Lords Record Office
Templewood Papers: Cambridge University Library

B. OFFICIAL PUBLICATIONS

Royal Commission on the Elementary Education Acts, C. 5485, 1888
Minutes of Evidence Taken Before the Royal Commission on Systems of Election, Cd. 5352
Report of Royal Commission Appointed to Enquire into Electoral Systems, Cd. 5163
Conference on Electoral Reform, Letter from Mr Speaker to the Prime Minister, Cd. 8463, 1917
Royal Commission on the Constitution (Kilbrandon Commission), Report, Cmnd. 5460; Memorandum of Dissent, Cmnd. 5460 – 1, 1973
Democracy and Devolution: Proposals for Scotland and Wales: Cmnd. 5732, 1974
Referendum on United Kingdom Membership of the European Community, Cmnd. 5925, 1975
Report of Royal Commission on Standards of Conduct in Public Life (Salmon Commission), Cmnd. 6524, 1976
Direct Elections to the European Assembly, Cmnd. 6768, 1977

C. PRINTED WORKS

Addison, Paul, *The Road to 1945*, Cape, 1975
Alderson, Stanley, *Yea or Nay? Referenda in the United Kingdom*, Cassell, 1975
Alford, Robert, *Party and Society*, John Murray, 1964
Andrae, Poul, *Andrae and His Invention: The Proportional Representation Method*, Philadelphia, privately published, 1926

Bibliography

Bagehot, Walter, *Collected Works* vols v and vi, ed. N. St John-Stevas, The Economist, 1974

Balfour, Arthur James, *Chapters of Autobiography*, Cassell, 1930

Beer, Samuel H., *Modern British Politics*, Faber, 1965

Bevan, Aneurin, *In Place of Fear*, Heinemann, 1952

Birch, A. H., *Representative and Responsible Government: An Essay on the British Constitution*, Allen and Unwin, 1964

Blewett, Neal, *The Peers, the Parties and the People: The General Elections of 1910*, Macmillan, 1972

Bogdanor, Vernon, *Devolution*, Oxford University Press, 1979

'The 40 per cent rule', *Parliamentary Affairs*, 1980

Boissevain, Jeremy, *Saints and Fireworks: Religion and Politics in Rural Malta*, Athlone Press, 1969

Boyd, C. W. (ed.), *Mr Chamberlain's Speeches*, 2 vols, Constable, 1914

Bryce, James, *Modern Democracies*, 2 vols, Macmillan, 1921

Buckle, G. E. (ed.), *The Letters of Queen Victoria*, 2nd series, 3 vols, John Murray, 1926

Butler, David, *The British General Election of 1951*, Macmillan, 1952

The Electoral System in Britain Since 1918, 2nd edn, Oxford University Press, 1963

and Uwe Kitzinger, *The 1975 Referendum*, Macmillan, 1976

and Austin Ranney (eds.), *Referendums: A Comparative Study of Practice and Theory*, American Enterprise Institute, 1978

(ed.), *Coalitions in British Politics*, Macmillan, 1978

and Dennis Kavanagh, *The British General Election of 1979*, Macmillan, 1980

Caldecote, Viscount, *Industry needs Electoral Reform*, Conservative Action for Electoral Reform, 1980

Campbell, John, *Lloyd George: The Goat in the Wilderness*, Cape, 1977

Carty, R. K., 'Politicians and electoral laws: the impact of localism and the electoral system in Ireland', *Political Studies*, 1980

Castle, Barbara, *The Castle Diaries, 1974–1976*, Weidenfeld and Nicolson, 1980

Cecil, Lady Gwendolen, *Life of Robert, Marquess of Salisbury*, 4 vols, Hodder and Stoughton, 1921–32

Cerny, Karl H., *Germany at the Polls: The Bundestag Elections of 1976*, American Enterprise Institute, 1978

Chamberlain, Joseph, *Imperial Union and Tariff Reform*, Grant Richards, 1903

Chester, Lewis, Magnus Linklater and David May, *Jeremy Thorpe: A Secret Life*, Fontana, 1979

Chubb, Basil, *The Government and Politics of Ireland*, Oxford University Press, 1970

Cole, M. I., *Beatrice Webb's Diaries, 1912–1924*, Longman Green, 1952

Cosgrove, Richard A., *The Rule of Law: Albert Venn Dicey, Victorian Jurist*, Macmillan, 1980

Curtice, John and Michael Steed, 'Electoral choice and the production of governments: the changing pattern of the UK electoral system, 1955–1979', unpublished paper delivered at Political Studies Association Conference, Hull 1981

Cyr, Arthur, *Liberal Party Politics in Britain*, John Calder, 1977

Dicey, A. V., *An Introduction to the Study of the Law of the Constitution*, 1st edn, Macmillan, 1885

'Ought the referendum to be introduced into England?', *Contemporary Review*, 1890

'The referendum', *National Review*, 1894

A Leap in the Dark, 2nd edn, John Murray, 1911

Disraeli, Benjamin, *A Vindication of the English Constitution*, Saunders and Otley, 1835

Duverger, Maurice, *Political Parties*, 2nd edn, Methuen, 1959

Ebsworth, Raymond, *Restoring Democracy in Germany: The British Contribution*, Stevens, 1960

Edwards, Sir Goronwy, 'The emergence of majority rule in English Parliamentary elections', *Transactions of the Royal Historical Society*, 1964

Fairlie, Henry, *The Life of Politics*, Methuen, 1968

Finer, S. E. (ed.), *Adversary Politics and Electoral Reform*, Anthony Wigram, 1975

The Changing British Party System, 1945–1979, American Enterprise Institute, 1980

Fraser, Peter, *Joseph Chamberlain*, Cassell, 1966

Gallagher, Michael, 'Candidate selection in Ireland: the impact of localism and the electoral system', *British Journal of Political Science*, 1980

Gooch, G. P., *Life of Lord Courtney*, Macmillan, 1920

Goodhart, Philip, *Referendum*, Tom Stacey, 1971

Full-Hearted Consent, Davis–Poynter, 1976

Gray, P. and F. A. Gee, *Electoral Registration for Parliamentary Elections*, HMSO, 1967

Grimond, Jo, *Memoirs*, Heinemann, 1979

Gwynn, S. and G. Tuckwell, *Life of the Right Honourable Sir Charles Dilke*, 2 vols, John Murray, 1917

Hanham, H. J., *Elections and Party Management: Politics in the Time of Disraeli and Gladstone*, Longman, 1959

Hansard Society, *Report of Commission on Electoral Reform*, 1976

Politics and Industry – The Great Mismatch, 1979

Hare, Sir Lancelot, *The Transferable Vote Explained in a Few Words*, P. S. King and Son, n.d.

Hare, Thomas, *The Machinery of Representation*, W. Maxwell, 1857

The Election of Representatives, Parliamentary and Municipal: A Treatise, Longmans, 1st edn 1859; 4th edn 1873

review of J. S. Mill, *Autobiography* in *Westminster Review*, 1874

Heard, Kenneth A., *General Elections in South Africa, 1943–1970*, Oxford University Press, 1974.

Herman, Valentine and Mark Hagger (eds.), *The Legislation of Direct Elections to the European Parliament*, Gower, 1980

Holme, Richard, *A Democracy which Works: an Analysis of the West German Electoral System*, Parliamentary Democracy Trust, n.d.

Hudson, Derek, *A Poet in Parliament*, John Murray, 1939

Humphreys, John H., *Practical Aspects of Electoral Reform*, P. S. King and Son, 1923

Hutchinson, Horace G., *Life of Sir John Lubbock, Lord Avebury*, 2 vols, Macmillan, 1914

Jay, Douglas, *Change and Fortune: A Political Record*, Hutchinson, 1980

Jenkins, Roy, *Sir Charles Dilke: A Victorian Tragedy*, Fontana edn, 1968

Jones, Andrew, *The Politics of Reform, 1884*, Cambridge University Press, 1972

Kellas, James, 'Political science and Scottish politics', *British Journal of Political Science*, 1980

Kelvin, Patricia, 'The development and use of the concept of the electoral mandate in British politics, 1867 to 1911', D.Phil. thesis, University of London, 1977

Kendall, M. G. and A. Stuart, 'The law of cubic proportions in election results', *British Journal of Sociology*, 1950

Kinnear, Michael, *The Fall of Lloyd George*, Macmillan, 1973

Knight, James and Nicolas Baxter-Moore, *Republic of Ireland: The General Elections of 1969 and 1973*, Arthur McDougall Fund, 1973

Kohn, Walter S. G., *Women in National Legislatures*, Praeger, 1980

Labour Party, *Proportional Representation and the Alternative Vote*, 1913

Lakeman, Enid, *How Democracies Vote*, 4th edn, Faber, 1974

Laver, Michael, 'On introducing STV and interpreting the results: the case of Northern Ireland 1973–1975', *Parliamentary Affairs*, 1976

Lemieux, Peter H., 'Political issues and Liberal support in the February 1974 British general election', *Political Studies*, 1977

Leruez, Jacques, 'A Frenchman looks at the Referendum Thistle: a few remarks on the March Referendum in Scotland against the background of French experience', unpublished paper read at Political Studies Association Conference, Warwick 1979

Loewenberg, Gerhard, *Parliament in the West German Political System*, Cornell University Press, 1966

Lowell, A. L., *The Government of England*, 2 vols, Macmillan, 1908

Lyman, Richard W., *The First Labour Government: 1924*, Chapman and Hall, 1957

Lyon, Elizabeth, *PR and Parliament: Round One 1886–1931*, Parliamentary Democracy Trust, n.d.

MacCarthy, Desmond (ed.), *H.H.A.: Letters of the Earl of Oxford and Asquith to a Friend*, 2nd series, 1922–1927, Geoffrey Bles, 1934

Mackenzie, Norman, (ed.), *Letters of Sidney and Beatrice Webb*, 3 vols, Cambridge University Press, 1978

Mackenzie, Norman (ed.), *Letters of Sidney and Beatrice Webb*, 3 vols, Cambridge University Press, 1978

McKenzie, Robert, *British Political Parties*, 2nd edn, Heinemann, 1964

McKibbin, Ross, *The Evolution of the Labour Party, 1910–1924*, Oxford University Press, 1974

Marquand, David, *Ramsay MacDonald*, Cape, 1977

Marshall, James Garth, *Minorities and Majorities: Their Relative Rights: A Letter to the Lord John Russell M.P. on Parliamentary Reform*, James Ridgway, 1853

Martin, A. Patchett, *Life and Letters of the Right Honourable Robert Lowe, Viscount Sherbrook*, 2 vols, Longman Green, 1893

Merkl, Peter H., *The Origin of the West German Republic*, Oxford University Press, New York, 1963

Middlemas, Keith and John Barnes, *Baldwin*, Weidenfeld and Nicolson, 1969

Mill, J. S., *Collected Works*, vols XV and XIX, University of Toronto Press, 1977

Miller, Kenneth E., *Government and Politics in Denmark*, Houghton Mifflin, 1968

Muir, Ramsay, *How Britain is Governed*, 4th edn, Constable, 1940

Ostrogorski, M., *Democracy and the Organisation of Political Parties*, 2 vols, Macmillan, 1902

Pelling, H. M., *Popular Politics and Society in Late Victorian Britain*, Macmillan, 1968

Penniman, Howard R. (ed.), *Ireland at the Polls: The Dáil Elections of 1977*, American Enterprise Institute, 1978

Israel at the Polls: The Knesset Elections of 1977, American Enterprise Institute, 1979

Pollock, James K., *German Election Administration*, Columbia University Press, 1934

Pugh, Martin, 'The background to the Representation of the People Act of 1918', Ph.D. thesis, University of Bristol, 1974

Electoral Reform in War and Peace 1906–1918, Routledge and Kegan Paul, 1978

'New light on Edwardian voters: the model elections of 1906–12', *Bulletin of the Institute of Historical Research*, 1978

'Political parties and the campaign for proportional representation, 1905–1914', *Parliamentary Affairs*, 1980

Pulzer, Peter, 'The German party system in the sixties', *Political Studies*, 1971

'Responsible party government and stable coalition: the case of the German Federal Republic', *Political Studies*, 1978

The Radical Programme, Chapman and Hall, 1885

Rokkan, Stein, *Citizens, Elections, Parties*, Universitetsforlaget, Oslo, 1970

Rose, Richard, *Do Parties Make a Difference?*, Macmillan, 1980

Russel, Trevor, *The Tory Party: Its Policies, Divisions and Future*, Penguin, 1978

Russell, A. K., *Liberal Landslide: The General Election of 1906*, David and Charles, 1973

Shaw Lefevre, G. J., 'The representation of minorities', *Contemporary Review*, 1884

Skidelsky, Robert, *Politicians and the Slump*, Macmillan, 1967

Smith, Paul, *Lord Salisbury on Politics*, Cambridge University Press, 1972

Spender, J. A. and Cyril Asquith, *Life of Herbert Henry Asquith, Lord Oxford and Asquith*, 2 vols, Hutchinson, 1932

Steed, Michael, *Fair Elections or Fiasco?*, National Committee for Electoral Reform, 1977

'Twelve into one: the effect of using diverse procedures for the first European Parliamentary Elections', unpublished paper

and David Faull, 'First past the post: the great British class handicap', Liberal Action Group for Electoral Reform, 1980

Steel, David, *A House Divided: The Lib–Lab Pact and the Future of British Politics*, Weidenfeld and Nicolson, 1980

Strachey, J. St Loe, *The Referendum*, T. Fisher Unwin, 1924

Tufte, E. R., 'The relation between seats and votes in two-party systems', *American Political Science Review*, 1973

Vallance, Elizabeth, *Women in the House*, Athlone Press, 1979

Walkland, S. A., 'The report of the Hansard Society Commission on Electoral Reform', *Parliamentary Affairs*, 1976

Wallas, Graham, *Human Nature in Politics*, Constable, 1908

Wambaugh, Sarah, *Plebiscites since the World War*, 2 vols, Carnegie Institute, Washington, 1933

Webb, Beatrice, *Our Partnership*, Longman Green & Co., 1948

White, Hope Costley, *Willoughby Hyett Dickinson: A Memoir, 1859–1943*, John Bellows Ltd, Gloucester, 1956

Williams, J. Fischer, *The Reform of Political Representation*, John Murray, 1918

Williams, Philip M. and Martin Harrison, *Politics and Society in de Gaulle's Republic*, Longman, 1971

Williams, R. J. and J. R. Greenaway, 'The referendum in British politics: a dissenting view', *Parliamentary Affairs*, 1975

Wilson, Harold, *Final Term*, Weidenfeld and Nicolson/Michael Joseph, 1979

Wilson, Trevor, *The Downfall of the Liberal Party, 1914–1935*, Collins, 1966

(ed.), *The Political Diaries of C. P. Scott: 1911–1928*, Collins, 1970

Index of subjects

Index of names

Index of names